The Artist in America

The Artist in America

Compiled by
THE EDITORS OF ART IN AMERICA

An Art in America Book

W · W · Norton & Company · Inc ·
New York

This book is dedicated
to the Archives of American Art
whose vast collection of documents
and photographs provided
the material for a large proportion
of the contents of this book.

First Edition

Library of Congress Catalogue Card No. 67-16609

Published simultaneously in Canada by
George J. McLeod Limited, Toronto

Printed in the United States of America
1 2 3 4 5 6 7 8 9 0

Contents

Introduction: What Is American?

One of the most American traits is our urge to define what is American. This search for a self-image is a result of our relative youth as a civilization and our years of partial dependence on Europe. But it is also a vital part of the process of growth. Just as an individual's understanding of himself helps him to grow, so should national self-knowledge.

National characteristics in themselves have no absolute value. The intrinsic values of art lie in its universal and timeless elements. But national character has an importance like that of the individual artist's personality in relation to his art. The essentials of a man's art come from his inborn gifts, his inner life and his relations to his world. Influences from other art cannot create his art; but they can change it, can help it to grow—or the reverse. Similarly, native elements in the art of a country contribute fundamentals, which can be modified by influences from other countries and other ages. So our problem is to define the elements in American art which are products of our land and society, and to see how they have been affected by the art of the world.

First, let us define our terms. "American" in what respect? In subject matter, in viewpoint, in emotional and intellectual content, in artistic concepts, in style? As to the first, native subject matter is obviously "American" by its very nature; on these grounds, artists like Copley, Mount, Homer, and Eakins are among the most "American." More to the point is the question of artists' viewpoints toward their native subject matter, and what they make out of it. Emotional and intellectual content is a deeper factor and takes in a wider range, not necessarily 'American" in subject—Ryder, for example. Then there is the matter of artistic concepts, the degree of artistic naïveté or knowledge; which in turn involves relations to world art. The question "What Is American in American Art?" could be discussed on any one of these levels. This essay is an attempt, perhaps foolhardy, to discuss it on all these levels. Since the factors have varied from period to period and artist to artist, the discussion will follow historical lines, with emphasis on individuals who have most clearly exemplified the issues.

Art developed in America amid conditions such as existed in no European nation. Instead of a civilized society inhabiting the same region for centuries, here was a group of colonies drawn from many countries. And for the first century and a half, conditions were unfavorable to the growth of any art. Up through the Revolution our people were too busy settling a continent and building a nation to have much time and energy for any but the utilitarian arts. There was no centralized government, no royal court, no cultured nobility. The simple churches had no need for religious art, and in New England there was the Puritan aversion to images. Historical art requires official patronage and a long background of history. Classical themes would have seemed even more foreign, and would have involved the forbidden motif of the nude. Pictures of daily life were of no interest to the mercantile aristocracy. Though there was some landscape painting of a naïve kind, a people engaged in fighting the wilderness had little use for the romantic sentiment for nature. And there was the fact that the colonists, especially the Anglo-Saxons, were more word-conscious than image-conscious. Up to the end of the eighteenth century, the only kind of art which people of wealth and position considered necessary was portraiture; and it was in portraiture that American artists made their first achievements. It is a tribute to man's innate creativity that in such conditions so many portraits were produced which were also fine as art.

Works of art are physical objects, existing in one place. From earliest days Americans possessed the great books of the world, but they owned no great art until the middle of the nineteenth century. There were engravings, but they were poor substitutes. In the absence of art schools, professional standards were represented by the few foreign-trained artists such as Smibert and Blackburn, who were themselves not the most successful practitioners in their own countries; "dukes do not emigrate." Many native-born artists began as craftsmen—house, sign, and carriage painters, carpenters and cabinetmakers. Not until the last quarter of the nineteenth century were American art schools to approach European standards; until then, many of our artists, including some of the best, were largely self-taught.

Hence early America had a larger proportion of folk art than Europe; and this remained true well into the nineteenth century. Created directly by innate talent out of local content, folk art contained the essence of native flavor on a popular level. Sometimes it included reminiscences of whatever art its producer might have seen—prints, textiles, porcelain, instruction books—but translated into folk language. This native flavor first appeared in a pure form in the limners who painted portraits in the colonies from the mid-seventeenth century on. While varying from colony to colony, they had in common the primitive virtues of first-hand observation, a sense of character free from professional glamor and, above all, the physical substance, the integrity of form and the instinct for color, line, and pattern that belong to the primitive the world over. Even when the artist was more sophisticated and adopted current European styles, the primitive structure remained, strong, vital, and visible, so that the rococo or neo-classic graces imposed upon it achieved that peculiar charm that one finds in Feke, the early Copley, William Rush, and the more elegant architecture of the period.

The tragedy of primitive virtues in the modern world is that they are inevitably doomed to disappear; their possessor aspires toward more conscious knowledge and skill, and in the process too often loses more than he gains. Inevitably, Europe had a magnetic attraction for the American artist. Over there were the masterpieces, the great old cities, the ordered landscape humanized and mellowed by centuries of cultivation. By contrast America was crude, raw, an artistic desert. So the irresistible course of development was toward closer contact with Europe, and with all that Europe represented artistically. An essential factor in the growth of American art has been the interaction—sometimes the conflict—between native creativity, relatively primitive but original and vital, and the powerful pull of European knowledge and skills. Some artists have matured through this interaction; some have been ruined by it; some have remained impervious or even totally oblivious.

Take the case of Copley. His art grew out of the colonial tradition of face painting, but raised to a higher level by his genius. His American portraits had all the primitive virtues combined with a richness of substance, a sculptural quality, and an architectonic sense that gave his work, with all its intense realism, a classic order. All this he owed more to native tradition and innate gifts than to the fashionable British portraitists. But Copley aspired toward their sophistication, was dissatisfied with provincial New England, resented the routine of portrait painting, and longed for the great world of Europe and for more imaginative themes. After he settled in London his native style gave way to a more knowledgeable elegance, but without the power of his American work. Thus America lost her greatest artist, to add another good painter to the British school. It is interesting to speculate on the course of art in America if Copley had returned. He would have been the unquestioned leader of our art, and with this prestige might have broken the yoke of portrait painting and initiated a broader range. Copley's case illustrates clearly the typically American conflict between the innocent eye and the mind aspiring toward more knowledge. In the America of his day the primitive virtues were not valued as we today have learned to value them.

As the United States emerged from colonialism into nationhood our more intelligent artists were drawn increasingly to Europe. When, unlike Copley, they elected to return here, many of them strove to expand the range of native art beyond portraiture. It was in London, in Benjamin West's studio, that the first American attempts at the grand style originated—in West's own innovations and in his pupils'. From his studio, Charles Willson Peale came home to paint his invaluable record of the Revolution and its leaders. While less gifted than Copley, Peale retained all his life a primitive strength of character and form, and became the foremost continuer of the colonial tradition. It was under West's teaching that John Trumbull painted his Revolutionary battle scenes, still the finest American historical paintings in the grand style. On his return Trumbull tried to make a career of history painting, but America was not ready for this; our federal government had advanced little beyond the colonies in recognition of art, and by the time Trumbull finally secured commissions for his Capitol murals, his youthful fire was gone.

The same fate overtook others who attempted like subjects; John Vanderlyn, coming home from Paris with the aspiration to rival the school of David but ending as an embittered provincial face-painter; and Morse, returning with the ambition to "revive the splendor of the fifteenth century," but reconciling himself to painting portraits—among our best—and finally abandoning art for invention. But the case of Allston most fully demonstrates the problem of the imaginative artist in early nineteenth-century America. The most richly cultivated mind in our early art, he spent his young manhood in Italy in contact with antiquity and the Renaissance; then seven years in London, painting his finest works. Beneath their old-masterish stylisms they revealed a born romantic poet, a lover of wildness and solitude. But Allston's romanticism was controlled by his reverence for the old masters. His ambitious religious and allegorical compositions, though lacking the romantic emotion of his landscapes, were among the most impressive attempts in the Anglo-Saxon world to revive the Renaissance tradition. But after his return to America in middle age, his art showed a progressive loss of vitality. An artist who needed contact with great art, in America he found none, nor any colleagues or connoisseurs with anything like his knowledge. And he was incapable of drawing artistic nourishment from the raw material of America, as his more provincial successors of the Hudson River School did. For years he labored in vain to finish his huge compositions. The sentimental nostalgia for Italy that marked his later work was clearly a reaction to the artistic barrenness of his native land. His case was the reverse of Copley's: with the latter, inborn realistic power was lost in acquiring European sophistication, while with Allston, romantic emotion and great intentions were starved by separation from Europe—the response of two opposite temperaments to Europe's magnetism.

So ended the first noble attempts to found an American school of great subject matter, and one based on the great art of the European past.

Colonial limitations continued into the early decades of the nineteenth century. In the absence of governmental or ecclesiastical patronage, the chief support for art came from the upper middle class, which to a considerable extent determined its range. Well into the century, portraiture retained its predominance and produced its masters. In the seventeen-nineties Stuart had brought back from England a technical skill, a subtlety and vivacity of characterization and a ripeness of artistry beyond any predecessor's, which had a wide and permanent effect. After Stuart, only folk painters could remain innocent of the British portrait style. Until the mid-century, portraiture was the branch of American art marked by the most widely diffused professional skill, the greatest realistic strength, and on the whole the most substantial achievements. In spite of the deadly dullness of the run-of-the-mill product, the school included a surprising variety, from Ralph Earl, who went to England a primitive and came back a unique and captivating blend of naïveté and maturity, to the cosmopolitan elegance of Sully. In this heyday of American portraiture our artists achieved all degrees of balance between native character, often grim enough, and worldly sophistication. After the mid-century, artistic values declined, perhaps under competition from photography, until Eakins revived portraiture as major art.

When national taste began to broaden in the eighteen-twenties and eighteen-thirties it was not in the direction of the grand style but in more familiar fields. With the advent of Jacksonian democracy came a new kind of nationalist consciousness. Westward expansion brought a realization of the vast scale and natural wonders of the continent. Increasing wealth was producing an urban bourgeoisie whose interest in art, though limited, went beyond the perpetuation of their own and their families' faces. Artists began to turn to native subjects, particularly in landscape and genre.

Some landscape had been produced since early days, but by folk artists or as the occasional recreation of portraitists. The first definite school of landscape appeared in the eighteen-twenties—the Hudson River School. The man who can be called its founder was not native-born—Thomas Cole, born in England but spending his youth in the forests of Ohio. To his celebration of the as-yet-unspoiled American wilderness, Cole brought a romantic imagination, a love of solitude and grandeur, and a dramatic power that were equal to his great theme. Sometimes his Byronic fantasy led him from the sublime to the ridiculous; but he was the first to picture the face of America with the passion of a poet, and to capture the wild beauty of this continent as it was a century and a half ago. As his friend William Cullen Bryant wrote after his death: "I well remember what an enthusiasm was awakened by these early works of his—the delight which was expressed at the opportunity of contemplating pictures which carried the eye over scenes of wild grandeur peculiar to our country, over our aerial mountain-tops, with their mighty growth of forests never touched by the axe, along the banks of streams never deformed by culture, and into the depths of skies bright with the hues of our own climate; skies such as few but Cole could ever paint, and through the transparent abysses of which it seemed that you might send an arrow out of sight."

The Hudson River painters formed a consciously native school, the first in our art. They were tremendously proud of America's natural beauties, and though most of them visited Europe to paint its immemorial picturesqueness, their admiration for their own land remained undimmed. In all simplicity they believed that the nobler the subject, the nobler the picture would be, and that the way to express nature's beauty was to represent her faithfully, leaf by leaf. The Hudson River valley was only the beginning of their exploration of America; some of them pushed westward to paint Niagara Falls, the Rocky Mountains, and the Grand Canyon. Their grandiosity culminated in the huge canvases of Church and Bierstadt exploiting the natural marvels of the Western Hemisphere—the volcanoes of Mexico, the jungles of South America, the icebergs of Labrador—paintings phenomenal in their scale, spectacular content, and technical proficiency.

The artistic limitations of the school were obvious enough. Though contemporaries of the French romantics and the Barbizon painters, they showed no awareness of the new trends; their romanticism took the form of literal representation of romantic subjects rather than expression of romantic ideas and emotions in the language of art. In relation to the French school, their artistic concepts were anachronistic. But their direct contact with nature and skill of eye and hand had their own values. In their less pretentious pictures, and in the works of other native landscapists such as Lane and Heade, the character of our country, its spaciousness and solitude, the clearness of our air, the brilliance of our light, our high remote skies, were pictured truly and with a romantic emotion that is still alive. In Heade particularly, the sense of loneliness, of all-embracing light, of crystalline clarity, attained a penetrating poetry. Such artists deserve honor not only as pioneer visual explorers of our continent, but as our first nature poets.

The rise of genre painting was a product of the Jacksonian era's new sense of the importance of the common man. To the new generation, the everyday life of the American people did not seem too vulgar for art. Soon our painters were covering many facets of that life: the humors and recreations of the old-fashioned Yankee farm, the vigorous, lusty picturesqueness of the Mississippi River and its people, the hardy, adventurous existence of the western pioneers. But as was natural in a nation still largely agricultural, the favorite theme was eastern country life. The farm was still the background of a large part of the population; and to dwellers in the ugly American cities of the time, the genre painters offered an escape into a simpler, happier world. This nostaglia for the country was an essential element of the nineteenth-century American mind, as was the parallel nostalgia revealed in the many childhood scenes. The bourgeois, facing the new America of railroads and factories, looked back on the farm and childhood as a golden age.

Our genre painting was pervaded by an optimism and an extroversion that are characteristic of one side of the American temperament. The emphasis was on action, on sports and festivities, on the pleasant aspects of rural life. There was much humor, of a good-natured sort, without satire. Sex was invisible, except as Victorian sentiment. By European standards, our genre art was singularly innocent. Of our sprawling cities, of industrialization, even of the epic of railroad-building, there was hardly a trace in our painting. For such matters one must turn to the illustrators and printmakers, who furnished the most complete pictorial record of nineteenth-century America up to the coming of photography. As artists, the genre painters were as *retardataire* in their relation to their contemporaries Millet, Daumier, and Courbet as our landscapists. But the best of them had virtues that were independent of current trends and that have made their work last: Mount's fresh eye and deft hand, Blythe's rich caricatural madness, and Bingham's large ordered design and golden serenity.

So in the second quarter of the nineteenth century the greatest growth of American art was in the discovery of native subject matter rather than of new artistic concepts. Until the mid-century our artists showed no awareness of new trends in Europe. The French romantic movement had little effect: only the internationalist John La Farge was fully aware of it, but not until the eighteen-sixties. More influential was the Barbizon School, but even this reached us late. In the eighteen-fifties several Americans visited Barbizon, particularly Inness, who was deeply affected by Corot; and Hunt, who returned to these shores to spread the gospel of Millet. The Barbizon influence was a liberating one, from literal representation toward subjective expression and a more painterly style. Inness's evolution after his discovery of Corot was from the Hudson River viewpoint toward a new concept of landscape: instead of the cult of the wilderness, a preference for the pastoral and civilized; instead of grandiosity, a love of nature's intimate aspects; instead of nature as external phenomena, a sense of her as a being whose changing moods are shared by man. While still retaining his native fidelity to facts, he developed a broader, richer, more chromatic style, concentrating on light, atmosphere, color, and tonal values. The most vital and many-sided American landscapist of his period, Inness ultimately revolutionized our landscape painting. In his later work he carried the Barbizon viewpoint further, into a dark, romantic form of impressionism. In his case, an external influence had been assimilated and transformed into a vitalizing force. His and Hunt's examples marked the beginning of the end of literal romanticism, and the emergence of subjective romanticism.

The early work of Homer and Eakins was both a continuation of the older genre tradition and the beginning of something new—naturalism. More mature than their predecessors, they were stronger in their realism, wider in range, deeper in content. Homer's early country subjects were much like Mount's or Johnson's, but seen with a new freshness and boldness, and a grave idyllic poetry. His innocent eye, his direct recording of outdoor light and color, curiously parallel to his younger contemporaries the French impressionists but without any possible influence from them, made him an indigenous forerunner of impressionism. In maturity he became the greatest pictorial poet of outdoor America—the sea, the forest, the mountains, and the men who inhabited them. In his energy, the pristine freshness of his vision, and his simple sensuous vitality, he embodied the extrovert elements of the American spirit as no preceding artist had. His art was completely personal and native, with no discernible outside influences; while allied in a general way to impressionism, it always retained the integrity of the object instead of dissolving it in luminous atmosphere.

Eakins, with uncompromising realism, built his art out of the middle-class city life of America in the late nineteenth century. His early genre paintings revealed a reserved but intense attachment to his community combined with utter honesty —a strong, original mind dealing directly with realities. His interest in science allied him with one of the dominant forces of his time, and in his two great paintings of surgical clinics he attacked a theme seldom approached in modern art. But his naturalism was too drastic for the American art world. With his strong sense of form and his anatomical knowledge he seemed destined to be a great painter of the human body; but the prevailing prudery, together with his own intransigent realism, thwarted his development in this direction. In middle age he abandoned his essays in the American scene, and concentrated on portraiture. In his portraits, with their powerful character and psychological penetration, he made within the limits of his subject matter the most solid and revealing pictorial record of the America of his period. In their austere concentration on sculptural form they ran completely counter to the current trend toward outdoor light and illusionism. On the other hand, his few paintings in which the nude or semi-nude figure played the central role showed potentialities as a plastic designer that he never fully realized. This frustration was a repetition of what so many of his predecessors had suffered in attempting a freer content. Yet Eakins made a monumental contribution. He was our first mature artist to accept completely the realities of American life and out of them to create powerful art. One may look upon him as the fulfiller of the native realistic tradition which Copley had first brought to full expression but which he had failed to continue because of his final expatriation.

Much the same relation as Homer's and Eakins's to native realism was that of Albert Ryder to that other characteristic strain in the American mind, romanticism. While Ryder never painted a specifically "American" subject, except his early farm scenes, he was as typically American as Melville or Emily Dickinson. Like the latter, his art was a product of an intense inner life, little influenced from without by either the world around him or the art of others. In his work all the deadwood of his romantic predecessors was eliminated—the nostalgia for the Old World that had enfeebled Allston, the literalism that had encumbered the Hudson River painters. As Ryder himself said: "What avails a storm cloud accurate in form and color if the storm is not therein?" He concentrated on the inward reality of the mind's eye and out of this unconscious world brought forth the purest poetic imagery in our art. He used nature far more freely than any American of his time, making her obey the rhythms of his instinctive design. In freedom and originality of form he was one of the purest creators of the nineteenth century, here or abroad; and in the authenticity of his inner vision, a true if belated child of the great age of romanticism. At the same time he was prophetic of certain modern tendencies—freedom from literalism, plastic creation, and discovery of the unconscious mind. Thus the imaginative faculty which had been starved or misdirected in many of Ryder's predecessors first found full expression, in stranger form but with greater intensity.

Homer, Eakins, and Ryder, like the earlier landscape and genre painters, lived most of their years in America and built their art out of American life or the subjective life of the mind. They had little or no connection with current foreign movements—impressionism, neo-impressionism, post-impressionism—and in relation to them could be considered anachronistic. Yet they were among the foremost creators in our history. This anomaly illustrates forcibly certain peculiarities in the development of our art through the nineteenth century. Many of the strongest, most vital contributions had been made by native artists with no relation to advanced trends abroad. In comparison with these advanced trends, much of this native contribution was limited in artistic concepts and language. American art so far had been marked more by vigorous naturalistic representation or romantic personal expression than by creation in more purely artistic language or by innovations in basic artistic concepts. Such innovations had mostly originated abroad and been imported by artists more knowledgeable and impressionable, who might or might not be as creative. In these importations there had been time lags of a generation or more. Sometimes, especially in early years, these imported seeds had fallen on stony ground. Sometimes, and more frequently as the years passed, they had proved fruitful, if not always to the individual carriers, to the development of our art as a whole. For primitive and provincial virtues must in the long run give way to greater knowledge, to widening international contacts, to changing concepts. Thus the development of American art through the nineteenth century can be seen in terms of these two forces: native creativity, growing out of American life and the artist's personal life, often limited, literal, lacking in free emotional expression, deficient in artistry and imagination, but making its fundamental contribution; and international influences, contributing the leaven of knowledge, skill, and new concepts. Both forces were necessary, and through their interaction American art gradually matured and approached closer to world standards.

Had there, so far, been characteristics which could be called "American"? It seems clear that there had been. In the native naturalistic tradition represented by the colonial limners, Copley, the genre painters, Homer and Eakins, there had been common elements of adherence to facts, avoidance of subjective emotion, directness and simplicity of vision, clarity, solidity, and traditionalism. In the Hudson River School and similar native landscapists these same stylistic qualities had been applied to romantic subject matter. Among the subjective romanticists there had been corresponding common elements of dark color, subdued light, veiled outlines, the creation of a twilight world; but even they, with the exception of Ryder, had spoken in traditional language.

But while such common characteristics could be isolated, there was as yet no original artistic language which could be called unmistakably American. There was no "American School" in the sense that there had been Florentine, Venetian, and French schools. These historic schools had been based on old cultures still lacking here. In considering French art, one thinks of qualities that can be called characteristic and continuing—realism, clarity, order, elegance, a sense of form, a rational sensuousness—which appear equally in Jean Fouquet in the fifteenth century, Poussin in the seventeenth, and Ingres in the nineteenth. And French art developed organically, as witness its history from David to the present, its progressive discoveries and revolutions within overall relationships that link Corot, Manet, and Braque, or Delacroix, Renoir, and Matisse.

Little such organic development can be traced in American art through the nineteenth century. Not that there was none. Group relationships, conscious or unconscious, can be seen—in portraiture, the limners, Feke, Copley, the Peales, Earl, Neagle, Eakins; in landscape, Cole, Durand, Kensett, Cropsey, Heade, Inness, Martin; in genre, Mount, Bingham, Johnson, Homer, Eakins; in still life, Raphaelle Peale, Harnett, Peto; in subjective romanticism, Allston, Page, Fuller, Newman, Ryder, Blakelock. And there was growth. Homer could be thought of as a more mature Mount, Eakins as a more profound Copley, Ryder as a more creative Allston.

But these lines of development were not in fundamental artistic concepts so much as in subject matter, viewpoints, and styles. In France the major figures were innovators, building on their predecessors but creating new concepts. Our major figures made no such basic innovations; their advances over their predecessors were more limited in scope, and continually superseded by more radical developments from abroad. Hence our artists had no strong influence on the following generation; they founded no schools. Compared to the Europeans they were isolated figures, with little direct connection with their own predecessors or successors. So while in France Renoir could look back to Delacroix, and Matisse to Renoir, in our country Inness looked back to Cole only in his youth, and in maturity turned to Corot. This was inevitable in an art as relatively young as ours, as much in process of learning. Let us recall that when France was producing Fragonard, we had advanced little beyond the provincial limners, and that even today our primitives go back only two centuries, those of France five centuries.

The end of the Civil War introduced a new era of material expansion, with increasing wealth, leisure, cosmopolitanism, and awareness of art. The new millionaires began their cultural pillage of Europe. Museums, art schools, and art magazines sprang into being. Women flocked to the art schools as never before, and while only a small minority persevered past matrimony, the feminine influence in our art world became more dominant than in any other nation. For artists, European study became *de rigueur,* with Paris now the center. Growing internationalism was shown in the fact that three leading Americans of the period, Whistler, Sargent, and Cassatt, expatriated themselves.

On the other hand, a typical time-lag occurred in the arrival in America of French impressionism. Although Mary Cassatt was a member of the Paris group from 1879 on, the movement had little direct effect over here until the late eighteen-eighties, through Robinson, Twachtman, Weir, and Hassam. Transplanted to our shores, impressionism was modified by native naturalism and sentiment to produce a variation that was distinctively American. Our impressionists were men of refinement rather than power, their contribution a pleasant lyricism which in Twachtman attained a delicate visual music. But impressionism's indirect influence was the widest of any European movement to date. Its emphasis on the outdoors, its love of sunlight and the smiling aspects of nature, its paganism, met a response in the optimism and idyllic side of the American temperament, especially to a generation enjoying a new freedom in outdoor life, sports, summer vacations, and country living.

By the turn of the century, the American art world had become predominantly academic. The generation of Homer, Eakins, and Ryder was old. The new generation's foreign study was mostly in the conservative schools of Paris, where its artists encountered no movements later than impressionism. Returning home, they combined American idealism with impressionism, Whistlerian refinement, and Sargent's brushwork, to produce an academic art which in its way was unmistakably and deplorably "American." Its chief features were idealism in subject and viewpoint, photographic naturalism, and manual dexterity. These were the days of the glorification of the American woman, pictured in every role and setting, but always decorative, leisured, and virtuous. With all its preoccupation with the feminine, this art was strangely sexless. At its best it achieved a zestful freshness with Chase, a wholesome, virginal vigor with Thayer, and an ethereal refinement with Dewing. But by and large its content was a tasteful vacuum. Focusing on gentility, it ignored the broader realities of American life. The city was seldom pictured, and then only Fifth Avenue. There was of course no social satire, or indeed any trace of humor. The landscapists selected the idyllic in nature, shunning factories and railroads and all such features that give the face of modern America its character. This academic art, in spite of its cosmopolitan veneer, was as provincial as the nineteenth-century genre school, but without its raciness.

This was the golden age of the Beaux-Arts architect and his colleagues, the Beaux-Arts muralist and sculptor. Under pressure of growing national wealth and ostentation, and the glittering example of the Chicago World's Fair of 1893, the federal, state, and municipal governments became large-scale art patrons. Almost all this new public art was academic. In murals, irreproachable ideals were embodied in pseudo-classic symbology, with nice American girls masquerading as the civic virtues. Avoiding the realities of modern America, this art was based on no vital beliefs or ideas. The result was some of the most frigid mural painting the world has ever seen.

Our sculptors in general did better. Since painting has more private uses, our leading painters produced for private clients, whereas the sculptors gravitated to public art. By the physical nature of their medium they were forced to think of substance, in a day when academic painters were pursuing illusionism; and substance involved relations to architecture and setting. Our public sculpture shared some of the defects of mural painting, and produced its real horrors, equal to the worst French Beaux-Arts work; but it also produced Saint-Gaudens, who combined idealism with vigorous naturalism and a genuine sense of the monumental, to create the finest American public art of his period.

About 1905 the academic calm was invaded by the group of young realist painters centering around Henri. Rebelling against sweetness and light, they turned to the teeming life of the modern city, which they loved as their nineteenth-century predecessors had loved the country. Their broad humor, social conscience, and feeling for the urban masses were new notes in our painting. In conscious reaction against impressionism they turned to the dark realism of Velázquez, Goya, and Daumier. Their radicalism lay not in their style, at first no more advanced than Manet's pre-impressionist phase of forty years earlier, but in their subjects and viewpoint. They broke down academic idealism and inaugurated a more robust interest in contemporary American life. All later art concerned with the American scene stemmed from their iconoclasm.

Almost simultaneously the European modern movements began to reach this country. American artists abroad had played a part in their beginnings. In the eighteen-nineties Prendergast had seen Cézanne's work in France and became his first American champion. From 1900 to 1906 a number of young Americans in Paris became converts of post-impressionism and fauvism: among others, Maurer, Karfiol, Halpert, Sterne, Weber, and Walkowitz. After 1906 their numbers increased. Never before had so many Americans been involved so early in European movements.

The United States to which these young men began to return about 1908 was building its early skyscrapers, but its technology was far in advance of its art. American dynamism was expressed by Parisian cubism and Italian futurism, but not by our established schools. The modernists had to struggle against academic domination for years. But the outcome was inevitable, thanks to the doughty help of the Henri group, the pioneer showmanship of Alfred Stieglitz, and the Armory Show in 1913.

Modernism was the most radical interruption so far to the provincial tendencies of our art. It reached us much earlier than any previous movement; where the Barbizon School had taken more than a generation, and impressionism almost twenty years, the various modern movements arrived within a few years after they were born—in some cases immediately, at Stieglitz's Fifth Avenue gallery. Within eight years of the birth of fauvism and five of that of cubism, the Armory Show presented a full panorama of the new movements to an outraged but curious public. With modernism, American art entered the mainstream of world art.

As they developed in this country the modern movements were marked by few radical American innovations. In Europe the innovators believed that the possibilities of representational art had been exhausted and that the only path was a search for a new visual language. But our art was far from having reached this stage; compared to the academy even Cézanne seemed revolutionary. So the fundamental changes continued to come from abroad; but they came more quickly—brought by artists who were themselves participants—and they were assimilated more rapidly.

There was less experimentation with basic form than in Europe. Cubism had a few exponents, but they tended toward expressionistic more than structural values. With its most inventive representative, Weber in his work from 1913 to 1917, color and free forms replaced the monochromatic geometry of cubism. But cubism had a much wider influence than its actual practice. Its severe concentration on form, its precision, its respect for the picture plane, affected artists who did not accept its degree of abstraction. The immaculate forms of Demuth, Sheeler, Dickinson, and O'Keeffe owed much to cubism. But they also expressed, for the first time in our art, the typically American predilection for machine-age technology and its precise perfection. Beyond these immediate effects, cubism helped our painting to throw off impressionist vagueness and return to the clarity that had characterized so much of our earlier art. And on a broader scale, cubism and its related movements had a wide influence on design in all fields.

Abstract art received a strong impetus from the Armory Show, and many early modernists experimented with it. But most of them returned after a few years to more representational styles, and by about 1925 this first wave of abstraction had passed, except for a few individuals. It had not been, as in Europe, the product of long historical evolution, and our art world was not yet ready for so extreme a departure from representation. More nativist trends intervened—the American scene and social-content schools. For more than a decade, advanced styles were much less practiced here than abroad. Not until the middle nineteen-thirties did the second wave of abstraction begin to gather force.

Futurism, not represented in the Armory Show, had few exponents aside from Stella, although one would have expected its doctrines of dynamism and speed to appeal to Americans. Neither dada nor surrealism found much of an echo here; it was in Paris that an American, Man Ray, played a significant part in them. But in time surrealism's exploration of the unconscious mind had a wide effect on artists who were not orthodox surrealists, freeing them from external realism in subject matter and releasing new elements of fantasy and free imagery.

By far the most widespread form of modernism in America from the Armory Show to World War II was expressionism. Expressionism is a broad word with ill-defined boundaries, but the only one to cover the myriad varieties of art which are not predominantly realistic on the one hand nor abstract on the other, and whose common element is the expression of emotions related in some degree to the real world. Expressionism's wide prevalence in this country can be linked to certain historic factors: the continuing tradition of romanticism in the American mind; our partiality for art which embodies emotions arising from specific realities; our preference for free personal expression as against formalism; and the increasingly important role played in our art by certain national and racial elements, especially German, Russian, and Jewish, particularly sympathetic to free emotional expression.

All these varieties of modernism were international. But in the mid-nineteen-twenties, partly in reaction against modernism, came a wave of nationalism, a conscious rediscovery and exploration of America, still an untouched continent for most twentieth-century American artists. This paralleled the literary explorations of Dreiser, Sherwood Anderson, Sinclair Lewis, Faulkner, and Wolfe. Regionalists such as Benton, Wood, and Curry returned to the rural Midwest and South, and immersed themselves in their people, landscape, and folkways. Articulate champions of native values, they celebrated the flavor and old-fashioned virtues of what they considered the heartland of America. At the same time, eastern painters of the American scene such as Hopper, Burchfield, and Marsh pictured the city and small town with a more drastic realism, a full acceptance of the ugly aspects of our country, but also with a deep emotional attachment. Their portrait of the city, compared with the good-humored gusto of the Henri group, revealed its elements of vulgarity, monotony, and human misery—new notes of pessimism and satire. Their version of the American landscape included all those characteristic and often grotesque man-made features shunned by their tender-minded predecessors the impressionists. In the work of such artists, aspects of the United States never touched before were assimilated into art. In a general sense, the American scene painters were a continuation of the interrupted tradition of nineteenth-century genre; but with little conscious influence, and with greater maturity, realism, and emotional depth.

The Depression of the nineteen-thirties, the rise of fascism, and increasing world tensions brought to artists as to everyone else a new realization of the ills of our times. A surge of social-protest art, ranging ideologically from socialist idealism to party-line conformity, swept the country, producing the first full-scale pictorial attack on our social system. This school dominated the art world of the mid-nineteen-thirties; in no other nation did artists say so frankly, loudly, and persistently what was wrong with their country. And many of them did so while on the federal payroll—an example of democratic freedom of expression unique in modern history. It is noteworthy that for the first time there appeared an influence from Latin America—in this case Mexico, through Rivera and Orozco.

Regionalism with its accompanying chauvinism and isolationism could not survive in the modern world; and as for the social-protest school, world events after 1939 rendered its message obsolete. They were replaced as dominant movements by the trend toward abstract art. But the American scene and social schools together achieved the most far-reaching visual exploration and evaluation of our civilization to date, and made an enormous contribution to our national self-knowledge. While the mass of their work is now of interest mainly as ideological history, the best of it ranks among the most vital achievements of American art, and I believe it will be more highly valued in the future than at present. Social content and the American scene are still important ingredients of present-day art, and individual exponents such as Hopper, Shahn, Evergood, and Levine are among our strongest figures. Not to mention the whole pop movement, which is as completely based on the American scene, although it speaks in a radically different artistic language.

In the mid-nineteen-thirties began a second abstract movement, which by the nineteen-forties had become the dominant trend in American art. Nationalism was giving way to internationalism, in art as in politics. In Europe, abstraction had never been eclipsed; it had grown and diversified, producing innumerable new concepts and masters. It was reaching the United States increasingly, not only in exhibitions and publications, but in the arrival of leading Europeans such as Hofmann, Albers, Moholy-Nagy, and Glarner, who made their homes here and greatly enriched our art. Aside from these influences from abroad, a younger generation of Americans had been exposed to the abstract creed and converted to it.

The word abstraction, like expressionism, covers a multitude of concepts and styles. In the early and mid-nineteen-thirties, the prevailing mode was geometric and precise, influenced to some extent by the leaders of the Bauhaus who had settled here after it was closed by the Nazis in 1933. But also, and perhaps more fundamentally, geometric abstraction was an expression of that side of the American mind that had produced precisionism—our involvement with the machine age. In those early years it seemed that a characteristically American variation of precise abstraction was in the making.

But at the same time appeared an opposite tendency: free-form abstraction. While owing debts to early Kandinsky and the "Blaue Reiter," and to Picasso, Miró, and the surrealists, free-form abstraction also stemmed from American expressionism in its subjectivity and instinctivism, its freedom and fluidity, and in the leading role it gave to color and to the direct sensuous impact of physical materials. Just as expressionism had prevailed over other tendencies of early modernism, free-form abstraction overwhelmed its geometric rival and dominated the American art scene of the nineteen-forties and nineteen-fifties.

The free-form abstractionists carried the revolt against tradition much further than had the early pioneers of modernism. They abandoned centralized composition in favor of open design, stressing space and movement. Forms were simplified to a few elements of extreme power. Sometimes there were no central elements at all, only space pervaded by colored light, as with Rothko, or filled with a network of vibrating lines, as with Tobey. With many artists, planned designing was superseded by purely instinctive methods, in which the physical action of painting determined the final forms. Conventional brushwork gave way to all kinds of revolutionary techniques, such as Jackson Pollock's method of pouring the pigment.

Even more radical innovations occurred in sculpture. With a few exceptions, American sculpture had been much less affected by modernism than our painting. But with the nineteen-forties all this was changed. Monumentality was replaced by open, fluid forms. Instead of resting on a pedestal, a piece of sculpture was as likely to be suspended. All kinds of new materials were adopted, as were new technical methods of shaping them, such as welding. An art that for centuries had been completely static took on physical motion, first with Calder's mobiles in the nineteen-thirties—a major break with sculptural tradition—then with an increasing number of kinetic sculptors. Color, long absent in sculpture, became an essential element. Light played a new role, not only in constructions designed primarily to catch light, like those of Gabo and Lippold, but in designs of moving colored light.

Compared to the pioneer abstract movement of 1913 to 1925, the second abstract movement was much more independent of European sources. There had been ample time for the principles of abstraction to become acclimatized, and for a whole generation to reach maturity within the abstract idiom. In these new art forms, in which traditional values were at a minimum and personal creativeness was the chief factor, Americans were more on a par with their European colleagues than in any preceding period. Compared to their modernist predecessors, these artists were conducting a more fundamental exploration of the physical and sensuous sources of art, and were producing bolder and more basic innovations. In their discarding of traditions and their drive to rebuild art from the ground up, they could be considered as a new manifestation of the indigenous and primitive forces that had been so strong in American art from the first. They were standing on their own feet more than any previous advanced school in this country. With the exception of the surviving pioneers of European modernism, they did not look to the current leaders abroad with the reverence that their predecessors had for the fauves and cubists. On the other hand, the new American school was the first to receive substantial recognition in Europe—a startling reversal of the international balance of art.

The decade of the nineteen-sixties has brought new developments, some as outgrowths of abstraction, some as reactions against it. In pure abstraction, optical art has used scientific principles to create dazzling visual effects in color and line, achieving a renaissance in the chromatic field. In reaction against the relative amorphousness of free-form abstraction, there has been a return to the logical planning and precision of geometric abstraction, but on a larger scale and with greater physical power than in the geometric abstraction of the nineteen-thirties. In sculpture, this tendency has produced primary structure: massive simplified forms, purely geometrical, constructed of sheet metal, plywood, or synthetic materials, frequently machine-fabricated, and often using strong primary colors. Here we see the American affinity with machine technology reaching its fullest expression so far.

Op and primary structure are developments within the abstract field. But other innovating tendencies are diametrically opposed to abstraction: in particular, pop art, or the new American realism. Where abstract art in its concentration on purely artistic values disregarded the external world and the actualities of present-day America, pop art uses the most common, banal features of daily life in the United States—comic strips, billboards, soft drinks, canned goods—to produce an art that is at once a devastating commentary on our mass culture, both bitter and funny, and the creation out of it of a new kind of artistic order. Like the regionalists and the American-scene school of the nineteen-twenties and the nineteen-thirties, the pop artists' attitude toward their native environment is ambivalent—a mixture of ridicule and fascination. The omnipresent, inescapable jungle of mass-produced things and slogans in which we Americans live is to them a treasure-house of raw material for art. Their inventive use of actual objects is producing a further revolution in the physical language of art. Whatever its ultimate value, pop in its own way is the most indigenous recent artistic embodiment of certain aspects of the United States.

The American art world today is probably the most diverse of any nation. The successive revolutions of the twentieth century, occurring in an artistic community that was conservative at the beginning of the century, have resulted in the phenomenon of an advance guard, a rear guard, and a middle guard all coexisting. Some of our strongest figures, like their nineteenth-century predecessors, have remained relatively little affected by changing movements. In spite of the current predominance of advanced trends, an interesting feature of American art today is the number and strength of representational artists. I do not mean academicians, who still cling to nineteenth-century viewpoints, but nonacademic artists who speak in more or less representational language. These believe that there need be no conflict between representation of reality and the creation of design, any more than there was in great art of the past.

In spite of this variety of contemporary American art, some generalizations are possible. The American art world is primarily individualistic; our art is produced for private collectors, museums, and the art public, with a minimum of governmental patronage or control. Whatever vital public art exists is mostly for business and industry. Although, as in any democracy, there is a tendency for artists to gather in schools, one of the outstanding characteristics of American art today is its individualism.

Our art has few deep roots in its own past. While some of our artists may consider certain native ancestors especially sympathetic (to Pollock, Ryder; to Hopper, Eakins), for the greater tradition they look to Europe, the Orient, or primitive cultures. Relationships to the American past are largely unconscious.

While it is still a question whether we have made basic innovations in artistic concepts equal to those of the European masters of modern art, there can be little doubt that in recent years we have begun to create concepts and forms that are original and vital, and totally independent of European example. Whether these innovations will stand the test of time is as problematical as ultimate value judgments applied to the contemporary art of any country. But to express a purely personal opinion, I believe that no other nation has more general artistic vitality, has produced more innovations, and shows more promise for the future—whatever that may bring.

To return to the original question: what qualities of our contemporary art can be called characteristically American? Obviously, those artists who devote themselves to the contemporary American scene, interpreted either naturalistically, semi-abstractly, or in the physical language of pop art, are expressing ideas and emotions that are peculiar to the United States, its life and people and culture. Their art ranges from Hopper's stark naturalism with its undertone of intense emotion, through Shahn's and Levine's biting, imaginative comment on our society, to the pop artists' obsessive love/hate.

But artists speaking in more abstract or semi-abstract language reveal equally "American" characteristics. In the recent past, we have had (to name only a few) John Marin's lyrics of New York and the Maine coast, as pure an expression of sensibility to our earth and air as the poetry of Walt Whitman or the painting of Winslow Homer; Max Weber's intense expression of the Jewish element in American life; Stuart Davis's powerful designs based on purely American themes, embodied in form and color that are as native as jazz; Alexander Calder's inventiveness in bringing motion into a hitherto static art; David Smith's creative use of machine-made forms; Jackson Pollock's revolutionary development of new techniques to produce the utmost physical immediacy. The combination of individual expression, technical inventiveness, and vital energy in these artists seems to define some qualities characteristically American.

Even the most purely abstract art of the past twenty years appears to me to embody essential aspects of the American spirit. Its return to primary physical sensation has parallels in many fields of our life. The artists' emphasis on creation as action is analogous to the free improvisations of jazz. Their open compositions, their sense of space, their largeness of forms, reflect the space and openness of America. Even the big scale of their works suggests the bigness of our land.

All these varied qualities seem as clearly products of our culture as the simpler virtues of our nineteenth-century art. As to any "American" common denominators, any quality or unified group of qualities underlying all, I do not believe that, if they exist, they can be isolated and identified by us who are so close to contemporary creation. The nearest that we can get to any such definition is that there are many diverse qualities that can be called characteristically American. Ours is a pluralistic art, the expression of a democratic society, which in spite of its standardization in material ways, mass-produced products, and mass communication, still allows freedom for wide-ranging individualism in artistic creation.

Foreword: Self-Portrait of the Artist

One has a right to be suspicious of self-portraits; they are often the image the artist would like to flaunt and are therefore flattering, or they are sometimes what the artist is afraid he might be and are thereby pejorative. But there is one quality about the self-portrait that is almost universal: the artist is looking himself straight in the eye and consequently straight at the man before his picture, whoever he may be. What follows here in this culling from the Archives of American Art is a composite self-portrait, a multiple image, contradictory in some respects but nonetheless a straight-in-the-eye and illuminating portrait of the American artist. He is set against a shifting landscape with many vanishing points and in the context of a rapidly expanding nation, and he is surrounded by a host of patrons who vary greatly in their degrees of sophistication and Philistinism and devotion.

At first the artist in America suffered the simplest but the most annoying of all irritations and frustrations. He had readily at hand no decent tools with which to work, and it took months to get them from Europe; even then he had to rely on the judgment of friends, as you will see that John Smibert had to. But there was another deprivation that was equally frustrating. There were no great paintings by the masters to look at, to base one's style upon, to study for subtleties; the best the artist could lay his hands on were engravings, tight little copies of works of great scale and bravura. They were a poor substitute, and they drove generations of American painters to take the long, slow, storm-tossed passage to Europe.

But these were not the painter's only frustrations. He found his compatriots prudish. Long before Thomas Eakins encountered the citizens of Philadelphia who caused his resignation from the Academy, the Sketch Club, and the Academy Art Club because he insisted on using nude models in his classes, another Philadelphia artist had encountered a similar situation. Art students, including young men, walked out on Charles Willson Peale, the founder of the Academy, because they found his insistence on nude models "indecent." When Peale borrowed a copy of the Venus de Medici from an English artist he was required to keep it locked up, and he showed it clandestinely to only a few close friends.

Prudery, however, was a minor enemy. "The tide of utility sets against the fine arts," Thomas Cole wrote in 1838. (He had less to complain about, so far as popular recognition goes, than almost any other American artist.) Materialism and industrialization seemed to walk hand in hand with Philistinism. When the sculptor Horatio Greenough came back from studying in Italy, he blamed the universal Philistinism he found in America on egalitarianism. "You are in a country," he wrote to James Fenimore Cooper, "in which every man swaggers and talks, knowledge or no knowledge, brains or no brains, taste or no taste. They are all *ex nato* connoisseurs, politicians, religionists, and every man's equal and all men's betters."

It is characteristic of an egalitarian society that everyone has an opinion about art, "taste or no taste"; critics are more likely to distrust this state of affairs than artists. One finds little hostility to everyman's taste in the following pages, although "respectable" opinion and the official opinions of academies are causes of sporadic aggravation in the nineteenth century and continual irritation in the twentieth.

Indeed, there is more hostility among artists than between artists and their patrons, real and potential. Robert Henri, when he said in the first decade of this century, "To hell with the artistic values," was only a few years later the target of those who wanted to upset the apple cart (or ash can)—the young men who perpetrated the Armory Show in 1913. They not only blew out the candle of The Eight but also blew out the gradually rising reputation of American painting and handed the art market over for about five decades to the European artists.

Until very recently Europe had always been a threat and a magnet to the American artist. Few of our artists have been chauvinists but almost every American artist in the last century and during most of this one wanted to get to Europe to study. How else could he see the great masters? Or study with the great teachers? Our early painters went to Rome and London, some to stay indefinitely; our sculptors went to Rome, and our architects wandered the whole European continent. The echoes of Europe are all through the comments of the artists and their friends in this self-portrait until the most recent entries, which reflect the fact that the art world has become truly international and that the winds of invention (and taste) blow as much from the west to east as they used to from London and Paris and Rome.

In reading the statements of the artists and their patrons which follow, one cannot but be impressed at how the tone of voice of the American artist changes, how much more socially conscious and philosophical it becomes, how much less worried the artist is about his craft and how much more worried he is about the nature of his art. He concerns himself less with pleasing his patron and more about pleasing his critics (granted that there were few serious nineteenth-century critics of painting and sculpture in America). In the nineteen-thirties he rode on a wave of social reform which gave way in the nineteen-forties to a concern with abstraction ("The human gesture and the human figure is very limiting in its possibilities," a sculptor is quoted as saying) and a concern with controlled accident. This in turn gave way to ". . . a whole new generation of young people . . . who were not second-string abstract expressionists, who were not anything, who were working in new materials and . . . new forms."

Fortunately, the self-portrait of the American artist constantly changes. It is a face that combines gravity with humor, style with insouciance, elegance with humanism, and inventiveness with daring.

I Origins of Native American Art

If the history of colonial America were recorded only in its paintings, the first one hundred and fifty years of English settlement would be seen today as a time of gentility dominated by divines, merchants, sea captains, officials, and pampered wives and children. The difficulties of existence and the struggle to carve out and preserve from the wilderness a replica of English society would be unknown. Only the replica itself is evident in many portraits.

We are often assured that until late in the eighteenth century Americans had no interest in art, no money to spend on it, and no technical skills to produce it. Yet thousands of portraits were painted here before the Revolution, more than four hundred of them during the seventeenth century alone. Most exhibit the technical ignorance and unsophisticated vision common to untrained painters, but this very scarcity of talent tells us something about life in the colonies. What artist of high attainment would be attracted to a harsh wilderness? John Smibert (1688–1751), the first well-trained painter in New England, arrived in Boston over one hundred years after the Pilgrims landed. Even he left the comforts of London in 1728 only because Dean George Berkeley of Dublin persuaded him to join the faculty of a projected university in the New World.

A few of the many early portraits of prosperous men and their families do exhibit remarkable strength. One thinks of Captain Thomas Smith's self-portrait, of an unknown painter's "Mrs. Freake and Baby Mary," of an equally unknown artist's characterization of Ann Pollard, a colonial crone who claimed to be over one hundred years old. Pioneer professionals such as Smibert and the native-born painters, Robert Feke (about 1705–1750) of Long Island and Joseph Badger (1708–1765) of Boston, paved the way for powerful younger men such as John Singleton Copley (1738–1815), Ralph Earl (1751–1801), and Gilbert Stuart (1755–1828). A sense of the continuity felt by the eighteenth-century American artists is gathered from the story of the time Charles Willson Peale (1741–1827) visited Smibert's studio and heard there of the brilliant young Copley.

In the period just preceding the Revolution, portrait painting rose from a moderately skilled level to a soaring height of professional competence. Copley, the outstanding genius of the colonial era, created a style which made him the leader of a developing school of portraiture. He knew that a generation dedicated to the ideals of liberty and equality could hardly be painted in the manner of Gainsborough's elegant courtiers. Men such as Paul Revere deserved likenesses which revealed personal character. Copley's realistic approach and skill as a draftsman encouraged younger men such as Stuart and John Trumbull (1756–1843) of Connecticut to break away from the stylized conventions of earlier colonial portraiture.

Of all the talented artists who came to maturity in the turbulent seventeen-sixties and seventeen-seventies, the most successful and influential was Benjamin West (1738–1820), who moved to London from Pennsylvania at the age of twenty-five. West soon attracted the attention of the powerful Archbishop of York, became court painter to George III, and served for twenty-eight years as president of the Royal Academy. His scenes from British history startled the public because of their verisimilitude in such things as dress and their avoidance of classical staging. His example and his generosity were an inspiration to two generations of Americans who studied under him in London.

Matthew Pratt (1734–1805), who accompanied West's fiancée to London in 1764, was among the first of these students. In 1765 he painted West instructing his American protegés, a scene which would be repeated in West's studio over the next fifty years. Despite West's warm friendship with the King, the artist took great pride in the accomplishments of the American revolutionaries. In 1775 Copley also settled permanently in London. Charles Willson Peale, three years younger than both Copley and West, studied under the latter but returned to the colonies, where he served as an officer in the Continental Army and painted portraits of military and political figures prominent in the new republic.

Gilbert Stuart, famous today for his oils of Washington, was the best of the post-Revolution portrait painters. He, too, studied abroad under West, and after a prosperous, gay, and eventually debt-ridden career in London and Dublin studios and taverns, returned to America in 1792. His portraits, unadorned by details of costume or background, are often penetrating character studies. John Trumbull learned historical painting from West and hoped to apply his knowledge to an official series of Revolutionary scenes. Trumbull's "Signing of the Declaration of Independence" and a few battle pictures were successful efforts, but an arrogant manner and declining artistic powers combined together to destroy his reputation toward the end of his life.

A few gifted artists of the Federal period also tried to bring historical painting to America. Washington Allston (1779–1843) produced romantic landscapes in Italian settings. He never entirely finished his enormous "Belshazzar's Feast," which he had hoped would be his great masterwork, and his smaller paintings were not accepted by the public beyond a small circle of admirers. John Vanderlyn (1775–1852) painted Greek mythological scenes whose European flavor found little sympathy among his compatriots. Samuel F. B. Morse (1791–1872), profoundly discouraged by what he regarded as the inadequate taste of Americans for historical painting, was obliged to produce portraits before turning to the telegraph. Rembrandt Peale (1778–1860), who like his father was a student under West, enjoyed a popular success with his melodramatic "Court of Death," but his reputation, too, was based chiefly on his portraits.

The melancholy and other-worldly canvases painted by Allston had little relation to a fixed environment. A native landscape art, soon to become the major school of American painting, was in an incipient stage in the Federal period. Although we know that some scenes had been painted by Smibert, if not by earlier figures, the style was completely overshadowed by portrait and historical art prior to 1825. Ralph Earl was the first important painter to turn to local settings with professional skill and a feeling for the American scene. The early work of Thomas Doughty (1793–1856) was an advance, and it provided an important inspiration to the founder of the Hudson River School, Thomas Cole (1801–1848).

The continuing vigor of portrait art followed an established colonial tradition. Efforts to create historical and classical art in the New World failed. The time was ripe by the eighteen-twenties for a new perception of American nature.

"Westward the course of empire takes its way;
The four first acts already past,
A fifth shall close the drama with the day;
Time's noblest offspring is the last."

Dean George Berkeley's famous lines from his poem, "On the Prospect of Planting Arts and Learning in America," look prophetically toward a brilliant future for the New World. It seems appropriate that America's first well-trained artist, John Smibert, should have come to New England in Berkeley's entourage. Berkeley returned to England in 1731, but Smibert stayed on to paint portraits of Massachusetts Bay Colony settlers and even did a few "Landskips" (landscapes), which are now unfortunately lost.

Writing from Boston on July 1, 1743, to Arthur Pond, his agent in London, Smibert listed his needs as the owner of a shop and his hopes as an artist. His letter indicates how dependent the colonial painter was on a source of supply:

John Smibert, a Scots painter who came to the Colonies in 1729, at 41, got his art training in London and Italy. His copies of European old masters became an inspiration and education to budding New England portrait artists. His self-portrait is a detail from Dean Berkeley and His Entourage (see p. 33), which Smibert painted after landing in Newport with Berkeley, a British philosopher-theologian whose never-executed purpose in coming to America was to start a university in the Bermudas.

. . . I have for a long time intended to send for ye pictures &c which my Nephew left with you, but delayed on act. of the war, which as there is no apearance of being over thinks it now best to have them over here again, for as you long ago wrote me you had sold none of them, nor thought it likely you should. I am in hopes I shal make something of them here so desires you wil order them to be carefully packed up in a god case & sent by the first opportunity for this Port & insure on the Virtu Cargo for £ 150. I must further trouble you to buy me 3 doz 3/4 Cloaths strained, & two whole Length Cloaths which pray order to be good & carefully rolled up & put in a case. Fann Paper ten Reams this is an article which we shal probably want considerable of so would desire you to write ye mans name you buy it of & where he lives that we may send to him directly without troubling you again. There are many women that paints fanns for the country use and as they buy the Collours of us the paper has of late come naturaly in to be an article in the shop let it be of the sort comonly used for cheap fanns & should be glad ye man would send a sheet or two of the different sorts of paper with ye prices. lake of the comon midling sort about two Guineas, and of good lake about two Guineas more. Prussian Bleu 50 l @ 2 shillings per pound. Do 6 l @ 20 shill. or a Guinea per pound. Do 6 l @ 18 shill. per pound. That may be had cheapest of ye maker Mr. Mitchell at Hoxton who you may send to by a peny post letter or a Porter. The old Cups & spoons are a Comision from my Wife who desires you wil be so good as to get her a Silver Teapott of the midle Size

As the self-portrait above, painted about 1760 and now in the collection of the H. F. du Pont Winterthur Museum, Winterthur, Delaware, suggests, John Singleton Copley created the most convincing portraits of the American 18th century. One such is that of Thomas Mifflin and Sarah (Morris) Mifflin, at left, an oil on bedticking, which Copley painted in 1773. It is now owned by the Historical Society of Pennsylvania, in Philadelphia. On the eve of the Revolution, at age 36, Copley left for Europe to escape the limitation of doing only portraiture. Settling in England, he produced a series of dramatic narrative pictures. The receipt shown acknowledges the payment, in 1782, by London engraver John Boydell of a balance still due Copley, who was paid £800 for his The Death of Major Pearson.

Recd Augst 17.1782 of Mr Boydell One
hundred & sixty four pounds five
shillings being the remainder of Eight
hundred pounds and in full for Painting
a Picture of the Death of Major Pearson
J.S. Copley

Charles Willson Peale's usual style when doing portraits of Revolutionary heroes was severely simple, but here, in The Staircase Group, he painted two of his artist-sons, Raphaelle and Titian, in life-size trompe l'oeil. Completed in 1795, it was first exhibited—with a wooden step projecting below the painted stairs—at the Columbianum Exhibition in 1795, where, legend says, the lifelike illusion caused President Washington to bow to the figures. Today it is in the collection of the Philadelphia Museum of Art.

but rather inclining to ye large & weighty ye fashion, she leaves entirely to you only would not have the top with hinges, but to take of. I have sent a sketch of ye arms which I know you wil take care to get done by a good engraver with proper Ornaments. I do not expect the old silver wil pay for the teapott which I would have a pretty one. What remains of ye money after paying for those articles and al charges . . . to lay out in gold leaf.

I am sory the state of ye Virtu is at so low an ebb, if the arts are about to leave Great Britain I wish they may take their flight into our New World that they may at least remain in some part of the British Dominions. remember me to al my old friends among ye painters. I would wilingly have acknowledged your favors by something from this Country but can think of nothing worth sending that is our own produce. amongst ye pictures with you my Nephew tells me he thinks you used to like ye Venus Nymphs &c by Poolenburgh, be so good as to accept of that picture to remember me by or any other of the pictures you like except ye Scipio, & if there be any of ye drawings that you fancy pray take them. when you write me let me know the state of Painting, who makes a figure, & what eminent ones are gone of ye stage. as for myself I have as much as keeps me employed, has my health better then I could have expected, having near 3 years ago recovered from a dangerous ilnes. but thank God has had no return of it. I am happy in 4 clever Boys & lives as easily as my friend could wish me, ye affairs of ye shop with my Nephew goes on well, he Joins me in respects to your Father & to Mess^s: Knaptons. I shal not make any further appologys for the trouble now given you only asures you, I wil not try your patience every year but only now & then.

During and after the Revolutionary period Americans were highly conscious of their new national responsibilities. Their views on the fine arts were colored by a sense of the need to achieve utilitarian successes. John Adams expressed this attitude perfectly in a letter to his wife in 1780:

Is it possible to enlist the *fine arts* on the side of truth, or virtue, or piety, or even honor? From the dawn of history they have been prostituted to the service of superstition and despotism. The useful, the mechanic arts are those which we have occasion for in a young country as yet simple and not far advanced in luxury, although perhaps much too far for her age and character. I could fill volumes with descriptions of temples and palaces, paintings and sculptures, tapestry, porcelain, etc., etc., if I could have time, but I could not do this without neglecting my duty . . . I must study politics and war that my sons may have liberty to study mathematics and philosophy. My sons ought to study mathematics and philosophy, geography, natural history and naval architecture, navigation, commerce and agriculture, in order to give their children a right to study painting, poetry, music, architecture, statuary, tapestry and porcelain.

The artists themselves devoted their skills to celebrating a nationalist mood. Even Benjamin West felt that painting Revolutionary scenes would be a privilege. Writing from London in 1783 to Charles Willson Peale, West made plain that the treaty, just signed, which proclaimed our independence, could be properly celebrated only on the canvases of our artists:

. . . lett me congratulate you and my Countrymen in general, on the event of the Peace and the fortitude they have shown during the unhapy war. Thier wisdom and unshaken perseverance, must enrole them for ever among the greates charactors of antiquity, and transmit that name which nothing but thier Virtues could have atcheved.

Benjamin West, whose self-portrait, of about 1771, is in the National Gallery of Art, Washington, D. C., was the first American painter to achieve international fame. Although he had been able to earn a living as an artist in the area of his birth, Philadelphia, he went to Italy to study old masters in 1759. On the way home three years later he stopped in London and never left. An immediate and lifelong success in England, where he was historical painter to George III and president of the Royal Academy, West ran a studio there that welcomed two generations of artists and was, in effect, the first American art school.

C W Peale having just finished a Painting of Christ at Bethesda, respectfully invites his friends to see it for a few days previous to its removal to the City

Belfield Mch 20. 1821

Before the rise of commercial galleries and dealers in the mid-19th century, artists promoted their own work. In this note of March 20, 1821, Charles Willson Peale, a prolific and versatile artist who fought in Washington's army and who, despite his talent and energy, was often in debt, is inviting his friends to his studio near Philadelphia for a look at his recently completed painting Christ at Bethesda.

In addition to being a painter, Charles Willson Peale was a writer, inventor (of a steam bath, chimney, and improved false teeth), an experimental farmer, a saddler, silversmith, and scientist. He was also one of the founders of the Pennsylvania Academy of the Fine Arts and a museum of natural history, both in Philadelphia, where Peale lived. This self-portrait, in his The Artist in His Museum, was painted by the artist at the age of 81. Peale's Museum was then in Independence Hall; the painting is now owned by the Pennsylvania Academy of the Fine Arts, Philadelphia.

Trumbull

You have given me great delight in saying you would by the next Oportunity, send me a whole length portrait of that greatest of all Charactors, General Washington. Weather the picture would meet with a sale here I cannot tell—but I am shure there are hundreds hear who would be curious to see the true likeness of that Phinominy among men—In this schem I must live you to act as you may judge best—But in what follows I shall esteem it a favor, you will indulge me. By Mr. Vaune (who will deliver this) you will receive a role of small prints— The portraits of the American worthys—which the publisher begs your acceptance of, he send them as a specimen of what he intends, which is, to give the world the likenesses of those men who have distinguished themselves in America during the late contest. he has been informed you have painted most of thier portraits and would you send him small picture of thier likeness's he will make you the recompense you may require . . . I have now a favor to ask for myself, which is, that you would procure me the drawings of small paintings of the dresses of the American Army, from the Oficer down to the common Souldier— Rifillmen &c. &c. and any other charactoristic of thier Armys or camps from which I may form an axact Idea, to enable me to form a few pictures of the great events of the American contest—To make up my mind for this work—(which I propose to have engraved). It will be necessary for your assistance in procuring me the materials (of which you will be a proper judge) so that the American armys may be charactorized from those of Europ—This work I mean to still the American Revolution—and I make no doubt you will be equally interested in the success with myself . . .

John Trumbull was a student of Benjamin West; his early promise developed into a mature gift for mastery of expressive movement and chiaroscuro. He painted the self-portrait above in 1801 while in England. It now belongs to the Wadsworth Atheneum, Hartford, Connecticut. In 1790 Trumbull painted Washington at Verplanck's Point, New York, opposite page, as a gift for Martha Washington, whose husband had become the nation's first President on April 30, 1789. It is now in the collection of the Henry Francis du Pont Winterthur Museum, Winterthur, Delaware.

To John Trumbull, son of the rich and influential governor of Connecticut, rather than to West, went the glory of making the first pictorial record of the American Revolution. But there could be no doubt of West's patriotism. In 1806, another artist, Samuel L. Waldo (1783–1861), wrote to Trumbull from London of the warm reception he had had in the studio of America's old master:

. . . My time has been passed very pleasantly in London & I have been highly favored with the friendly instruction of Mr. West, whom I sincerely venerate, & esteem. I feel myself almost incompetent, even to begin the first rudiments of the art in the presence of so great an artist.

I have been drawing in chalk most of the time, & think it will eventually be most to my advantage. I have painted a few portraits, some I have been paid for & some I have given away but I do not apprehend that I shall take enough this year to find me in pocket money. My expenses could not be less than they are, in any part of America where there is an opportunity of studying the art. If my improvement answers the expectations of my instructor, I shall be very happy . . .

Washington Allston was another American painter who went to London. He became, in spite of himself, an admirer of West's style, as a letter written in 1801 to a South Carolina friend, the miniature painter Charles Fraser, makes clear:

You will no doubt be surprised that among the many painters in London I should rank Mr. West as first. I must own I myself was not a little surprised to find him such. I left America strongly prejudiced against him; and indeed I even now think with good reason, for those pictures from which I had seen prints would do no credit to a very inferior artist, much less to one of his reputation. But when I saw his gallery and the innumerable excellences which it contained, I pronounced him one of the greatest men in the world. I have looked upon his understanding with indifference, and his imagination with contempt; but I have

Gilbert Stuart's self-portrait below hangs at the Redwood Library in the town where the artist was born, Newport, Rhode Island. Stuart painted it in 1778 when he was only 24 and was living and working in Benjamin West's London studio. Stuart returned from abroad in 1792 after eighteen years away and soon became celebrated for his paintings of prominent men and women of the time; above 1793 portrait of Mrs. Richard Yates, now in the National Gallery of Art, Washington, D.C., is a good example.

now reason to suppose them both vigorous in the highest degree. No fancy could have better conceived and no pencil more happily embodied, the visions of sublimity than he has in his inimitable picture from Revelation. Its subject is the opening of the seven seals, and a more sublime and awful picture I never beheld. It is impossible to conceive anything more terrible than death on the white horse, and I am certain no painter has exceeded Mr. West in the fury, horror, and despair which he has represented in the surrounding figures. I could mention many others of similar merit, but were I particular on each I should not only weary you but write myself asleep. . . .

By the by, how long do you suppose Trumbull was about his "Gibraltar?" It is truly a charming picture; but he was a whole year about it therefore it ought to have been better. I have no idea of a painter's laboring up to fame. When he ceases to obtain reputation without it, he becomes a mechanic. Trumbull is no portrait painter. By this picture alone he has gained credit. But it is indeed credit purchased at a most exhorbitant interest.

I have lately painted several pictures; but am now about one that will far surpass anything I have done before. The subject is from the passage of Scripture, "And Christ looked upon Peter." It contains twenty figures, which are about two feet in height, on the whole making the best composition I ever attempted. The two principal groups are Christ between two soldiers, who are about to bear him away, the high priests, etc., and Peter surrounded by his accusers. The other groups are composed of spectators, variously affected, men, women, and children.

Among others who followed in West's train to Europe was John Vanderlyn, the Kingston, New York, painter who was a precursor of the Hudson River School. Writing from Paris to his friend John R. Murry, a New York lithographer, in July 1809, Vanderlyn pointed out that he was hard at work:

As you as well as some other of my friends may wonder at my not returning home, or be curious to know what I am about, I will take the liberty to disclose you my answers to these supposed questions, though more to comply with the request of the gentlemen who proposes to be the bearer thereof than my own impulses—for I fear I may again commit a breach or species of ill manners, which I reproach myself as being too apt to fall into, and of which I am more anxious to correct myself than to apologize for, but as I have now raised your curiosity by this long parley the least I can do is to make my apology that it is for *si peu de chose* and naturally will bring to your mind the fable of the mountain in labor, but to begin I will tell you that I have the little project on my return to America to make a small exhibition of my own pictures and with that view I wish to remain here in order to provide myself with a couple more pictures to add to that of "Marius." From the success a foreign artist Mr. [Adolph Ulrich] Wertmuller (1751–1811) met with in exhibiting a picture of "Danae" in Philadelphia a few years ago, as I am informed, I have reason to form similar expectations, and I have been more encouraged to believe so from opinions I have consulted from those last from America, and I trust you may not think differently. I am now engaged with copying a picture in the gallery here intended for that purpose. The one I have chosen is "Antiope Asleep with Cupid and Jupiter in the Form of a Satyr." You probably recollect the picture . . . In my opinion it is the best picture of Correggio's in the collection here—possessing in a greater degree the excellencies which distinguish him than any I have yet seen. That breadth of light and shadow, and insensible artful unison, one with the other joined to exquisite harmony and delicacy of tint, is here seen in a most conspicuous manner.

(continued on page 41)

John Smibert: Dean George Berkeley and His Entourage, oil, 1729.
Yale University Art Gallery, New Haven, Connecticut.

Benjamin West: Conference of the Treaty of Peace with England, oil, 1783.
H. F. du Pont Winterthur Museum, Winterthur, Delaware.

Robert Feke: Brigadier General Samuel Waldo, oil, about 1748.
Bowdoin College Museum of Art, Brunswick, Maine.

Matthew Pratt: The American School, oil, 1765.
Metropolitan Museum of Art, New York.

Thomas Smith: Self-Portrait, about 1675.
Worcester Art Museum, Worcester, Massachusetts.

John Singleton Copley: Mrs. Seymour Fort, oil, 1785.
Wadsworth Atheneum, Hartford, Connecticut.

Anonymous: Ann Pollard, oil, 1721.
Massachusetts Historical Society, Boston.

Washington Allston: Rising of a Thunderstorm at Sea, oil, 1804. Museum of Fine Arts, Boston.

n Vanderlyn: Ariadne, oil, 1814.
ansylvania Academy of the Fine Arts, Philadelphia.

Gilbert Stuart: The Skater, oil, 1782.
National Galley of Art, Washington, D. C.

As do many artists, Vanderlyn had an eye on the public:

I aim at making a *good* copy, not a tolerable one. I will feel mortified if I don't succeed. The subject may not be chaste enough for the most chaste and modest Americans, at least to be displayed in the house of any private individual, to either the company of the parlor or drawing room, but on that account it may attract a greater crowd if exhibited publicly, and the subject may thus invite some who are incapable of being entertained by the merits the picture may possess as a work of art.

John Trumbull, usually remembered as a disappointed and crusty old man, could be perceptive. According to a legend, he chanced upon a landscape painting in a New York shop window. The picture impressed him so much that he inquired after the artist. "This youth," he pronounced, "has done what all my life I have attempted in vain."

Trumbull could also be kind, and he proved it when he wrote from New York to the Baltimore collector Robert Gilmor, on November 14, 1825, of the young and as yet unrecognized artist whose painting he had encountered:

A young man of the name of T. Cole has just made his appearance from the interior of Pennsylvania who has surprised us with landscapes of most uncommon merit. We shall therefore have some interesting novelties for your next visit.

OIL PAINTINGS, PRINTS, &C.

NEW-YORK, DEC. 1844

SIR:—

Your attention is respectfully invited to the inspection of a few PAINTINGS, mostly by the pencil of COL. JOHN TRUMBULL, which will be sold at Auction on Tuesday, Dec. 10, at 11 o'clok, by W. H. FRANKLIN, No. 15 BROAD STREET, NEAR WALL, where they may now be examined. Sale without reserve, to close his estate.

CATALOGUE.

1. HOLY FAMILY—Mother and Child—copy from Vandyke, by Col. T.
2. LADY DRESSING—Copy from Murillo by Col. T., a fine painting.
3. THE CHASTITY OF SUSANNAH—or Susannah and the Elders, by Col. T.
4. HEAD OF GOVITUS—Copy from the original in the Royal Gallery in London, by Col Trumbull, a very valuable Painting.
5. SPANISH LADY—Original, by Valasquez, procured by Col. Trumbull in London.
6. LANDSCAPE—Near Bath, England, by Col. T.
7. Do. do. do. do. to match.
8. Do. do. do. do. do.
9. Do. unknown, by Col. T.
10. DRAWING in India Ink—Study of the Picture of Peter the Great at Neva—original in the Trumbull Gallery at New-Haven, by Col. T.
11. Two Drawings in India Ink—Sketches of Pasaic Falls, N. J. by Col. T.
12. ONE SKETCH in India Ink, of Niagara, by Col. T.
13. PORTRAIT of a Revolutionary officer, unknown, by Col. T.
14. PORTRAIT of Dr. Smalley, one of the commissions under Mr. Jay's Treaty With Col. T., by himself.
15. PORTRAIT of Sir Grenville Temple, well known in Boston—by Col. T.
16. PORTRAIT of Ralph Hickley, a servant to Sir Joshua Reynolds through life—a fine head, by Col. T., taken from Life in London.
17. PORTRAIT of Mr. Ellis, an English Merchant, a fine Picture, by Col. T.
18. PORTRAIT of Mrs. Trumbull, Wife of Col. T., by himself. 15 x 12, a fine Painting.
19. PORTRAIT of Mrs. Mitchell, Wife of an English Clergyman, by Col. T.
20. PORTRAIT of Mr. Palmer an Artist of London, by Col. T.
21. PORTRAIT of Mr. Elis, now a member of Parliament, taken when young, in London.
22. PORTRAIT of Dr. Edward Marcelin.
23. PORTRAIT of a Matron Lady—Supposed mother of the late Doctor Hossack
24. PORTRAIT of Mrs. Trumbull, small size, by Col. T.
25. MINIATURE of Gen. Green, of the Revolutionary army of the U. S,
26. MINATURE of Col. Trumbull, do. of Mrs. T.
27. LARGE PORTFOLIO containing 8 Prints from Raphael's Frescoes in the Vatican, very fine engravings, and scarce.
28. PROOF Prints of the Declaration of Independence—these proofs are scarce and the plates destroyed.
29. PRINTS of the Battle of Bunker Hill, and death of Gen. Warren.
30. PRINTS of the attack on Quebec, and death of Gen. Montgomery.
31. SORTIE of Gibralter, engraved by Sharp, whose works are rare, and much prized in England—fine prints.
32. PRINTS, full length, of Gen. Washington.
33. Two Portfolios, containing old Engravings of Battles, sketches &c., &c.
34. SEVERAL Volumes of Autobiography, Reminiscences and letters of Col. J. Trumbull, from 1756 to 1841, by himself
35. PRINTS of Judge Jonas Platt.
36. PRINTS of Chief Justice Oliver Elsworth, from Paintings by Col T.

Art auctions began in the U.S. in the latter part of the 18th century and were an established institution by 1844, when John Trumbull's estate was sold. This announcement of the Trumbull sale, which took place in New York on December 10, a year after the artist's death, includes an estimated value for each lot.

II The Opening of the West

Although Coronado marched across the plains of Kansas as early as 1541—nearly seven decades before Jamestown was founded—the pictorial record of the trans-Mississippi West did not begin until the last quarter of the eighteenth century. Then artists aboard English, French, and Spanish ships exploring the Pacific coast began to picture the land they saw and the people they met on trips ashore in California and in the Pacific Northwest.

John Webber (1752–1793) was the London-born and Paris-trained son of a Swiss sculptor. In 1778 he accompanied the English mariner and explorer Captain James Cook on a visit to Nootka Sound on the west coast of Vancouver Island. For the first time and with remarkable accuracy, Webber drew the Nootka Indians and scenes of their domestic life in their large wooden houses. In his published narrative, Captain Cook explained why he had taken an artist on this prolonged and dangerous voyage of discovery. "Mr. Webber was pitched upon and engaged to embark with me for the express purpose of supplying the unavoidable imperfections of written accounts, by enabling us to preserve, and to bring home, such drawings of the most memorable scenes of our transactions, as could only be executed by a professional and skillful artist." And so John Webber became the first in a long line of artist-illustrators to explore the American West.

Not until after the United States purchased Louisiana from France in 1803 did American artists discover that vast and colorful panorama of the western interior beyond the Mississippi. In the West's bright sky, its grassy plains, hot deserts, deep canyons, craggy summits and snow-capped peaks, flowered mountain valleys and dense forests of pines, firs, cedars, and giant redwoods—as well as in its shallow rivers, calm mountain lakes, and swift-flowing streams—artists found not one but many challenging environments, all quite different from the familiar landscapes of the settled East and of Europe.

No less exciting to the majority of the more than two hundred artists who traveled in the West during the nineteenth century were the native peoples: the Indians of more than one hundred tribes and a half-dozen cultures—all fine physical specimens whose nearly naked bodies reminded artists of the Grecian ideal, and whose strong features, natural dignity, and picturesque costumes provided appealing subjects for portraiture. The Plains Indians had still other attractions. Their skill as horsemen and as big-game hunters intrigued more civilized sportsmen. Their mobile warfare, exotic dances, and savage religious rituals were powerfully dramatic.

The first American artist to feel the lure of the West strongly was Charles Willson Peale of Philadelphia; everything about the newly-acquired Louisiana excited him. He was then past sixty and too old to go West himself, but he avidly sought natural history specimens and Indian artifacts collected by the Lewis and Clark Expedition across the continent, and displayed them prominently in his popular Peale's Museum in Independence Hall, Philadelphia.

In 1806, a delegation of handsome western Indians on a tour of the East, after meeting their Great White Father in Washington, visited Peale's Museum. Peale cut silhouettes of them and sent a set of the likenesses to his friend President Jefferson. Peale used a mechanical device, the physiognotrace, to make an exact outline of his sitter's face. (The French emigrant portraitist Charles Balthazar Julien Fevret de Saint Mémin (1770–1852) had used this method to make crayon portraits of Osage leaders who, in 1804, were the first Indians from beyond the Mississippi to visit Washington.)

Peale obtained for his twenty-year-old son Titian Ramsay Peale (1799–1860) the post of assistant naturalist on Major Stephen H. Long's official explorative expedition of 1819–1820. Another Philadelphian, Samuel Seymour (about 1796–1823), was selected as artist for that expedition. The two pioneer artist-explorers of the Great Plains divided their work: Peale rendered pencil and watercolor sketches of the birds, animals, and insects new to science, while Seymour executed watercolors of the landscape, including the first known views of the Rocky Mountains. Both did a few Indian scenes as they traveled up the Missouri, wintered above what is now Omaha, then journeyed up the south branch of the Platte River to the Rockies, and returned eastward down the Arkansas to the frontier post of Fort Smith.

By the eighteen-twenties, farsighted Americans foresaw that as the white man's settlements pushed westward, the Indian population there would be decimated by wars and disease and their traditional cultures destroyed, much as had been the fate of the Red Men of the eastern forests in earlier years.

In a desire to preserve likenesses of some of the finest examples of the Indian race, the War Department established an Indian Gallery in Washington. From 1821 to 1838, Charles Bird King (1785–1862) was commissioned to paint oil portraits of prominent chiefs who visited Washington. At times there were so many chiefs in the nation's capital that King called upon his student George Cooke (1793–1849) to assist him. Among the more than one hundred portraits in the Indian Gallery were likenesses of the leaders of some fifteen Plains Indian tribes.

The sight of a delegation of painted and feathered Indians from the wilds of the West passing through Philadelphia on their way to Washington aroused in George Catlin (1796–1872), a self-taught portraitist, the determination to travel widely among the Indian tribes beyond the frontiers of settlement and to devote some time to becoming their "historian."

Catlin spent about six years among western tribes. He first crossed the Mississippi in 1830, and his travels in the West ended in 1836; there was a brief,

Charles Willson Peale cut this silhouette of Pagesgatse, a Pawnee member of an Indian delegation that visited his museum in Philadelphia in 1806. Sending a set of the Indian silhouettes to President Thomas Jefferson, Peale commented: "Some of these Savages have interesting characters by the lines of their faces." The silhouette is in the Smithsonian Institution.

The drawing of the physiognotrace, the device Peale used to trace the outline of the head, is in the Library of Congress, Washington, D. C.

George Catlin painted this self-portrait at the age of 29, before he headed West to paint Indians. First crossing the Mississippi in 1830, the subsequent six years of travel among the tribes were enough to generate an enthusiasm that lasted a lifetime. He was still copying his earlier Indian studies at the age of 72, a few years before his death. This self-portrait, completed by Catlin in 1825, is in the Thomas Gilcrease Institute of American History and Art, Tulsa, Oklahoma.

inconsequential trip westward in the eighteen-fifties. His finest Indian portraits, and many of his best scenes of buffalo hunts, Indian dances, and ceremonies were executed during the summer of 1832 when he spent three months among the tribes of the Upper Missouri (from Fort Pierre northward). It was a period of feverish activity and, wielding the fastest pencil and brush in the West, Catlin made studies for more than one hundred paintings that included a majority of his best-known works. On his trips to southwestern Oklahoma in 1834 and to the Upper Mississippi in 1835 and 1836, he added substantially to what was to become his famous Indian Gallery that was exhibited in the major cities of the East and in Europe.

Catlin's Indian works reveal clearly his extraordinary ability to catch a likeness with a few deft strokes of his brush, as well as his innocence of basic principles of perspective and his limitations in drawing the human body in action. Yet many of his hastily rendered scenes have the freshness and vitality of on-the-spot observation.

Catlin's Indians suffer when they are compared with the meticulous watercolors of the young, thoroughly trained Swiss artist Karl Bodmer (1809–1894). Bodmer spent a year (1833–1834) among the tribes of the Upper Missouri in the employ of Prince Maximilian of Wied-Neuwied, the able German scientist. He illustrated Maximilian's published account of his travels and observations. Bodmer's ability to render both the forms and the quality of materials in sharp focus allies him with the later *trompe l'oeil* artists. His superb accuracy of detail has endeared him to anthropologists, who regard him as *the* master painter of the American Indian.

The publication of Catlin's and Bodmer's pictures in 1841 encouraged other artists to go West and to paint Indians. The best-known painters of Plains Indians during the mid-nineteenth century decades were Seth Eastman (1808–1869), John Mix Stanley (1814–1872), Paul Kane (1810–1871), Charles Wimar (1826–1862), and Bodmer's Swiss friend Rudolph Friederich Kurz (1818–1871). The works of Catlin, Bodmer, and their followers contributed substantially to the emergence of the equestrian, war-bonneted Plains Indian as the symbol of the American Indian in the imaginations of later generations of civilized Easterners and Europeans.

Only one artist, Alfred Jacob Miller (1810–1874), knew the rugged mountain men in their heyday as Rocky Mountain trappers. He was also the first artist to picture the movement of a wagon train up the North Platte valley and over the Continental Divide along the route that was to become the well-worn emigrant road to Oregon, the Mormon settlements in Utah, and the California gold mines. With Sir William Drummond Stewart, his employer, Miller camped at the trappers' annual rendezvous on Green River in western Wyoming and visited the lakes of the Wind River Mountains to the north. This was a heady experience for the city-bred artist, so we may forgive him if some of his lively watercolors and sepia drawings, executed on his sole excursion into the West, are more romantic than real.

During the eighteen-forties, the artists' frontier was extended into both the Oregon Country and the Southwest. Father Nicholas Point (1799–1866), the French-born Jesuit who assisted Father Pierre Jean De Smet in founding the first Catholic mission in the Northwest in 1841, was also the pioneer artist of the Northern Rockies. His miniature watercolors of the Flathead, Coeur d'Alene, and Blackfoot tribes painted in the years 1841–1847 have a charming old-world style; yet they depict aspects of the life of "his Indians" which no other artist portrayed. Meanwhile, in 1845–1846, British army officer Captain Henry J. Warre (1819–

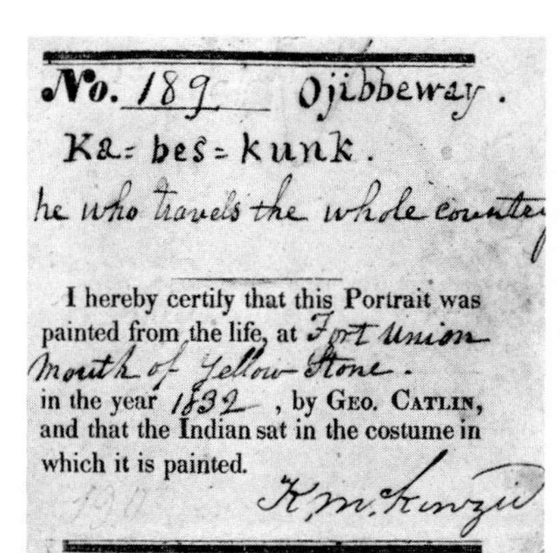

No. 189 Ojibbeway.
Ka-bes-kunk.
he who travels the whole country

I hereby certify that this Portrait was painted from the life, at Fort Union Mouth of Yellow Stone. in the year 1832, by Geo. Catlin, and that the Indian sat in the costume in which it is painted.

K. McKenzie

George Catlin painted both Bear Dance of the Sioux and Tobacco, an Oglala Sioux chief, near Fort Pierre on the Upper Missouri during the summer of 1832. The above label affixed to Catlin's oil portrait of "Kabes-kunk, he who travels the whole country," testifies that in 1832 at Fort Union, at the mouth of the Yellowstone, he painted "from the life" this Ojibwa Indian, who "sat in the costume in which it is painted." The Smithsonian Institution, Washington, D. C., owns these illustrations.

1898), while exploring the valley of the Columbia as high as the Willamette, made interesting landscape sketches which were developed into handsome, hand-colored lithographs published in London.

In 1846–1847, Lieutenant James W. Abert explored New Mexico. He illustrated his published report with his own sketches of the abandoned pueblo of Pecos, the inhabited pueblos of the Rio Grande valley, and the fabulous sky-city of Acoma atop its high mesa. In 1847 the Kern brothers of Philadelphia, Edward (1823–1863) and Richard (1821–1853), accompanied Lieutenant James H. Simpson from Sante Fe to the Navaho Country and drew portraits of the Navaho as well as scenes of the rich ceremonial life of the pueblos. They also made the earliest known drawings of Pueblo Bonito and the ruins of other large masonry apartment-like houses that were abandoned nearly two centuries before Columbus. During the early and middle eighteen-fifties, the artists' record was extended into the deserts of Arizona and Southern California. As artist-cartographers they traveled with Pacific Railway and Mexican Boundary Surveys and pictured the scantily clad Yuman and Mohave tribes and their hot, dry homeland. Official reports of these explorations presented colored lithographs of some of the field drawings by Heinrich Balduin Möllhausen (1825–1905) and Arthur Schott (about 1813–1875).

A pictorial interpreter of the Northwest, and the most versatile artist on the northern railway survey directed by Major Isaac I. Stevens (an experienced military engineer who was appointed first governor of the newly created Territory of Washington), was German-born Private Gustavus Sohon (1825–1903). He made excellent drawings of the lands traversed; his is the first panoramic view of the lofty main chain of the Rocky Mountains in what is now Montana. Sohon was also a gifted linguist and served as an interpreter in dealings with the Indians, of whom he made many expressive likenesses. He is especially known for his sketches and pen-and-ink drawings of the first treaty councils with the powerful Blackfoot, Nez Percé, Flathead, and numerous other tribes of the Northwest. Equally important, historically, are Sohon's sensitive portraits of the Indian chiefs who signed the treaties with the United States in 1855.

Two western artists of the mid-nineteenth century, working more than two thousand miles apart, created detailed genre paintings which interpreted the vitality and humor of frontier life. George Caleb Bingham (1811–1879) was born in Virginia. He is remembered for his jolly river boatmen and his witty visual commentaries on small-town politics in his adopted state of Missouri. Charles Christian Nahl (1818–1878) was born in Germany and trained in Paris. His hands were hardened in the diggings at Rough and Ready Camp on the Yuba River. On canvas, he precisely documented intimate phases of mining-camp life during the California gold rush.

Artists knew many of the areas west of the Mississippi before the Civil War. Their illustrations on paper or canvas recorded the character of the land and the cultures of the Indian tribes. But many of their works were known only because they were reproduced in technical reports of scientific explorations. And there was still much grandiose scenery that had not been a subject for the artist's brush or pencil.

Albert Bierstadt (1830–1902) first saw and became enamored of the Rocky Mountains in 1859. His mammoth oil paintings, developed from numerous field sketches, were exhibited in the early eighteen-sixties. In great demand in this country and abroad, the paintings informed the world that the grandeur of our Rockies rivaled that of the Alps. Bierstadt quickly gained international fame and his works, despite their contrived theatrical qualities, commanded the highest prices paid to an American artist.

Often heroic in scale, Albert Bierstadt's paintings, opposite page, of the mountains aroused national pride in our "American Alps." His View from the Wind River Mountains, Wyoming, painted in New York in 1860 from field sketches made the previous summer, is in the Museum of Fine Arts, Boston. The Free Public Library of New Bedford, Massachusetts, owns his 1861 Sunset Light, below, which appears to be the artist's first version of a scene he expanded into his enormous The Rocky Mountains, in the Metropolitan Museum, New York. The latter painting, truly a Bierstadt spectacular, covers more than sixty square feet of canvas. The public loved it when it was first shown in 1863; some of the art critics were noticeably less enthusiastic.

Frederic Remington, painter, sculptor, illustrator, war correspondent, and writer, is shown, opposite page, in his New Rochelle, New York, studio in 1903. He died in 1909, at age 48. His creative output—more than 2,700 paintings and drawings, at least 15 bronzes, and several books—is something of a record for so brief a life. This photo is in the Remington Art Memorial, Ogdensburg, New York.

Before Bierstadt's popularity waned, Thomas Moran (1837–1926) explored the wonderland of the Upper Yellowstone as guest artist with the Hayden Survey of 1871. He discovered a riot of color in its canyon and hot springs and its spouting geysers. Moran's pictures helped to convince Congress that this unique region should be preserved for the benefit of all the people as the world's first national park. Moran's subsequent paintings of other breathtakingly beautiful areas in the West, such as the Grand Canyon, Yosemite Valley, and the Tetons, encouraged the establishment of other national parks.

The second half of the nineteenth century was marked by intermittent, widely scattered, but bitter, Indian wars. The Red Men, disillusioned by broken treaties and continued white settlers' encroachment upon their hunting grounds, challenged the might of the United States Army. Few artist-reporters witnessed this dramatic warfare. Sohon participated in the Indian War of 1858 in the Columbia Valley and made some pencil sketches of the action. Theodore R. Davis (1840–1894), a veteran Civil War artist-correspondent for *Harper's Weekly,* drew informative pictures of General Hancock's futile campaign against the Cheyenne and Sioux on the plains of Kansas in 1867. They included a gruesome sight of massacred and mutilated soldiers. William Simpson (1823–1903) pictured the final stages of the Modoc War in the lava beds of southern Oregon for the *Illustrated London News* in 1873.

Frederic Remington (1861–1909) rode with the army chasing elusive Apaches in Arizona in 1886. He was also with the army in the Dakotas when the Ghost Dance—a five-day ritual of the messianic religion instituted by Wovoka, a Paiute, who taught his followers that their performance of the Ghost Dance and other rituals could cause the whites to disappear, the buffalo to return, and the Indians to be reunited with their dead relatives as in the old way of life—excited the Sioux to the uprising of 1890 that culminated in the last tragic battle of the Indian Wars on December 29, 1890, at Wounded Knee Creek. The robust, good-humored Remington was well liked by army officers; he repaid their friendship with many well-drawn pictures of the Indian-fighting army in the field.

Before the turn of the century, the Old West of frontier days had passed into history. Buffalo were exterminated. The proud, breech-clouted warrior of the open plains became a dejected, trouser-clad, reservation-bound Indian standing in line to receive government rations. The wood palisades of once-active fur-trading posts had rotted away, and solitary ghost towns were mute reminders of once-prosperous mining camps. The open range was fenced, and more and more grasslands were converted to fields of waving wheat.

In 1880, Charles M. Russell (1864–1926) left his St. Louis home and began his life as a Montana cowboy. He taught himself to draw and paint range and ranch life with great facility. Working independently, Russell and Remington continued to pay tribute to the memory of an earlier, exciting, and action-packed West in thousands of paintings, book and magazine illustrations, and small sculptures. The West of the Indian, the explorer, the fur-trader, the Indian-fighter, the bad man, and the open-range cowboy was vividly re-created in their art. They knew, too, the appeal of rampaging red- or white-skinned horsemen long before Hollywood began to produce the horse operas still enjoyed today. Remington and Russell founded a historical action school of popular western art to which Charles Schreyvogel (1861–1912), Frank Tenney Johnson (1874–1939), William R. Leigh (1866–1935), and a host of lesser artists have made more recent contributions. The continued popularity of Remington's and Russell's story-telling pictures is manifest in the high prices paid for their original paintings in today's art market and in the large sales of reproductions.

Preliminary to creating a series of historical paintings of the Lewis and Clark expedition of 1803–1806, Charles M. Russell sketched his concept of York, Captain William Clark's servant. At the time no description of York was in print. The only Negro on the expedition and the first of his race the remote tribes had ever seen, York amazed the Indians—some of whom thought he was a white man covered with black paint. This ink sketch, about 1903, is in the Russell Memorial, Great Falls, Montana.

Frederic Remington's Buffalo Horse, a bronze sculpture in the Thomas Gilcrease Institute of American History and Art, Tulsa, Oklahoma, is dated 1907 and is believed to be the only cast of this work.

But toward the end of the century there were other, quieter trends in western art, and a more idealistic interpretation of the Indian found expression. Frankly disinterested in western history, George de Forest Brush (1855–1941) deliberately posed his Indian models through whom he sought to recapture the Greek ideal of beauty. However, Guy Pène du Bois (1884–1958) recognized the basic fallacy in Brush's visual poetry; his late nineteenth-century Indians, stripped to their breech-clouts and moccasins, were not noble savages but mere men who displayed "many civilized graces, and airs of conscious Olympian athletes."

Even though the Old West was disappearing, the placid Pueblo Indians of the Southwest still maintained their traditions. As had their ancestors, they lived in multi-storied apartment houses, cultivated maize, and performed ceremonial dances to bring rain and abundant crops. In 1893, an artist from Cincinnati, Joseph Henry Sharp (1859–1953), visited Taos, a pueblo fifty miles north of Santa Fe. The clear sky and brilliant sunlight, the surrounding mountains, and the ancient architecture of Taos, as well as the Indians there, impressed him.

Five years later, Sharp persuaded Bert G. Phillips (1868–1956) and Ernest L. Blumenschien (1874–1960), two of his fellow students at the Académie Julien in Paris, to settle in Taos. They were later joined by E. Irving Couse (1866–1936), Oscar E. Berninghaus (1874–1952), Walter Ufer (1876–1936), Victor Higgins (1884–1949), and others. These artists developed the first art colony in the American West. There—with conservative yet contemporary Indians at their doorsteps and the eternal mountains on the horizon—they believed they had found the ideal setting for a uniquely American art.

Why did so many artists leave the comforts and security of civilized life to accept the hardships and hazards of travel in an Indian-infested western wilderness? All these paint-brush pioneers were curious and courageous, energetic and enthusiastic. But we cannot generalize or succinctly summarize the complex motives that drew or impelled them to their adventures in the West. Some, but not all, were young men. Some were disenchanted with their familiar surroundings and sought fresh inspiration in the little-known West. Some were confirmed lovers of the out-of-doors. But others were pale, city-bred and studio-bound artists, unaccustomed to an outdoor life. Although Remington and Russell were horsemen from boyhood, Thomas Moran never rode a horse until he explored the Yellowstone. For the soldier and the missionary who contributed to the artists' record of the Old West, drawing and painting were attractive sidelines to their performance of other duties. Yet many artists went West solely or primarily to picture what they saw there. Rousseau's ideal of "the noble savage," and the Greek ideal of the beauty of the lightly-draped human form, made the Indians especially attractive subjects for many artists; but so did the thought that these Indians were doomed to cultural extinction. And there were other artists who preferred the grandeur of the western landscape.

If we are to understand the varied motives that inspired leading artist-interpreters of the American West, we must let each one speak for himself.

George Catlin arrived at Fort Union at the mouth of the Yellowstone River on June 16, 1832. He was aboard the first steamboat to reach the remote trading post; the journey of more than two thousand miles up the Missouri from St. Louis had taken three months. His letter to the editor appeared in the New York Commercial Advertiser on July 24, 1832:

The Fur Company has erected here, for their protection against the savages,

George Catlin was 72 years old when above photo was taken, and he was even then repainting his Indian works for showings in both the United States and Europe. Actually, Catlin hung his last exhibition—his "Cartoon Collection"—in the Smithsonian in February 1872. An illness that began the following summer while he was living in one of the towers of the old Smithsonian building preceded his death in December 1872. The Smithsonian Institution, Washington, D. C., owns this old photograph.

Rudolph Friederich Kurz's sketches of Indians almost cost him his life. In 1851, soon after his arrival at the small trading post of Fort Berthold on the Missouri, a cholera epidemic broke out among the nearby Hidatsa Indians. The superstitious Indians remembered that a smallpox epidemic had followed visits by artists George Catlin and Karl Bodmer, and attributed the cholera plague to Kurz's "bad medicine." His drawings were quickly withdrawn from sight. The Historical Museum in Berne, Switzerland, has the original drawings.

a very beautiful Fort, and our approach to it, under the continued roar of cannon for half an hour, and the shrill yells of the half affrighted savages who lined the shores, presented a scene of the most thrilling and picturesque appearance. . . .

I am here in the full enthusiasm and practice of my art. That enthusiasm alone has brought me into this remote region, three thousand five hundred miles from my native soil, the last two thousand of which have furnished me with unlimited models, both in landscape and the human figure, exactly suited to my feelings. I am now in the full possession and enjoyment of those conditions on which alone I was introduced to pursue the art as a profession, and in anticipation of which alone, my admiration for the art could even be kindled into a flame. I mean the free use of Nature's undisguised models, with the privilege of selecting for myself. . . .

I have, for a long time, been of the opinion that the wilderness of our country afforded models equal to those from which the Grecian sculptors transferred to the marble such inimitable grace and beauty; and I am more confirmed in this opinion, since I have immersed myself in the midst of thousands and thousands of these knights of the forest, whose whole lives are lives of chivalry, and whose daily feats, with their naked limbs, might vie with those of the Grecian youths in the beautiful rivalry of the Olympian games. . . .

In addition to the knowledge of human nature and of my art, which I hope to acquire by this toilsome and expensive undertaking, I have another in view, which, if it should not be of equal service to me, will be of no less interest and value to posterity. I have designed to get portraits of several distinguished and well selected Indians of both sexes, from every tribe of Indians in North America, painted in their native costumes, accompanied with pictures representing their villages, domestic habits, amusements, and the landscape of the country they inhabit, with as much anecdote of their lives as I can obtain and attach to them. . . .

If I should live to accomplish my design, the result of my labors will, doubtless, be interesting to future ages, who will have nothing else left from which to judge of the original habits of that noble race of beings, who require but a few years more of the march of civilization and death to deprive them of all their native customs and character.

At the age of seventy-five, in the twilight of his long career as an exhibitor of his Indian paintings in the larger cities of the United States and of Europe, George Catlin hung his last show in the Smithsonian Institution in Washington. This Cartoon Collection included many small-scale compositions he had previously painted in Belgium from his field sketches of the eighteen-thirties. In the Catalogue Descriptive and Instructive of Catlin's Indian Cartoons, published in New York in 1871, the following expressed the artist's modest hope that viewers would

. . . find enough of historical interest, excited by faithful resemblance to the physiognomy and costume of these people, to compensate for what may be deficient in them as works of art.

The American wilderness cast its romantic spell on the mind of Rudolph Friederich Kurz, a young artist in far-off Switzerland. He explained this powerful attraction in the opening pages of the Journal of Rudolph Friederich Kurz, in which he wrote of his six years of travel (1846–1852) in the American West:

From my earliest youth, primeval forest and Indians had an indescribable charm for me. In spare hours I read only those books that included descriptions and adventures in the new world. . . . I longed for the quietude of immemorial woods where no paupers mar one's delight in beauty, where neither climate, false modesty, nor fashion compels concealment of the noblest form in God's creation; where there is neither overlordship of the bourgeois nor the selfishness of the rich who treasure their wealth in splendid idleness, while the fine arts languish.

When I was allowed to devote myself to painting, these longings became the more intense for the reason that, from the moment I determined to become an artist, my life purpose was fixed; I would devote my talents to the portrayal of the aboriginal forests, the wild animals that inhabited them, and to the Indians. From that moment I had an ideal—a definite purpose in life to the attainment of which I might dedicate all my powers.

Kurz clung to his romantic ideal even when superstitious Hidatsa Indians near Fort Berthold on the Upper Missouri threatened his life; they believed his picture-making had caused a death-dealing cholera plague among them. On August 12, 1851, when the epidemic was at its height, Kurz confided to his Journal:

Primitive conditions exert an irresistable charm upon me. Here I may clothe the figures only so far as to make any picture acceptable to the greater number of people. The most beautiful of garments can not serve the purpose of art as well as the perfect human form; garments are beautiful, in an artistic sense, only when they reveal to advantage the human form.

In the summer of 1837, Alfred Jacob Miller had a unique opportunity to meet, to observe, and to picture the Rocky Mountain trappers during their month-long annual rendezvous on Green River. His description of these rugged mountain men appears in The West of Alfred Jacob Miller by Marvin C. Ross:

Encircled with danger, they wander far and near in pursuit of "sign" of beaver. Ever on the alert, a turned leaf, grass pressed down, or the uneasiness of his animals, are signs palpable to him of proximity to an Indian foe, and places him on guard.

. . . Under privations of all kinds, the universal resort of the Trapper was the pipe of tobacco; this is suspended in a *gage d'amour* from his neck; he carries also tinder and flint, with which to strike a light in a moment; with this he solaces every affliction and it gives him stamina (one would suppose) to combat any trouble;—it is his universal medicine.

. . . The trappers in the sketch are *en repose,* the peculiar caps on their heads are made by themselves, to replace felt hats, long since worn out or lost, their fringed shirts, leggings, moccasins &c., are made by the Indian women, and sewed throughout with sinew instead of thread, which they do not possess.

City-bred Alfred Jacob Miller executed this self-portrait, now in the Joslyn Art Museum, Omaha, Nebraska, before he became famous for his portrayals of trappers and Indian life in the hazardous Rocky Mountain wilderness. Miller's watercolors provided an impressive record of trappers and the first pictures of the Wyoming mountains.

When the trappers' raucous rendezvous was over, Miller's party visited the quiet mountain lakes of the Wind River Range in Wyoming. He was the first artist to describe (as quoted by Marvin C. Ross in his The West of Alfred Jacob Miller) and to paint the wild and beautiful scenery of that region:

We reached this point about sunset on our way to the Lakes, and from fatigue rested here for the night; it gave me ample time to obtain a sketch from the bluff rock to the left, which completely overlooked one of the Lakes, the object of our pilgrimage.

Solitude brooded over the scene, and with the exception of our party, the eye wandered in vain to discover a living being, or a sign of habitation. . . . The rays of the declining sun glimmered on the distant tops of the snow-covered peaks, while darkness had already begun to cast its pall on the valley below,—the air being sensibly colder as the night advanced. . . .

The most favorable time to view these Lakes (to an artist especially) was early in the morning or towards sunset;—at these times one side or the other would be

Karl Bodmer's drawing of Pehriska-Ruhpa, leader of the Hidatsa Dog Dancers, who posed for him near Fort Clark in 1834, exemplifies the high degree of accuracy in the rendering of costume detail for which Bodmer was famous. This sepia, redrawn by Bodmer from his original field sketch in preparation for reproduction, is in the Glenbow Foundation, Calgary, Alberta, Canada.

George Caleb Bingham's Fur Traders Descending the Missouri, now in the Metropolitan Museum, New York, is that artist's earliest extant genre painting. It was painted in 1845, before Bingham's election to the Missouri legislature and before he created such famous political scenes as The Verdict of the People and Stump Speaking.

Two of the many watercolors Alfred Jacob Miller painted during his western trip with Sir William Drummond Stewart in 1837 are Chain Lake and Fort William, with an Indian encampment near its gates. This fort, later renamed Fort Laramie, was an important trading post on the North Platte. The U.S. Army bought it in 1848 to protect emigrants on the Oregon Trail. Both paintings are in the Joslyn Art Museum, Omaha, Nebraska.

George Caleb Bingham's self-portrait, on view in the William Rockhill Nelson Gallery of Art, Kansas City, Missouri, probably was painted in 1877, the year he became the first professor in the newly established department of art at the University of Missouri.

thrown into deep purple masses, throwing great broad shadows, with sharp light glittering on the extreme tops,—while the opposite mountains received its full complement of warm, mellow & subdued light—thus forming a *chiaro obscura* and contrast most essential to the picturesque in color.

George Caleb Bingham's concern for grass-roots democracy was solidly founded on personal experience. He had represented Saline County in the Missouri legislature before he began to paint his well-known series of political scenes. How—in his dual roles of politician and artist—he handled a rather unusual problem that arose when he was working on one of his famous canvases, "Stump Speaking," is told in a letter written to a friend, James S. Rollins, on December 12, 1853:

A new head is continually popping up and demanding a place in the crowd, and as I am a thorough democrat, it gives me pleasure to accommodate them all. The consequence of this impertinence on one side and indulgence on the other, is, that instead of the select company which my plan at first embraced, I have an audience that would be no discredit to the most populous precinct of Buncomb. . . .

In my orator I have endeavored to personify a wiry politician, grown gray in the pursuit of office and the service of his party. His influence upon the crowd is manifest, but I have placed behind him a shrewd clear headed opponent, who is busy taking notes, and who will, when his turn comes, make sophisms fly like cobwebs before the housekeepers broom.

Albert Bierstadt's enthusiasm for both the Rocky Mountains and the Indians knew almost no bounds, as proved in his letter dated July 10, 1859, written shortly after he had reached the Wind River on the first of his many painting expeditions into the western high country. It appeared in the September 1859 issue of The Crayon:

If you can form any idea of the scenery of the Rocky Mountains and of our life in this region, from what I have to write I shall be very glad; there is indeed enough to write about—a *writing* lover of nature and Art could not wish for a better subject. I am delighted with the scenery. The mountains are very fine; as seen from the plains, they resemble very much the Bernese Alps, one of the finest ranges of mountains in Europe, if not in the world. They are of granite formation, the same as the Swiss mountains and their jagged summits, covered with snow and mingling with the clouds, present a scene which every lover of landscape would gaze upon with unqualified delight. As you approach them, the lower hills present themselves more or less clothed with a great variety of trees, among which may be found the cotton-wood, lining the river banks, the aspen, and several species of the fir and pine, some of them being very beautiful. And such a charming group of rocks, so fine in color—more so than any I ever saw. Artists would be delighted with them—were it not for the tormenting swarms of mosquitoes. In the valleys, silvery streams abound, with mossy rocks and an abundance of that finny tribe that we all delight so much to catch, the trout. We see many spots in the scenery that reminds us of our New Hampshire and Catskill hills, but when we look up and measure the mighty perpendicular cliffs that rise hundreds of feet aloft, all capped with snow, we then realize that we are among a different class of mountains; and especially when we see the antelope stop to look at us, and still more the Indian, his pursuer who often stands dismayed to see a white man sketching alone in the midst of his hunting grounds. We often meet Indians, and they have always been kindly disposed to us and we to them; but it is a little *risky*, because being superstitious and naturally distrustful, their

(continued on page 65)

Charles M. Russell: The Medicine Man, oil, 1916.
Collection of C. R. Smith.

George Catlin: Comanche Village, Women Dressing Robes, oil, 1834.
Smithsonian Institution, Washington, D. C.

Charles Bird King: Indian Chief Shaumonekusse, oil, about 1821.
The White House Collection, Washington, D. C.

Henry Lewis: Mississippi River Panorama (detail showing Nauvoo, Mormon capital in Illinois), lithograph, 1846–48. Western Americana Collection, Yale University Library, New Haven, Connecticut.

Karl Bodmer: White Castles on the Missouri, watercolor, 1832.
Northern Natural Gas Company Collection, Joslyn Art Museum, Omaha, Nebraska.

Alfred Jacob Miller: Trappers, watercolor and gouache, 1837.
Walters Art Gallery, Baltimore, Maryland,

Frederic Remington: Fight for the Water Hole, oil, 1908.
Museum of Fine Arts, Houston, Texas.

Thomas Moran: The Musquito Trail in the Rocky Mountains of Colorado, lithograph of a watercolor painted about 1871. Western Americana Collection, Yale University Library, New Haven, Connecticut.

friendship may turn to hate at any moment. We do not venture a great distance from the camp alone, although tempted to do so by distant objects, which, of course, appear more charming than those nearby; also the figures of the Indians so enticing, travelling about with their long poles trailing along on the ground, and their picturesque dress, that renders them such appropriate adjuncts to the scenery. For a figure-painter, there is an abundance of fine subjects. The manners and customs of the Indians are still as they were hundreds of years ago, and now is the time to paint them, for they are rapidly passing away, and soon will be known only in history. I think that the artist ought to tell his portion of their history as well as the writer; a combination of both will assuredly render it more complete. . . .

The mountains here are much higher than those at home, snow remaining on portions of them the whole season. The color of the mountains and of the plains, and, indeed, that of the entire country, reminds one of the color of Italy; in fact, we have here the Italy of America in a primitive condition.

Thomas Moran's first ride on a horse was taken in July 1871 when, as guest artist with portfolio in hand, he explored the Yellowstone with Dr. Ferdinand V. Hayden's scientific expedition. He was struck by the region's natural colors and formations. Moran's watercolors of the hot springs, waterfalls, geysers, and canyon—supplementing William H. Jackson's photographs—supported Dr. Hayden's plea to Congress to preserve this wonderland for all the people. On March 1, 1872, President Ulysses S. Grant signed the bill creating Yellowstone National Park. This photo of Moran, by Jackson, is in the East Hampton, New York, Free Library.

Ten years after he began to paint the high mountains and colorful canyons of the West, Thomas Moran (in G. W. Sheldon's American Painters) explained his artistic objectives and how he sought to realize them in two of his best-known landscapes:

I place no value upon literal transcripts from Nature. My general scope is not realistic; all my tendencies are toward idealization. Of course all art must come through Nature; I do not mean to depreciate Nature or naturalism but I believe that a place, as a place, has no value in itself for the artist only so far as it furnishes the material from which to construct a picture. Topography in art is valueless. The motive or incentive of my "Grand Canyon of the Yellowstone" was a gorgeous display of color that impressed itself upon me. Probably no scenery in the world presents such a combination. The forms are extremely wonderful and pictorial, and while I desired to tell truely of Nature, I did not wish to realize the scene literally, but to preserve and to convey its true impression. Every form introduced into the picture is within view from a given point, but the relations of the separate parts to one another are not always preserved. For instance, the precipitous rocks on the right were really at my back when I stood at that point, yet in their present position they are strictly true to pictorial Nature; and so correct in the whole representation that every member of the expedition with which I was connected, declared, when he saw the painting, that he knew the exact spot which had been reproduced. The rocks in the foreground are so carefully drawn that a geologist could determine their precise nature. I treated them so in order to serve my purpose. In another work, "The Mountain of the Holy Cross," the foreground is intensely realistic also; its granite rocks are realized to the farthest point that I could carry them; and the idealization of the scene consists in the combination and arrangements of the various objects in it. At the same time, the combination is based upon the characteristics of the place. My purpose was to convey a true impression of the region; and as for the elaborated rocks, I have elaborated them out of pure love of the rocks. I have studied rocks carefully and I like to represent them.

Frederic Remington prided himself on his knowledge of horses, and he shared this knowledge in an article, Horses of the Plains, published in the January 1889 issue of Century Magazine. After his years of extended travel among Indians of the Great Plains, he wrote an exceedingly accurate description of the now-extinct Indian pony—the homely little horse that helped make the Plains

Indians such effective light cavalrymen during the Indian wars of 1851–1877:

He may be all that the wildest enthusiast may claim in point of hardihood and power, as indeed he is, but he is not beautiful. His head and neck join like the two parts of a hammer, his legs are as fine as a deer's, though not with the flat knee-cap and broad cannon-bone of the English ideal. His barrel is a veritable tun, made so by the bushels of grass which he consumes in order to satisfy his nature. His quarters are apt to run suddenly back to the hips, and the rear view is decidedly mulish from the hocks. The mane and tail are apt to be light, and I find that the currycomb of the groom has a great deal to do in deciding on which side of the horse's neck the mane shall fall; for an Indian pony it is apt to fall on the right and the left, or stand up in the middle in perfect indecision.

When he was asked to write about himself for the March 18, 1905, issue of Collier's Weekly, designated Remington Number in his honor, Frederic Remington recalled how, as early as 1881 on his first trip West, he had become painfully aware of the passing of the Old West he loved:

I had brought more than the ordinary schoolboy enthusiasm to Catlin, Irving, Gregg, Lewis and Clark, and others on their shelf, and youth found me sweating along their tracks. I was in the grand silent country following my own inclinations, but there was a heavy feel in the atmosphere. I did not immediately see what it portended, but it gradually obtruded itself. The times had changed.

Evening overtook me one night in Montana, and I by good luck made the camp-fire of an old wagon freighter who shared his bacon and coffee with me. I was nineteen years old and he was a very old man. Over the pipes he developed that he was born in Western New York and had gone West at an early age. His West was Iowa. Thence during his long life he had followed the receding frontiers, always further and further West. "And now," said he, "there is no more West. In a few years the railroad will come along the Yellowstone and a poor man can not make a living at all." . . .

The old man had closed my very entrancing book almost at the first chapter. I knew the railroad was coming—I saw men already swarming into the land. I knew the derby hat, the smoking chimneys, the cord-binder, and the thirty-day note were upon us in a resistless surge. I knew the wild riders and the vacant land were about to vanish forever, and the more I considered the subject the bigger the Forever loomed.

Sitting before his easel in his log-cabin studio in Great Falls, Montana, in 1920, Charles M. Russell contemplates his Salute of the Robe Trade, an Indian trading scene at Fort Lewis in the Blackfoot country during the 1840's. This historical painting was the first work his shrewd wife, Nancy, sold for more than $10,000. Russell found it hard to believe his paintings would bring what he called "dead men's prices." This photograph is in the collection of the Russell Memorial in Great Falls.

Although popularly known as "the Cowboy-Artist," Charles M. Russell was very modest about his career as a cowboy as well as his artistic talent. One item at the Russell Memorial in Great Falls, Montana, where Russell's log cabin studio has been restored, is a biographical note, A Few Words About Myself, which the artist penned but a few months before his death on October 24, 1926. He wrote:

The papers have been kind to me—many times more kind than true. Although I worked for many years on the range, I am not what the people think a cowboy should be. I was neither a good roper nor rider. I was a night wrangler. How good I was, I'll leave it to the people I worked for to say—there are still a few of them living. In the spring I wrangled horses, in the fall I herded beef. I worked for the big outfits and always held my job. . . .

My friends are mixed—preachers, priests and sinners. I belong to no church, but am friendly toward and respect all of them. I have always liked horses and since I was eight years old have always owned a few.

I am old-fashioned and peculiar in my dress. I am eccentric (that is a polite way of saying you're crazy). I believe in luck and have had lots of it.

To have talent is no credit to its owner; what a man can't help he should get neither credit nor blame for—it's not his fault. I am an illustrator. There are lots better ones, but some worse. Any man that can make a living doing what he likes is lucky, and I am that. Any time I cash in now, I win.

The American West's first non-urban art colony was founded at Taos, north of Santa Fe, New Mexico, in 1898 by Joseph Henry Sharp, Bert G. Phillips, and Ernest L. Blumenschien. Sharp's 1919 painting of Taos Pueblo, below, in the University of Cincinnati collection, dramatized the brilliant colors of its setting. In 1932 the Taos Society of Artists included, left to right, lower row: Sharp, Blumenschien; middle row: E. Martin Hennings, Phillips, E. Irving Couse, Oscar E. Berninghaus; top row: Walter Ufer, W. Herbert Dunton, Victor Higgins, Kenneth Adams. The group photo, taken by C. E. Lord, is in the Museum of New Mexico, Santa Fe.

In 1883, when he returned to the United States from his studies under Gérôme in Paris, George de Forest Brush of Tennessee proceeded westward to paint Indians. Two years later his article, An Artist Among the Indians, appearing in the May 1885 issue of Century Magazine, explained why he had chosen Indians as subjects for his art:

All that Rembrandt asked of the human figure was that it might exhibit light and shade; he never looked for pretty people, but found in this aspect of things a life-work. It is not necessary that an Indian learn to spell and make change before we see that his long locks are beautiful as he rides against the prairie winds. A hawk is cruel, yet who has not loved to watch its spiral course in the summer heavens?

It is also a mistake to suppose that Indians are all homely. A really handsome squaw is rare, but there are more superb and symmetrical men among them than I have seen elsewhere, their beardless faces reminding one always of the antique; these are not rare but are to be seen at every dance, where they are mostly naked, decorated in feathers and light fineries. Their constant light exercise, frequent steam-baths, and freedom from overwork develop the body in a manner only equalled, I must believe, by the Greek. . . .

But in choosing Indians as subjects for art, I do not paint from the historian's or the antiquary's point of view; I do not care to represent them in any curious habits which could not be comprehended by us; I am interested in those habits and deeds in which we have feelings in common. Therefore, I hesitate to attempt to add any interest to my pictures by supplying historical facts. If I were required to resort to this in order to bring out the poetry, I would drop the subject at once.

Half a century after he had helped to found the art colony at Taos, New Mexico, Joseph Henry Sharp was still active. His letter to his friend Ruel P. Tolman, Director of the National Collection of Fine Arts in Washington, D.C., was dated Pasadena, California, February 20, 1947:

. . . We are here 4–5 months each year. . . . Taos is near 8,000 ft. alt. Mrs. Sharp has to come down on account of heart. Good for every one not born in mountains to get down a few months.

At 87 I am still on deck; tho' feel the age a bit in eyes and bones. Work in studio (in Taos outside also) every day—maybe not so much steam, but same enthusiasm. Just now working on a 36″ Sioux Scalp Dance which I had a glimpse of 40 odd years ago. . . . In Taos can get my models to correct drawing.

I'm almost cleared out of Indian stuff last two years. Gilcrease Fd'n, Okla. got the last 75 portraits of the old Custer and other warriors, some large historical and other figure pieces. Now over 200 of the old heads (good many pictures) are in museums or some such institutions and I am satisfied.

III The Voice of the Folk Artist

During the eighteenth and nineteenth centuries the northern colonies—and later, the states—provided fertile seed-ground for the folk artist; there his productions were eagerly sought and gratefully received. The years that marked the establishment of the new states were the years of the country painter's greatest prosperity. The end of this era was finally and decisively marked by the arrival of the daguerreotype, ironically introduced to America by a painter, Samuel F. B. Morse. The tradition of the self-taught carver is one of the most continuous in American art; despite the development of machine methods, the handcrafting of decoys, store figures, and toys continued well into this century.

In the country that grew from the towns along the Atlantic seaboard up the rivers to new farms and settlements, the folk sculptor or painter followed soon after the frontiersman. His creations were often useful, but broad, vigorous handling of two- or three-dimensional design made usefulness secondary to esthetic worth. The variety of production was endless. Besides portraits and ornaments for house and garden, the folk artists created landscapes, religious and historical scenes, weathervanes, whirligigs, toys, circus and carousel sculpture, cigar-store figures, ship carvings, and sacred objects.

Many artists were known by name: John Durand, Captain Simon Fitch, Nathaniel Wales, John Brewster, Jr., Eunice Pinney, Jacob Maentel, Ammi Phillips, Winthrop Chandler, Ralph Earl, Rufus Hathaway, James Sanford Ellsworth, Charles Hofmann, J. N. Eaton, Erastus Salisbury Field, and Edward Hicks are among those who attained high repute. They were outnumbered, however, by anonymous legions whose circumstances were as varied as their performances–soldiers and sailors, housewives, blacksmiths, tinsmiths, coppersmiths, lumberjacks, hunters, farmers, and itinerant craftsmen. All of these contributed to a torrent of folk art. For some, handcrafting was a livelihood; for others, a pastime for their leisure.

A general definition of folk art identifies it as the creation of self-taught men and women working for their peers in the country and in small towns. Thus, the greatest number of works were made in the Northeast, in areas originally settled by the English, Dutch, and Germans and dominated by the middle class. From these states, outcroppings later appeared in Ohio and in the Southern Highlands.

In New England, New York, New Jersey, and Pennsylvania the painters and carvers were inspired by the medieval symbols and designs of British and North European country art. The artists of the New World transformed their source material into typically American expressions. Their honest creations emphasized bold form, fluid movement, and rough-hewn texture rather than delicate detail and fine delineation. The picture of the folk artist that emerges is that of a craftsman gaining skill as knowledge of his materials increases; it is the picture of a respected member of a small community performing a valuable service in a vivid, attractive, and often, highly realistic way.

Unlike his academic brother schooled in the uses and complexities of art, the untutored folk limner or carver was content to remain within his own society. While Benjamin West went to Italy to learn the lessons of the Renaissance, and later attracted whole generations of budding American artists to his studio in London, most of the folk artists, who learned through their own trials, stayed close to relatives and neighbors and to the cultures of which they were a part. In the years of their greatest prosperity they were important citizens of their limited world, admired for their ability to make useful and decorative objects and to take accurate—often disturbingly accurate—likenesses of their patrons. By the standards of the economies in which they flourished, they were handsomely paid. While Samuel F. B. Morse, the professor who had briefly tutored one of their ranks, was compelled to turn in bitterness from painting to the invention of the telegraph, his pupil, Erastus Salisbury Field, could make a greater profit at portrait painting than could his cousin who ran a favorably located tavern.

In Europe and America the trained painter sought help beyond the tantalizingly small black-and-white engraving that echoed the grandeur of English and European painting. But his country cousin took not only the engraving but every Bible illustration, every children's book, and every instruction manual as a point of departure from which he might take flight in grandiose fantasy and on which he enlarged, improved, and enriched.

To the folk artist, at one with his society, Europe was not nearly so great a temptation as the houses of relatives and friends, beyond the hill or over the river in the next community. There he could create a new esthetic object in the most essential and direct terms (though he did indulge his urge to use one splendid dress in portraits of sisters-in-law or cousins). It was a job to be done. Here was a need to remember a face for oneself or for posterity, a need to decorate one's house and barn; and here, in the person of the self-taught artist, was the means for fulfilling the need.

While the academically-trained artist avoided abstraction and design, the folk artists of the Northeast, limited by their difficulties in expressing perspective and anatomy, depended on these devices to develop their compositions. Fittingly, the scale of folk artists' creations tended to be as magnificent as their dreams. Giants appeared on canvas, emperors of their country world. Biblical tales transplanted to the Pennsylvania countryside became contemporary parables in which creatures of prophesy symbolized the artist's state of mind. The results were noble, devout, funny, outrageous, and splendid.

The new romanticism of the nineteenth century touched the artist who learned for himself as deeply as it influenced the romantics led by the great academic landscape painters. Because he catered to country patrons, the folk artist, along with his farmer subjects, saw and appreciated that acres hard-won and not easily tamed were fully as beautiful as growing forests and rustic glens. For, in fact, the paths of the tutored and the self-taught crossed frequently. Most often, it was as the folk artists saw a crumb to snatch and set as a feast at his own table; less frequently, it was an embittered artist who, chagrined at his tottering career in the city, marveled at the prosperity his less-skilled rural contemporary enjoyed. Their worlds overlapped but seldom did the two move together. Each must have noted and wondered what his life might have been had he chosen the other's life and way.

The hard, dry line sometimes mentioned as typical of John Durand's work is apparent in his The Children of Garrett Rapalje, opposite page, painted about 1768 and now owned by the New-York Historical Society. But the bright-eyed subjects do possess a gayety and charm also characteristic of Durand.

Shem Drowne (1683–1774), born in Kittery, Maine, spent most of his long life in Boston as a maker of weathervanes and figureheads. An accident and subsequent repair of Drowne's most famous vane—the grasshopper that still flies atop Boston's historic "cradle of liberty," Faneuil Hall—is mentioned in a contemporary's note quoted by J. Rayner Whipple in Old-Time New England, in October 1940, the bulletin of the Society for the Preservation of New England Antiquities:

Shem Drowne made it May 25, 1742. To my brethren and fellow Grasshopper: Fell in ye year 1753 Nov.18, early in ye morning by a great earthquake by my Old Master above. . . . Again like to have met with my Utter Ruin by fire [1761], but hopping Timely from my Public Scituation cam of with Broken bones and much Bruised. Cured and Fixed . . .[by] Old Master's son Thomas Drowne June 28, 1768, and though I will promise to Discharge my Office, yet I shall vary as ye wind.

Jacob Maentel, a German settler in Pennsylvania who preferred painting to farming, was himself painted in 1816 by a fellow artist, Lewis Miller of York, Pennsylvania. During the early- and mid-19th century Maentel did many of the portraits formerly attributed to another folk artist, Samuel Andredi Stettinius. The Historical Society of York County owns the Maentel portrait.

The group portrait of "The Children of Garrett Rapalje" was painted in 1769 by John Durand, who made numerous expert and skillful portraits in New York, Connecticut, and Virginia between 1766 and 1782. However, the year before Durand painted the winsome children, he did try to interest New Yorkers in historical painting. His plea for backers for a series of historical subjects (which apparently went unheeded) was outlined in The New-York Gazette or Weekly Post-Boy for April 11, 1768:

John Durand.—The Subscriber having from his Infancy endeavored to qualify himself in the Art of historical Painting, humbly hopes for the Encouragement from the Gentlemen and Ladies of this City and Province, that so elegant and entertaining an Art, has always obtain'd from People of the most improved Minds, and Best Taste and Judgment, in all polite Nations in every Age. And tho' he is sensible, that to excell (in this Branch of Painting especially) requires a more ample Fund of universal and accurate Knowledge than he can pretend to, in Geometry, Geography, Perspective, Anatomy, Expression of Passions, ancient and modern History, &c. &c. Yet he hopes, from the good Nature and Indulgence of the Gentlemen and Ladies who employ him that his humble Attempts, in which his best Endeavours will not be wanting, will meet with Acceptance, and give Satisfaction; and he proposes to work at as cheap Rates as any Person in America.

To such Gentlemen and Ladies as have thought but little upon this Subject, and might only regard painting as a superfluous Ornament, I would just observe, that History-painting, besides being extremely ornamental, has many important uses. It presents to our View, some of the most interesting Scenes recorded in ancient or modern History; gives us most lively and perfect Ideas of the Things represented, than we could receive from an historical account of them; and fre-

quently recals to our Memory, a long Train of Events, with which these Representations were connected. They shew us a proper Expression of the Passions excited by every Event, and have an Effect, the very same in Kind, (but stronger) than a fine historical Description of the same Passage would have upon a judicious Reader. Men who have distinguished themselves for the good of their Country and Mankind, may be set before our Eyes as Examples, and to give us their silent Lessons, and besides, every judicious Friend and Visitant shares with us in the Advantage and Improvement, and increases its Value to ourselves.

Mary Ann Bacon (1787–1869) was the daughter of Asabel and Hannah Franch Bacon of Roxbury, Connecticut; her portrait and those of her parents and younger brother Charles were recorded in 1795 by the Connecticut folk artist William Jennys, who was active from 1790 to 1805. All the portraits are owned by the Abby Aldrich Rockefeller Folk Art Collection in Williamsburg, Virginia. In 1802, Mary Ann and her father traveled on horseback to Litchfield, Connecticut, so that the girl might enter Miss Sarah Pierce's school. Excerpts from Mary Ann's journal of her days there were first published in Emily Vanderpoel's Chronicle of a Pioneer School (Cambridge University Press, 1903). In the diary the gentle sweetness that characterizes her childhood portrait is confirmed:

. . . we stopped at Mr. Mosley about three oClock where we refreshed our selves and mounted our horses about four and rode in solitude saw many beautiful meadows and the little birds warbling sweet notes seeming to enjoy the sweet pleasures of life it rained a little before we reached Litchfield which was about Six oClock in the afternoon. Papa got me into Board at Mr. Andrew Adams's. After staying a short time we parted and being much fatigued I retired to rest soon after tea.

Friday June the 11—I returned to the house where breakfast was almost ready at nine oClock went to school with Miss Cornelia Adams drew and heard the Girls read history, at Noon studied my Dictionary and devoted the afternoon to reading drawing and spelling and spent the rest part of the day with Mrs. Adams and her daughter and retired to rest at Nine oClock.

Wednesday August 11th—Miss Pierce drew my landscape.

Wednesday August 25— . . . in the afternoon read worked on my picture studied my spellings and spelt after school the Boarders all moved the South Chamber and my time was spent in writing in graret and I was forgot and licked to lost my tea however I did not go up raret again with out partisioning to some one to caul me meal times the evening was spent in reading till Nine and after that went down and went to Mr. Chappins to get some beer.

"View of Quebec" by Mary Ann Bacon is one of two similar versions of the scene by the same artist; both are in the Litchfield Historical Society's collections. Undoubtedly the schoolgirl used a print or drawing book as the source for her composition; it is this subject that she twice mentions in her journal, writing that her schoolmistress, Miss Sarah Pierce, had helped her draw at least one of the landscapes.

John Stevens III of Newport, Rhode Island, was the third of his name to work as a stonecutter (between 1769 and 1789) in the shop established on Thames Street in 1705. The tradition of fine stonecutting formulated then is carried on to this day in the John Stevens Shop directed by Esther Fisher Benson and her son, John E. Benson. In the Newport Historical Society Bulletin of October 1963, Mrs. Benson first published excerpts from the eighteenth-century account books of the three Stevens—grandfather, father, and son; the ledgers of the

The design on the 1771 gravestone of Mercy Buliod and her son is an example of the graceful work done by John Stevens III, whose family was famous as stonecutters in Newport, Rhode Island, during the 18th century. The gravestone rubbing is by Ann Parker and Avon Neal of Brookfield, Massachusetts.

At 8 years, Mary Ann Bacon of Roxbury, Connecticut, possessed a serene beauty captured in 1795 by William Jennys. Her portrait and those of her parents, Asabel and Hannah Franch Bacon, and of her brother Charles, are in the Abby Aldrich Rockefeller Folk Art Collection, Williamsburg, Virginia.

original John Stevens Shop are owned by Mrs. Benson. Among the most amusing entries are those written by John III in the first book. At thirteen, he wrote: "John Stevens that long scorpion measures five feet eight inches tall, two foot four inches and a half round. December 7, 1767." Young John seems to have been an avid reader with a spelling problem and catholic tastes. In an account book for 1767, he recorded the "Books Read by Me. John Stevens Begun January the 1th 1767":

The 2nd Vols of the Supposed Daughter or the Innocent Impostor; The Wars of England &c in Reign of King Charles the 1th; The Unfortunate Young Nobleman in 2 Vol; The English Rogue or Witty Extravergant; Paradice Lost. A Poem in 12 Books (the Author John Milton); The Travels of Cyrus in 8 Book all in one Vollom; The 2 Last Vol. of the Naval History of Great Britain; A Genuine History of the Irish Rogues Papparees w z [word not clear]; A Discourse Addressed to The Sons of L I B E R T Y at a Solemin Assembly, near Liberty Tree, in Providence Feb.14 1766; [two notations not clear]; A History of the Seven Wise Masters of Rome; The Cronacols of the Kings of England; De Laune's Plea for the Non-Conformists; The Daventures of the Count De Vinevil; The History of Jack Conner in 2 Volloms; The Memories of Charles Goodville in 2 Volloms.

On a ledger page dated Feb.23 1727 and headed with a simple entry "By Cash Received—By Cash—3 Shillings" appears a patriotic poem of uncertain origin but most probably the composition of an earlier Stevens:

The nation free, dispotic rule that craves,
And gives up Liberty to link to slaves,
Where cruel Kings and havoc decrees oppress,
In vain shall mourn and hope in vain redress.—

Combine! ye sons of freedom, ah, combine!
The people are invincible, who join:
Factions and feuds will overturn the state,
Which union renders flourishing and gereate.—

Treat not a forefinger with barb'rous pride,
Mock not his accent, or his garb deride:
For peace at home that people ne'er shall find,
Who wage a war with all mankind.

In 1802, at the age of fifty-seven, Ephraim Starr (1745–1809) of Goshen, Connecticut, was portrayed by Captain Simon Fitch (1758–1835) of nearby Lebanon. More than fifty years later Simon Fitch's brother-in-law, the Reverend Dan Huntington, published in his Memories, Counsels and Reflections (Cambridge Press, 1857) the only printed account of the artist's work, an anecdote rediscovered by William L. Warren in preparing the 1961 exhibition of Fitch's work at the Connecticut Historical Society in Hartford. Huntington's story of Fitch's trials in achieving verisimilitude, and his frenzy over defeat, is a tale worthy of Washington Irving:

Simon Fitch, portrait-painter, married Wealthy Huntington, my sister. He was employed by a class in Yale College to take the portrait of President Dwight, in which he succeeded well in the main; but in finishing one of the hands, he could not suit himself; the more he worked upon it, the less he was satisfied, till, in a state of hopeless frenzy, he mounted his horse, and, without being blamed

With the probable aid of her schoolmistress, Mary Ann Bacon (1787–1869) painted this View of Quebec, in which the lively delineation of hills, trees, shrubs, and livestock imitates needlework—a stylistic device the young folk artists of the period often used for their watercolors. This 1802 landscape and a similar version by Mary Ann belong to the Litchfield, Connecticut, Historical Society.

This portrait of Ephraim Starr of Goshen, Connecticut, painted in 1802 by the rather eccentric Captain Simon Fitch, is considered the best work by this Lebanon, Connecticut, artist. At the time a sizable 57 years, Ephraim amply fills the chair and canvas; it has been said that the star-patterned floor was a pun on his name.

This figure-studded mansion that stood on High Street in Newburyport, Massachusetts, in 1806 housed what its master, self-styled "Lord" Timothy Dexter, called his "mouse-rum." The restored six-and-one-half foot William Pitt, left, is presumably the "mister pitt" mentioned by Dexter, who named Joseph Wilson as the carver of Pitt and the other figures. The carving is in the Smithsonian Institution, Washington, D. C.

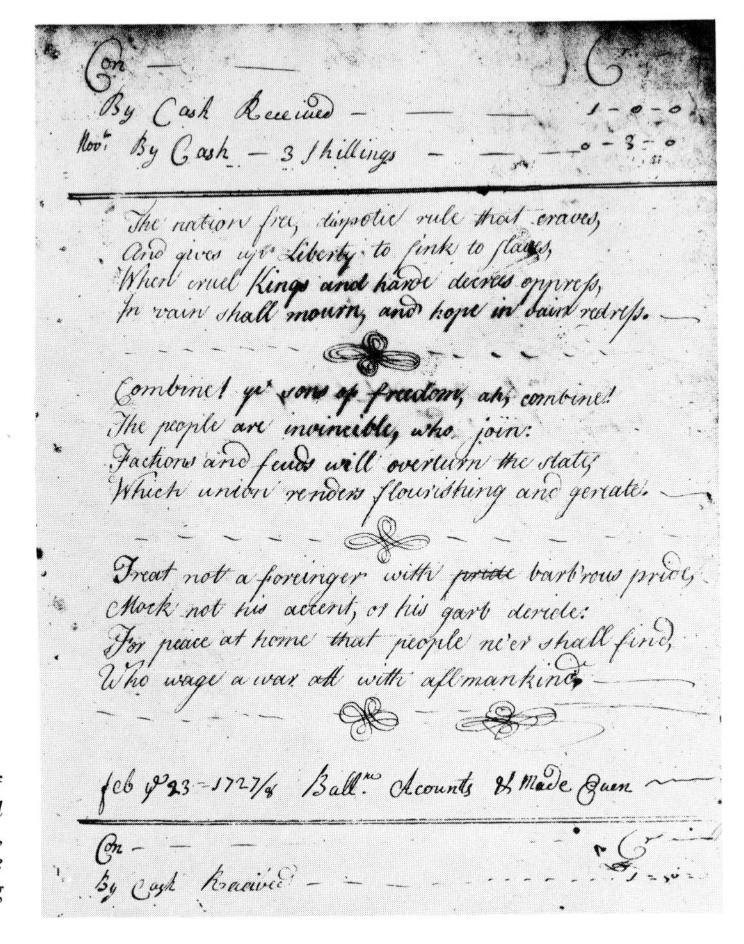

Con —

By Cash Received — 1-0-0
Nov. By Cash — 3 Shillings — 0-3-0

The nation free, despotic rule that craves,
And gives up Liberty to sink to slaves,
Where cruel Kings and harsh decrees oppress,
In vain shall mourn, and hope in vain redress.

Combine! ye sons of freedom, ah, combine!
The people are invincible, who join:
Factions and feuds will overturn the state,
Which union renders flourishing and great.

Treat not a foreinger with ~~pride~~ barb'rous pride,
Mock not his accent, or his garb deride:
For peace at home that people ne'er shall find,
Who wage a war all with allmankind

feb y 23 - 1727/8 Ball. Acounts & Made Even

Con —
By Cash Received —

One of the earlier John Stevens of Newport, Rhode Island, is believed the author of this patriotic poem, found in the ledger books of the family of stonecutters famous during the 18th century.

by any one, or mentioning his trouble to others, he set his face homeward. Coming to Durham woods, he heard some one trying his skill upon a tin trumpet. Supposing it was intended for him, he leaped a fence into the forest, where he wandered about till morning, and the next day made his way safely home, but could never be persuaded to finish the portrait, or meddle in any way with his palette and brush. It must have been a temporary derangement, the effect of a keen sensibility, peculiar to artistic genius.

Fitch and [John] Trumbull, in their boyhood, contemporaries at the Brick School (Tisdale's) it was said were at that time nearly upon a par, as competitors in the occasional trials of their skill, in the opinion of good judges; and at times Trumbull was known to have the generosity to ascribe the palm to his rival. . . . The portrait was hung up, among others, in the College Library, and was thought well of. I remember once standing before it, in company with Dr. Dwight. He spoke of the defect in the hand as hardly worth noticing, and appeared to be otherwise satisfied with the performance.

Again in 1802, the year the Starr portraits were painted in Connecticut, a completely eccentric, self-styled lord, Timothy Dexter of Newburyport, Massachusetts, had printed the first edition of A Pickle for the Knowing Ones. In the fourth edition, published in 1848 by Blanchard and Sargent of Newburyport, a "View of Lord Dexter's Mansion, High Street, Newburyport, 1806" was one of the illustrations, and Timothy Dexter, Esq., himself explains his motives in erecting his mansion—"mouserum"—and ordering the carving and placement of the figures, both "two Leged and fore Leged":

Now I be gin to Lay the Corner ston with grat Remembrence of my father Jorge Washington the grate herow 17 sentreys past before we found so good a Father to his children and Now gone to Rest Now to shoue my Love to my father and grate Carieters I will shoue the world one of the grate Wonders of the World in 15 months. . . such A mouserum on Earth will announce O Lord thou knowest to be troue fourder. . . Now to see good Lord what has bin in the world grat wase back to own fore fathers Not old plimeth [Plymouth] but stop to Addom & Eve to shoue 45 figers two Leged and fore Leged becose we Cant Doue well without fore Legd in the first plase they are our foude in the Next plase to make out Dexters mouseum I want 4 Lions to defend thous grat and mistry men from East to wist from North to South. . . . if Agreabel I forme A good and peasabel govement on my Land in Newburyport Compleat I take 3 presedents hamsher [Hampshire] govener all to Noue York and the grate mister John Jay is one, that makes 2 in that state the king of grat britton mister pitt Roufus King Cros over to france Loues the 16 and then the grate bonnepartey the grate and there segnetoure Crow biddey—I command pease the gratest brotherly Love and Not fade be Linked to gether with that best of troue Love so as to govern all nasions on the fass of the gloub not to tiranize over them but to put them to order if any Despout shall A Rise as to boundreys or Any maturs of Importence it is Left france and grat britton and Amacarey to be settled A Congress to be always in france all Despouts is to be thare seteled and this may be Dun this will balless powers and then all wars Dun A way . . . .

At the time he was painting the portrait of Middletown residents Nathan Sage and his wife, the Connecticut folk artist, Nathaniel Wales, who was active from 1806 to 1815, listed his talents and qualifications in an advertisement in The Witness—dated Litchfield, Feb. 4, 1806:

Nathaniel F. Wales Informs the citizens of Litchfield and the towns adjoining,

One Shoe Off, inscribed in pencil on the original stretcher, is by John Brewster, Jr., a deaf-mute folk artist who probably painted it in Connecticut, where it was found. It is dated June 4, 1807, and is now owned by the New York State Historical Association, Cooperstown. The tie of the shoe worn by the child repeats the design motif of the stenciled floor.

that he (now residing at Mr. Jonathan Bull's one hundred rods north of the Court house) intends to carry on the Sign Painting Business, in all its various branches; Tavern Signs may be had, with different devices, glass Signs, neatly enamelled, with gilt letters; or any common gilt or plain Sign, as may best suit the employer. Those persons who will favor him with their work may depend on having it done with neatness and dispatch.

Also LIKENESSES painted on Canvas or Glass, for Eight Dollars each; and if not approved as Likenesses, no pay will be requested.

In 1960, Nina Fletcher Little explored the career of an astonishingly creative folk artist, John Brewster, Jr. (1766–1854)—a career even more dramatic since he was both deaf and mute. In preparing the catalogue for the first major exhibition of his work, at the Connecticut Historical Society, Hartford, she discovered many contemporary references to Brewster, who traveled along the New England coast from Connecticut to Maine pursuing his vocation in spite of his double affliction. The Reverend James Cogswell of Windham, Connecticut, mentions this folk artist in his diary (now in the Connecticut Historical Society's manuscript collection):

December 13,1790: . . .Doctor Brewster's Son, a Deaf & Dumb young man came in in [sic] the Evening. he is very Ingenious, has a Genius for painting & can write well, & converse so that he may be understood in many Things. he lodged here.

On February 7, 1791, a second reference was made:

Brewster, the Deaf & D. young Man was at my House when I came Home. he tarried and dined here—he appears to have a good Disposition & an ingeneous Mind. I could converse little with Him, being not quite enough acquainted to understand his Signs. I pity Him—& feel thankful to God for the Exercise of my Senses.

In 1817, at the age of fifty-one, John Brewster became a student in the country's first school for the deaf, established in Hartford. Before 1837 he was one of only two students who were able to pay their own way at the Connecticut Asylum for the Education and Instruction of Deaf and Dumb Persons.

Eunice Pinney (1770–1849) is the most skilled and creative of the lady amateurs who painted for their own pleasure. All her paintings date to the years of her second marriage, when her children had grown up and left home. Notes, letters, and even lines of verse often accompanied the watercolors she sent as gifts to her friends and relatives.

On a Wednesday midnight in October 1826, Eunice Pinney wrote a long and affectionate note to her daughter Emeline Minerva Pinney, a teacher of painting at a school near Brunswick, Virginia. The artist's closing lines are on the reverse of a charming landscape with figures, and they demonstrate her intention that her daughter use the composition as a guide for her girl students:

. . . for I suppose you won't wish your picture to be scribbled all . . . if you can alter it any way for the better . . . do it. It wants more skill [and] the leaves of the tree darkening and if I have written any thing you don't [wish] your scholars should see you can sew or bast or paper over the back side of it. And now it is night for I have got a dismal light. Write soon I pray And come you home without delay EP Oct 13 1826 Wednesday night 12 O Clock.

Although his career as a folk artist lasted for half a century in eastern New York and western Connecticut and Massachusetts, Ammi Phillips's long life as a

[illegible] are many reasons why but have not time to explane them now. Norman says
[illegible]rite so often as you would wish that you are the less dear to my heart. No no Emeline to my sor[illegible]
[illegible]s and sleepless nights I have had on your account since your departure you'd not accuse me of in[illegible]
you yes you are my wish by day my dream by night How much we all long to see you
you to return when your year is expired, And I am sure I shall not consent to your going so
[illegible]per, must forbare. Your unkle Elisha & Aunt D. were here last August said Lydia was teach[illegible]
could get six hundred as well as two hundred. Think you have been impos'd upon. But if
you get home alive I shall think but little of that. May the winds and waves prove prop[illegible]
and waft you safe home to my arms Then will this conflict of my mind be ber And we
hope, shall meet to part no more. You see I am very poettical. But I must hasten to tell you
all the news I can recolect and conclude my letter, for I suppose you wont wish your pa[illegible]
scribbled all over. And now prepare for a dreadfull shock. You have lost Luke Prouty he has
married for some weeks to the amiable Miss Louisa Eno. Julia Holcomb is likewise ma[illegible]
one Phelps Turkey Hills. And last sunday Mrs Clapp was published to a black man, the
ugliest & most disgusting creature you ever saw. Several people in Turkey Hills have die[illegible]
this summer past, amoung others are the following personages Esquire Owen Erastus
Roots Alson Hoskins Mr Roswell Chancy Barker & Sally his sister. And last mo[illegible]
cousin Catherine Owen. of a billious fever, she lived but four days after she was taken
& those 4 days in great distress indeed I was at her funeral stay'd all night they appear'd qu[illegible]
resign'd indeed much more so than I expected Chloe sends her love to you. Sophia & Ann [illegible]
same I was greatly shock'd at the news of the death of Indiana Mead. Poor dear girl I hope
shes gone to a better world. Had she all the fine qualities you tell me no wonder you
regret the loss no wonder you deplore her. But tho in youth she bid adue to time
Still let us hope she's found a happier clime. Norman told me of her death befor
you wrote. But I must quit this subject Tis very late and I am very cold. When ne[illegible]
you write to me inclose it in one to Norman he can pay the postage & send it to
me. He thinks this the best way. He was here last saturday night & Mr Scoll with
him. You, Dr Barns & C have become very sociable. I hope you treat them with sivili[illegible]
& politness as I think every person intitled to common sivility. Dont try to m[illegible]
yourself enemies I beg of you. Cinro has now they say a number of scholers from
Redhook among the rest Alexander Hoofman & Frances Livingston.

Relatives and friends benefited by the practice of one of the early 19th century's few women folk artists, Eunice Pinney; she often sent watercolors as gifts and added her personal messages, written on the reverse side. Above is a landscape (now in the collection of Edgar William and Bernice Chrysler Garbisch) painted in 1828. With its accompanying letter on the back, it went to her daughter Emeline Minerva.

painter (1788–1865) has been thoroughly explored only in this decade, by Barbara and Larry Holdridge of Baltimore, Maryland, who made a scholarly investigation of his work. In the course of their research, which was first published in Art in America (No. Two 1960), they found a letter at the Senate House, Kingston, New York, from John Vanderlyn to his nephew John Vanderlyn, Jr. In his letter dated September 9, 1825, the well-known artist twice mentioned Ammi Phillips—his contemporary whose fame was purely local:

I heard with pleasure that you had made some very clever attempts in portraits where you are and which had given much satisfaction. A couple of years more spent in N. York must improve you in this occupation if you pay the least attention to it and in being only a little superiour to the Philips [sic] who was here some years since, you may gain more money than you could by any Mechanical business, which you must know, is far more labourious and less genteel and considered. Were I to begin life again, I should not hesitate to follow this plan, that is, to paint portraits cheap and slight, for the mass of folks can't judge the merits of a well finished picture, I am more and more persuaded of this. Indeed, moving about through the country as Philips did and probably still does, must be an agreeable way of passing ones time. I saw four of his works at Jacobus Hardenburgh's the other day painted a year or two ago, which seemed to satisfy them.

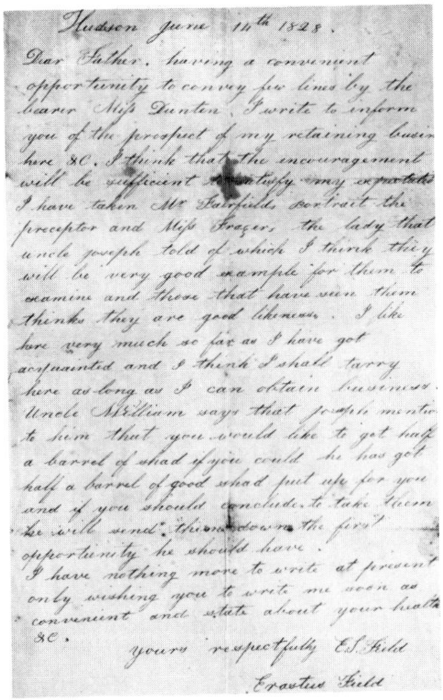

Hudson June 14th 1828.
Dear Father. having a convenient
opportunity to convey few lines by the
bearer Miss Dunton, I write to inform
you of the prospect of my retaining business here &C. I think that the encouragement
will be sufficient to satisfy my expectations
I have taken Mr Fairfield's portrait the
preceptor and Miss Frazer, the lady that
uncle Joseph told of which I think they
will be very good example for them to
examine and those that have seen them
thinks they are good likeness. I like
here very much so far as I have got
acquainted and I think I shall tarry
here as long as I can obtain business.
Uncle William says that Joseph mention
to him that you would like to get half
a barrel of shad if you could he has got
half a barrel of good shad put up for you
and if you should conclude to take them
he will send them down the first
opportunity he should have.
I have nothing more to write at present
only wishing you to write me soon as
convenient and state about your health
&C.
yours respectfully E.S. Field
Erastus Field

The letter sent by Erastus Salisbury Field is believed the only one known from his early years. Under a June 14, 1828, date he told his father that he had found Hudson [New York] a place where "the encouragement will be sufficient to satisfy my expectations" and said he'd "tarry as long as I can obtain business." Belatedly, he has been identified as the artist who painted the portrait of Lauriette Ashley, opposite page, his cousin, in 1828. The house beyond the window is probably the Ashleys' home on Prospect Hill in Hudson. The portrait is now in the City Art Museum of St. Louis.

Erastus Salisbury Field (1805–1900) was gainfully employed as a portrait painter in the late eighteen-twenties and eighteen-thirties as he traveled across Massachusetts, Connecticut, and eastern New York State. Often his services were recommended to prospective patrons by his relatives. On June 14, 1828, he wrote the following to his father; it is the only letter known from his early career. It is owned by Mrs. Carey S. Hayward of Pittsfield, Massachusetts:

Dear Father, having a convenient opportunity to convey few lines by the bearer Miss Dunton, I write to inform you of the prospect of my retaining business here &C. I think that the encouragement will be sufficient to satisfy my expectations. I have taken Mr. Fairfield's portrait the preceptor and Miss Frazers the lady that uncle Joseph told of which I think they will be very good example for them to examine and those that have seen them thinks they are good likenesses. I like here [Hudson, New York] very much so far as I have got acquainted and I think I shall tarry here as long as I can obtain business. Uncle William says that Joseph mentioned to him that you would like to get half a barrel of shad if you could he has got half a barrel of good shad put up for you and if you should conclude to take them he will send them down the first opportunity he should have. I have nothing more to write at present only wishing you to write me soon as convenient and state about your health &C. Yours respectfully E. S. Field Erastus Field

The portrait of the sizable family of the Reverend John Atwood of Concord, New Hampshire, is all the more remarkable for having been painted by Henry F. Darby of North Adams, Massachusetts, when the artist was only sixteen years old. In Henry Darby's Journal the artist wrote about his early career in art:

It would be difficult to find a spot where there was such destitution in aids to Art as the place where I was born. My Mother had a little portrait, of some connection, done in water colour and the only other pictures I have except prints were two poor portraits of my Grandmothers. I have wondered if all the inhabitants there were the first settlers, who escaped from somewhere, glad to leave everything behind them except their skins, or were they created on that spot, and

Newly acquired by the Abby Aldrich Rockefeller Folk Art Collection in Williamsburg, Virginia, this portrait of Edward Hicks was painted in 1839 by a cousin, Thomas Hicks, then 16. The setting was Edward's shop in Newtown, Pennsylvania.

Edward Hicks's favorite among his close to sixty versions of The Peaceable Kingdom was the one dated 1844. He sent it to Joseph Watson, his neighbor in Newtown, Pennsylvania, along with a letter that called it "one of the best paintings I ever done" and mentioned the price—$21.75 for painting and "fraim"—adding, "thee can pay the money to Isaac [his son] who can give thee a receipt if necessary."

Art had not yet reached them. I saw a drawingbook for the first time when I was sixteen, and by that time newcomers to the town had brought some portraits with them. . . . Up to this time my study had been of engravings mostly—tracing them on the window pane roughly and then going over them with more care. I had never heard of any principles of drawing or proportion until I was thirteen when there came a portrait painter who allowed me to see him paint a portrait from life. From him I learned what "tools" to use, and how to begin a head—and I painted my own portrait under his supervision.

From this time I was an "artist" painting in oil. Sometimes I attempted miniatures—on cardboard, on polished wood, and on pieces of ivory (got perhaps from a fine toothed comb.) My acquaintances did not know more of Art than I, so I must have made many queer portraits, and the sum I received for them was appropriate in amount. . . . I was led by the impulse which has been the moving power of all my life, and I was up in the centre of New Hampshire. Soon I found myself at Concord the Capital. It was a pleasant family "the Atwoods" I painted, all on one canvas. The father was represented sitting in the midst of his admiring wife and children expounding his Bible. I lived in this pleasant family and in the beautiful town, one summer. Mr. Atwood was State Treasurer, and I saw other State Officials—who intelligently encouraged me.

Religion and history were subjects as pleasing to self-taught folk artists as the faces of their contemporaries: Edward Hicks (1780–1849), a famous Quaker preacher and skilled sign and coach painter, was an inspired folk artist as well. His favorite subject, "The Peaceable Kingdom," is known today in about sixty versions, each slightly different from the other. His 1844 version, on a theme that had deep personal and symbolic meaning for the artist, was—even to Hicks's ambivalent way of thinking—one of his "best paintings." He said as much in the letter that accompanied the "Kingdom" when he sent it to his Newtown, Pennsylvania, neighbor, Joseph Watson, in 1844:

I send thee by my son one of the best paintings I ever done (& it may be the last) The price as agreed upon is twenty dollars with the additional sum of one dollar 75 cents which I give Edward Trego for the fraim. . .with ten coats of varnish. . . .With gratitude and thankfulness for thy kind pattronage of the poor painter & a greatful rememberence of many favours from thy kind parents—I bid the dear child affectionate farewell.

Hicks died in 1849, five years after completing his 1844 "Kingdom." His own attitude toward his "fondness for painting" was a changing one; some of his contradictory thoughts concerning it are recorded in his Memoirs, printed in Philadelphia in 1851, two years after his death:

In addition to a constitutional weakness, I quit the only business I understood, and for which I had a capacity, viz. painting, for the business of a farmer, which I did not understand, and for which I had no qualifications whatever. I verily thought then, and still think, farming more consistent with the Christian, and was willing to sacrifice all my fondness for painting. But it would not do, for notwithstanding I worked hard, I went behind hand daily. The cruel moth of usury was eating up my outward garment, soon to expose me a poor naked bankrupt; for my father, who I thought had given me forty acres of land in the vicinity of the village, altered his mind and took it from me, leaving me with only twenty acres, for which I had given eighty-six dollars per acre at public sale, and which I had to sell for forty dollars. Thus ended my farming speculation.

If the Christian world was in the real spirit of Christ, I do not believe there would be such a thing as a fine painter in christendom. It appears clearly to me

Talent beyond his years—the artist was 16 at the time—is evident in this portrait of the Reverend John Atwood and his family, painted by Henry F. Darby (active from 1831–1880) about 1845. The setting is the Atwoods's home in Concord, New Hampshire. Both the portrait and Henry Darby's Journal are owned by the Museum of Fine Arts, Boston.

Captain Samuel Chandler, painted about 1780 by the captain's younger brother Winthrop Chandler (1747–1770), is considered one of the finest works by this artist, who spent his last, sadly debt-ridden years in Worcester, Massachusetts. In the portrait, which is in the National Gallery of Art, Washington, D. C., collection of Edgar William and Bernice Chrysler Garbisch, a Revolutionary battle in which the captain may have taken part appears beyond the window.

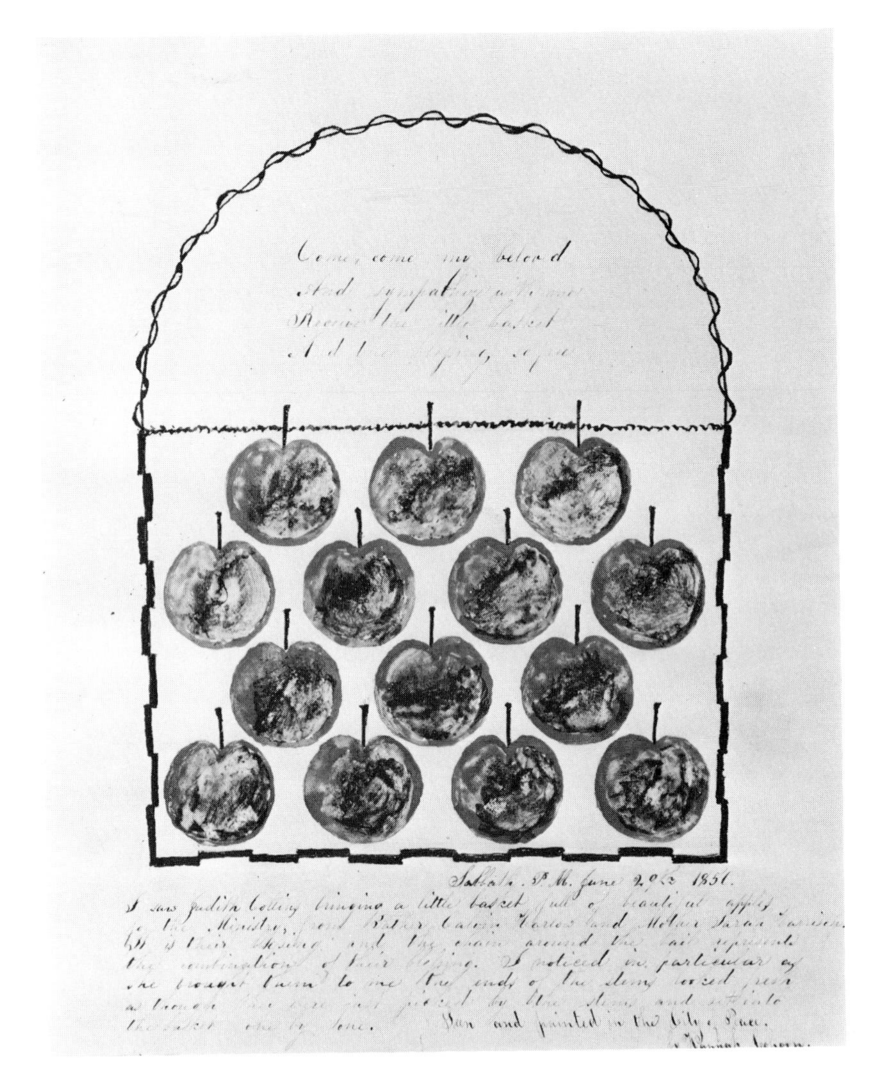

Basket of Apples is a watercolor painted in 1856 by Hannah C. Cohoon, who, as a "believer" in the Hancock Shaker Community at Pittsfield, Massachusetts, felt that these "spirit drawings" were truly recordings of visions received from Heaven. She inscribed the Apples as "seen and painted in the City of Peace."

Ralph Earl's impressive and careful portrait of Oliver Wellsworth, jurist, statesman, and Chief Justice of the United States from 1796–1799, with Mrs. Ellsworth, was painted in 1796. It is in the Wadsworth Atheneum, Hartford, Connecticut.

to be one of those trifling, insignificant arts, which has never been of any substantial advantage to mankind. But as the inseparable companion of voluptuousness and pride, it has presaged the downfall of empires and kingdoms; and in my view stands now enrolled among the premonitory symptoms of the rapid decline of the American Republic. But there is something of importance in the example of the primitive Christians and primitive Quakers, to mind their callings or business, and work with their own hands at such business as they are capable of, avoiding idleness and fanaticism. Had I my time to go over again I think I would take the advice given me by my old friend Abraham Chapman, a shrewd, sensible lawyer that lived with me about the time I was quitting painting; "Edward, thee has now the source of independence within thyself, in thy peculiar talent for painting. Keep to it, within the bounds of innocence and usefulness, and thee can always be comfortable."

The otherwise unidentified Lady with Pets might have lived somewhere near Duxbury, Massachusetts, about 1790, when this portrait was painted by Rufus Hathaway; his archaic style suggests earlier dates than the ones cited. Now at the Metropolitan Museum, New York, collection of Edgar William and Bernice Chrysler Garbisch, it is noted for the chiseled quality of the face, its color, design, and multiplicity of details.

Inspiration for a series of watercolors made in the Shaker communities of Massachusetts and New York in the eighteen-forties and early eighteen-fifties came not from an earthly muse but were recordings of "visions" received from Heaven. Chief among the Shaker scribes was Hannah Cohoon of the Hancock Community in Massachusetts. In that "City of Peace" in the summer of 1856, watercolors and words were used to describe what she saw:

Sabbath. P. M. June 29th 1856. I saw Judith Collins bringing a little basket of beautiful apples for the Ministry, from Brother Calvin Harlow and Mother Sarah Harrison. It is their blessing and the chain around the bail represents the combination of their blessing. I noticed in particular as she brought them to me the stems looked fresh as though they were just picked by the stem and set into the basket one by one. Seen and painted in the City of Peace by Hannah Cohoon.

Another of the visions "Seen and received by Hannah Cohoon in the City of Peace Sabbath Oct. 9th 10th hour A.M., 1845," was her "The Tree of Light or Blazing Sun."

The catalogue (about 1905) of the Dentzel Carrousel factory in Philadelphia illustrates a typical horse produced there. The change in the design of merry-go-round carvings from the Dentzel factory is credited to the arrival in 1903 of Salvatore Cernigliaro, a skilled Italian woodcarver of considerable renown in the early twentieth century. He describes the Dentzel shop in his long letter to Frederick Fried of New York City:

Feb. 18–63 Los Angeles 920½ So. Berendo

My own story relanted in connection to the G. Dentzel manifacturer of Carrousel. The first job I got was in Phila. P.A. there was a Mr. Morris a wealty man who manifacterred marry go round. not for sale but for his own use or his own parks. It was a new job for me carving wood horse for marry-go-round as I was carver for furniture. But I didn't go lost very quickly and got equantance with the new work and I like it very much. After tree month summer came Mr. Morris close his shop and open his park so I was out work I asked some-body if there was any other carrousell shop in Phila. They told me of Mr. Dentzell shop on Germantown near Erie Ave Phila. I manage and I find the place. Facing Germantown Ave was Mr. Dentzel house where he live on side the house was a drive way taking inside a large yard where a little factory was. . . . when I was geting inside the yard Mr. Gustavo Dentzel was in front the house and stoped me. That time I could not speak english only I say tree word—me, woodcarver, job.—Mr. Dentzel notice I was an emigrant and taking to me in German language wich I could not understud eter. So after he taked to me I understud

The carousel horse is the work of Italian-born Salvatore Cernigliaro, who came to work at the Dentzel Carousel Factory, Philadelphia, in 1903.

The wooden cigar-store Indian, by an unknown carver, dates back to the early 19th century; it belongs to the New York State Historical Association, Cooperstown.

The Skater is attributed to the John and Simeon Skillin workshop, which was active in Salem, Massachusetts, during the late 1790's and early 1800's. Here an English porcelain figurine representing Winter has been translated into wood. It is owned by the Abby Aldrich Rockefeller Folk Art Collection, Williamsburg, Virginia.

Shem Drowne, Boston's famous maker of weathervanes and figureheads during the 1700's, made the copper weathervane described as "An Indian chief, gilded all over [who] stood during the better part of a century on the cupola of the Province House, bedazzling the eyes of those who looked upward, like an angel in the sun."

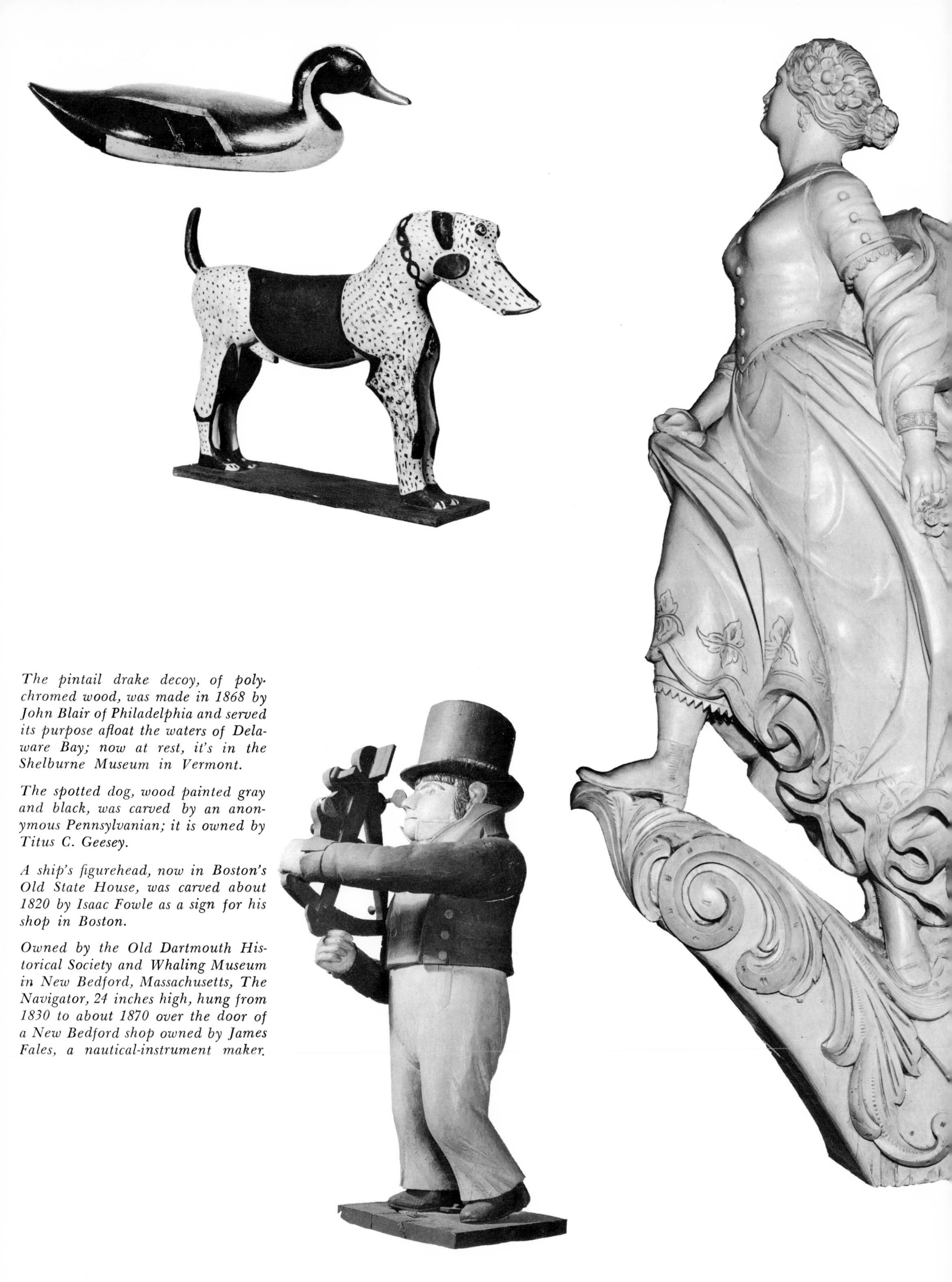

The pintail drake decoy, of polychromed wood, was made in 1868 by John Blair of Philadelphia and served its purpose afloat the waters of Delaware Bay; now at rest, it's in the Shelburne Museum in Vermont.

The spotted dog, wood painted gray and black, was carved by an anonymous Pennsylvanian; it is owned by Titus C. Geesey.

A ship's figurehead, now in Boston's Old State House, was carved about 1820 by Isaac Fowle as a sign for his shop in Boston.

Owned by the Old Dartmouth Historical Society and Whaling Museum in New Bedford, Massachusetts, The Navigator, 24 inches high, hung from 1830 to about 1870 over the door of a New Bedford shop owned by James Fales, a nautical-instrument maker.

Aaron Mountz, who died in a Pennsylvania almshouse in 1949, carved this elongated, stylized crane in the Milton Flower collection.

there was no job for me and I walked way. After one week I was still out work. Appened that still looking round for job and find my self near Dentzel shop where one block far from his shop there is S. Stefano church I whent in church and I pray. I said Mr. Lord I have only $4.00 in my pocket it is last pay for my board and if I don't find job now and and I can't pay my board sure they will trow me out. I came out of the church. it was a very hot day and I was very very thirst. I remember that a week ago when I was taking with Mr. Dentzel a notice that in middle of his yard was a artisian well so I decided to go there and get drink there Appened that when I reached Mr. Dentzel shop again there was Mr. Dentzel in front of his house He saw me and reconized me so he start tak to me again in German but I could not understand not one word of what he was saying so before I got I repeated my tree word to him again—*me, woodcarver—job*—Mr. Dentzel was a very good man he feel some kind pity for a poor emigrant. So he invited me to follow him and we went inside the shop. There was a man from Cirdo a very good wood carver who could speak few italian word his name was Boory true him as an entrepetre Mr. Dentzel told me that week ago when I saw him the first time he gave me the job but I din't come. I told that I could not understand him and I was very very glad that he told me to bring my tool there and start at work immediately. . . . I went again in S. Stefano church and I thank Lord.

. . . I start work for Mr. Dentzel 1903 The Mr. Dentzel shop was in full operation manifacturing merry-go-round. In fact that time 1903 Mr. Dentzel had a very larg carousell running in woodside park in Phila another on Willow Grove Phila and another in Atlantic City N.J. That time his shop was not very large in accont the work done there On the first floor there were all the machine need to manifactured the carrousels even a large carving machine on the second floor there were the carving room and on the thirt floor there were the paint shop were there painted all horse and animal and rest of the carrousels. . . . In fact after a short time I was working there Mr. Dentzel as he had plenty ground there he enlarge the factory and made nice big building with plenty room for work. On the first floor there was Harry Earnest Dentzel son of Mr. Gustavo Dentzels old brother. He operated all the machine there to cut the wood . . . Then on second floor they carved the horse or animal head and the legs separated to be assembled on the body and carved it. Then that go on the tird floor to be painted and finish.

Dr. Milton E. Flower has documented the lives of two carvers, Wilhelm Schimmel (1817–1890) and Aaron Mountz (1873–1949), who lived in his home town, Carlisle, Pennsylvania. Schimmel was born in Germany in 1817. Not long after the Civil War he appeared in the Cumberland Valley and for the next several decades roamed and worked there as a woodcarver. At his death this extraordinary small notice appeared in the Evening Sentinel of August 7, 1890:

Old Schimmel the German who for many years tramped through this and adjoining counties, making his headquarters in jails and almshouses, died at the almshouse on Sunday. His only occupation was carving heads of animals out of soft pine wood. These he would sell for a few pennies each. He was apparently a man of very surly disposition.

When Schimmel died, another Carlisle woodcarver, Aaron Mountz, was still in his teens. Many of the fewer than fifty pieces that comprise Mountz's total production reflect the influence of "Old Schimmel." There is a visible stylistic difference, however, between the quick, strong, rough work of Schimmel and the painstaking orderliness of Mountz. Mountz, broken in mind and body, died in

(continued on page 97)

Anonymous: Mrs. Freake and Baby Mary, oil, about 1674.
Worcester Art Museum, Worcester, Massachusetts.

Anonymous: The Prodigal Son Reveling with Harlots, watercolor, about 1790.
Abby Aldrich Rockefeller Folk Art Collection, Williamsburg, Virginia.

James Sanford Ellsworth: Mr. and Mrs. C. T. Gunn, watercolor, about 1845.
Museum of American Folk Art, New York.

Jacob Maentel: General Schumacker, watercolor and ink, about 1812.
Collection of Edgar William and Bernice Chrysler Garbisch.

Anonymous: The Colden Family, oil, about 1795.
Abby Aldrich Rockefeller Folk Art Collection, Williamsburg, Virginia.

Anonymous: Meditation by the Sea, oil, about 1855.
Museum of Fine Arts, Boston, M. and M. Karolik Collection.

J. N. Eaton: William and Mary, oil on wood, about 1845.
Abby Aldrich Rockefeller Folk Art Collection, Williamsburg, Virginia.

Edward Hicks: Peaceable Kingdom, oil, 1844.
Abby Aldrich Rockefeller Folk Art Collection, Williamsburg, Virginia.

arles Hofmann: View of the Montgomery County Almshouse Buildings, oil, about 1878.
by Aldrich Rockefeller Folk Art Collection, Williamsburg, Virginia.

Anonymous: Fruit in a Wicker Basket, oil on wood, about 1855.
Abby Aldrich Rockefeller Folk Art Collection, Williamsburg, Virginia.

Ammi Phillips: Harriet Leavens, oil, about 1816.
Fogg Art Museum, Harvard University, Cambridge, Massachusetts.

1949 at the same almshouse in which Schimmel had died; shortly before the end, Dr. Flower visited him in a Pennsylvania mental hospital. Mountz did not speak, and the only glimmer of response came when Dr. Flower asked if he had once been a carver; the old man simply lifted his hands and studied them as though asking himself the same question.

A fitting climax to the history of the early American folk artist is "The Historical Monument of the American Republic." Painted by Erastus Salisbury Field to commemorate the one hundredth anniversary of American independence, it was completed in 1876. That same year Field wrote an eleven-page "Descriptive Catalogue of the Historical Monument of the American Republic," which was printed in Amherst, Massachusetts. It is clear from the opening paragraphs that the aging artist wistfully dreamed that the "Monument" might actually be built:

A professed architect, on looking at this picture, might have the impression that a structure built in this form would not stand. The idea is this, to build after this model (supposing such a thing took place), it would be necessary to fill up with stones or concrete in one solid mass, all but the center and the entrance through each Tower, on account of each succeeding section receding. The center in each Tower could be sufficiently large for circular stairs to reach to the top. The entrance from each side to the center, and also from the center to each of the platforms on each section, might be arched over, and also there might be spacious rooms arched over in many of the sections, for various purposes, and still the structure would be sufficiently solid. . . . I am not a professed architect, and some things about it may be faulty. Be that as it may, my aim has been to get up a brief history of our country or epitome, in a monumental form. . . . The columns represent the Colonies and the States, which are frequently repeated, and they vary in their style to accord somewhat with the time and circumstances. . . . The lower part of the structure is intended as one whole or base, on which the eight Towers that are seen, stand.

Throughout the years from 1876—when he completed his Historical Monument of the American Republic—to 1900 (he died on June 28), Erastus Salisbury Field hoped that the cluster of colonnaded towers he had linked together symbolically as a tribute to his country would somehow be built. The ambrotype likeness of Field shown above was made during the 1840's and was possibly colored by the artist himself. His Monument is in the collection of the Museum of Fine Arts, Springfield, Massachusetts.

IV Romantic America

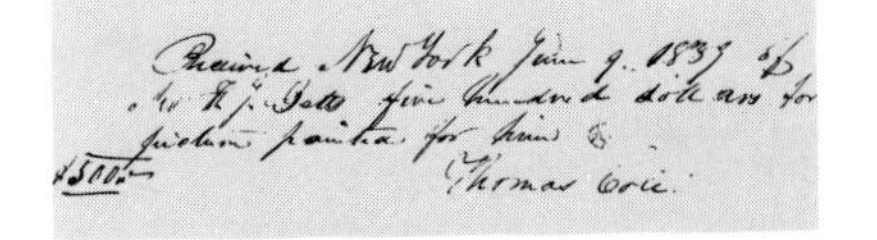
Received New York June 9. 1839 of
Mr F. J. Betts five hundred dollars for
pictures painted for him &c.
$500
Thomas Cole.

Thomas Cole commanded high prices in the late 1830's. This June 9, 1839, receipt shows that New York collector F. J. Betts paid the top Hudson River School painter $500 for a commissioned work.

In the eighteen-twenties Thomas Cole and James Fenimore Cooper brought to the American public a new vision of uncorrupted nature. Cooper's romantic concept of the forest, the noble Red Man, the simple frontiersman, reappears in Cole's rugged Catskill gorges, storms, and waterfalls. American society, ready for a departure from Old World cultivation and classical allusion, eagerly embraced this celebration of its own environment.

Cole's dramatic view of nature and his skill in presenting it inspired the first truly native school of artists. The Hudson River School painter, in the words of one late joiner of the movement, wanted to create an "expression of his impressions of Nature." No coherent body of doctrine was ever drawn up to define this aim, but its chief features were rather consistent: a relatively literal rendition of leaves, rocks, water, and atmospheric conditions organized in either extremely wild or exaggeratedly tranquil settings. An acceptance of and an affection for the surrounding universe pervades these canvases. The drama of Cole's scenes and the repose found in those of his followers, Asher B. Durand (1796–1886), John F. Kensett (1816–1872), and John W. Casilear (1811–1893), all reflect a poetic response to a specifically American landscape.

The Hudson River School enjoyed an immediate and widespread approval among a public newly awakened to a sense of national purpose by the War of 1812 and by Jacksonian expansion. Ironically, the steamboat and railroad which came into use in this period ultimately eliminated the romantic wilderness so celebrated by Cole and his followers. The very popularity of the Hudson River painters among the new urban middle class foreshadowed a nostalgia for what would soon be despoiled. Cole himself traveled to Europe in 1829 and returned to devote his talents to elaborate allegories of mankind and civilization; they had rather over-dramatized titles such as "The Voyage of Life" and "The Course of Empire." His disciples avoided the temptations of allegory and carried a more natural landscape tradition into the eighteen-fifties, when an even more talented generation picked it up.

One of the most interesting painters of the outdoors in the early nineteenth century had no connection with the Hudson River School. This was John James Audubon (1785–1851), who studied with Jacques Louis David before immigrating to Philadelphia from Paris in 1803. He hated his business life in America and spent most of his time hunting, tramping through the forest, and collecting bird specimens. In 1819 he reverted to the more congenial life of an artist, and a few years later the literal accuracy and natural settings of his *Birds of America* established a reputation still undiminished.

Primitive art in America had thrived in the eighteenth century when art instruction and access to original paintings were limited to a few city dwellers. In later years the isolated character of rural life continued these limitations for most Americans. Anonymous and often charming early nineteenth-century still lifes, landscapes, and figures painted with a doll-like innocence have been brought to light by the hundreds in our own day. In the period before the Civil War, obscure and untrained painters such as Joseph H. Davis of New Hampshire, Eunice Pinney of Connecticut, and Mary Ann Willson of Greenville, New York, developed a vigorous technique for rendering neighborhood and historical scenes. The outstanding American primitive was Edward Hicks, a Pennsylvania Quaker whose intense religious feelings are reflected in his many versions of "The Peaceable Kingdom," and his views of his neighbors' farms show his instinct for local environment.

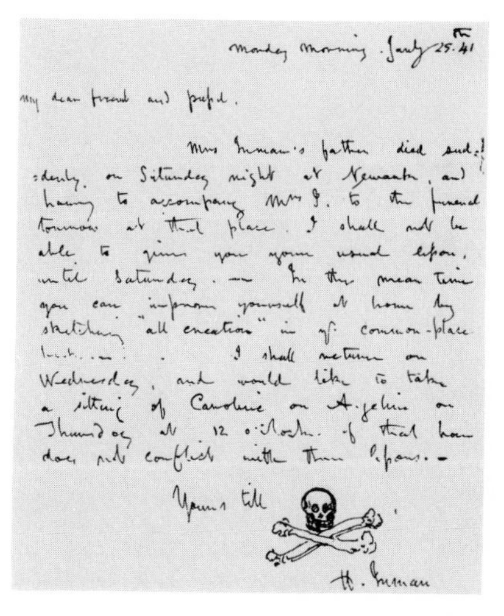

Monday Morning. Jany 25th 41

My dear friend and pupil.

Mrs Inman's father died suddenly on Saturday night at Newark, and having to accompany Mrs I. to the funeral tomorrow at that place. I shall not be able to give you your usual lesson until Saturday. — In the mean time you can improve yourself at home by sketching "all creation" in yr. common-place book... . I shall return on Wednesday, and would like to take a sitting of Caroline or Angelina on Thursday at 12 o'clock. if that hour does not conflict with their lessons. —

Yours till

H. Inman

Henry Inman (1801–1846), a New York portrait and genre painter, who helped found the National Academy of Design in New York in 1825, wrote this illustrated letter to a student in January 1841. It postpones a lesson because of the death of Inman's father-in-law, an event the artist emphasized with a skull and crossbones.

An active school of genre painting appeared in the years following 1825. It was led by William Sidney Mount (1807–1868) of Long Island, John Quidor (1801–1881) of New York, and George Caleb Bingham of Missouri. Mount never stirred from his own neighborhood, and his scenes of Long Island barns, banjo players, and fishermen have an appealing if somewhat artificially anecdotal tone. Quidor was a fantastic creator of wild, improbable scenes and grotesque figures out of Washington Irving's novels. Bingham painted the life of the west represented by river boatmen, fur traders, and small-town political rallies. Despite little formal training, a fresh vision and luminous coloring give his genre work a significance which transcends the subject matter itself.

This was also a period when American sculptors took advantage of Italy's trained workmen and cheap marble. An earlier sculptor, William Rush (1756–1833) of Philadelphia, had carved wooden figureheads as well as portraits and allegorical works, but John Trumbull's remark made in 1820 that "nothing in sculpture would be wanted in this country for a hundred years," expressed the general view of the Federal period. The neo-classicists, Horatio Greenough (1805–1852) of Boston, Hiram Powers (1805–1872) of Cincinnati, Thomas Crawford (1814–1857) of New York, and Harriet Hosmer (1830–1908) of Boston produced smooth marble portraits and neo-classical figures in Florence and Rome. It remained for anonymous and obscure wood- and stone-carvers at home to produce a more lively folk scúlpture in the form of ships' figureheads, cigar-store Indians, and decorative ornamentation.

If a native landscape art was the chief contribution of the second quarter of the nineteenth century, the discouragement of historical painting was an important secondary one. As the New York art critic Charles Frederick Briggs pointed out to William Page (1811–1885), a New York and Boston portrait painter who felt an urge to paint Biblical scenes in 1845, "Why bother yourself with Judiths, and Ruths and Jephthas? There are plenty of Sarahs and Marys and Josephs alive and breathing. You need not paint Scripture pieces because other artists have, but if you will do so, follow the plan of Rafaelle and paint your neighbors but christen them after the Saints."

With the exception of a few major artists famed for their portraiture—men such as Rembrandt Peale (1778–1860) and Thomas Sully (1783–1872)—talented artists turned to nature, and portrait painting rather declined in quality. Among those who found inspiration in the calm of lakes and countryside or the turbulence of oceans were Thomas Doughty, Martin Heade, Jonathan Fisher, and Thomas Birch. The Civil War was long over before the powerful works of Thomas Eakins brought a renaissance to this field.

The self-portrait of Samuel Lovett Waldo (1783–1861), painted around 1813, belongs to the Metropolitan Museum of Art, New York. Waldo went to London from Connecticut in the early 1800's to study with Benjamin West and John Singleton Copley. When he returned to America in 1809 he set up a studio in New York and, in partnership with his former assistant, William Jewett (who often painted the backgrounds in Waldo works), became a popular portraitist. He was one of the founders of the National Academy of Design.

The career of Thomas Cole proves that there was a handsome living to be made by chronicling the beauties of the Hudson and Connecticut valleys. Cole not only never lacked patrons; he was befriended again and again by representatives of both new urban and old established wealth. A New York wholesale grocer, Luman Reed, and William Patterson Van Rensselaer of the patroon dynasty from the Hudson valley, were particularly impressed. In few other periods was the relationship between American artist and patron more intimate—and rewarding.

Although the Hudson River School succeeded in bringing respect and popularity to native scenes and native artists, the attraction of European travel and European influences continued to draw American painters. Not long after Cole's early shop-window recognition by Trumbull, Washington Allston heard that someone—Cole, unmistakably—was thinking of studying in Europe. Writing from Boston to the Salem poet, Henry Pickering, on November 23, 1827, Allston commented:

As you have not mentioned for what part of Europe your friend means to embark, I suppose you have left it for me to advise on this point. If so, I would recommend his going first to England where I would have him remain at least half the time he proposes to pass abroad. The present English school comprises a great body of excellent artists, and many eminent in many branches. At the head of your friend's department, he will find Turner, who "take him all in all," has no superior of any age . . . I advise this disproportionate stay in England because I think it important that the first bias he receives should be a good one, inasmuch as on this not a little of the future tone of his mind will depend. . . .

You say that your friend is a "passionate admirer of nature." Let him never lose his love of her. This may, perhaps, seem to him impossible. But there are artists, as well as connoisseurs, who, as Sir Joshua Reynolds says, "have quitted nature without acquiring art." To avoid this, the young artist should study pictures and nature together: he will find they mutually reflect light on each other. In studying the works of other men we are in effect appropriating to ourselves their experiences; in this way we may be said to multiply our eyes, and to see a thousand things that might otherwise elude us; in studying nature we are enabled to separate in art the true from the factitious; thus we become learned in both. In no other way can a sound critic be formed, much less a sound artist. . . .

I think it is Young who says, "an undevout astronomer is mad." This may well also apply to the painter. It has been my happiness to know many artists who were no less estimable for their moral and religious characters, than distinguished for their genius. I hope your young friend may be added to their number. He has chosen a profession in itself innocent, and if properly pursued—that is, for its own sake—in a high degree elevating. Indeed it seems as if no one could *truly* love nature without loving its divine author, who in all His works, even in the

Long Island-born William Sidney Mount was a master of the everyday scene. He found his genre subjects in the rural life around him and recorded them with a natural ease and lucidity of style that almost conceals his great skill. In The Painter's Triumph, 1838, from the collection of the Pennsylvania Academy of the Fine Arts, Philadelphia, Mount included himself showing his work to a farmer.

John Trumbull's 1826 portrait of a fellow painter, Asher B. Durand, hangs in the New-York Historical Society. Durand's friendship with Trumbull had begun years before when he engraved a reproduction of Trumbull's oil, The Declaration of Independence. A native of New Jersey and a resident of New York, Durand had studied abroad and became one of the first and most important members of the Hudson River School.

horrible, if rightly understood, no less than in the beautiful, speaks only in the language of love.

Thomas Cole knew to whom to turn for financial assistance for his European expedition. On January 5, 1829, he wrote from New York to Robert Gilmor, Jr., of Baltimore, the son of a rich merchant and art patron and the subject of a portrait by Gilbert Stuart:

I believe you are acquainted with the strong desire I have long had to visit Europe for the purpose of studying the works of the great masters, and know the advantages young artists may derive from that study. For a few years past I have labored unceasingly that I might obtain means for the accomplishment of my desire; hitherto I have been unsuccessful. Owing to the exigencies of my family my expenses have been equal to my income, and I am brought reluctantly to the conclusion that my purpose must be abandoned, except I have other means of accomplishing it than I now possess.

Your former favor and kindness have encouraged me to ask if you will assist me. My "Garden of Eden" and "Expulsion" are not yet sold. May I venture to propose that you would take them into your hands, and advance me a sum that shall enable me to visit Europe, which you should be repaid in money or pictures, when and as you shall think best. I will not dwell on the greatness of the favor you would confer by granting my request, but hope if it be an improper one you will find an excuse for me in my earnest desire for improvement in my art.

Gilmor was a generous patron, and Cole felt obliged to protest what seemed to him an unnecessarily generous sum. A few weeks later he wrote to Gilmor again:

I think you have mistaken the amount I wished you to advance. I did not expect more than five or six hundred dollars, which sum, added to that which I hope to raise from my own resources, with economy would enable me to acomplish my purpose . . . If my assiduity and frugality (which I hope I am thought to possess) had not been rendered unavailing by untoward circumstances I should have visited Europe before this. . . . I am an only son, and my parents are advanced in years. To their support as well as that of my sisters I have found it my duty to contribute.

In Florence almost three years later Cole was dreaming of the series of paintings that became "The Course of Empire." (Finally commissioned by Luman Reed, the series now hangs in the New-York Historical Society.) In a January 1832 report to Gilmor, Cole describes his approach:

Although I have seldom written you since I have been in Europe, I have not been forgetful how much I am indebted to your kindness; and I now write to offer you something in return for the pecuniary obligation under which you have placed me. A variety of circumstances have concurred to render this so tardy; but I hope the lateness of it will not render it less acceptable. I have sent to the National Academy of Design, New York, a picture the making of which has occupied the greater part of the seven months that I have been in Florence, and is by far the most labored, if not the best of my works. I offer it for the three hundred dollars you advanced me; and your acceptance will be considered a favor. . . . The picture was intended for the first of a series that I have long contemplated and in order that you understand the subject it is necessary that I give you the plan of the series, and if you will allow me, shall extract from my memorandum book some first thoughts on the subject:

A series of pictures might be painted that should be the history of a natural scene, as well as an epitome of Man: showing the *natural* changes of landscape and those effected by man in his progress from barbarism to civilization—to the

The self-portrait of Samuel F. B. Morse, painted about 1814, is in the collection of the Addison Gallery of American Art, Phillips Academy, Andover, Massachusetts. Morse was an idealist who wanted to paint romantic, imaginative compositions, but finding few commissions for these he turned to portraiture and finally stopped painting altogether, convinced that Americans were not ready for the best art. Best known for inventing the telegraph, Morse was also the main organizer of the National Academy of Design.

Dear Mrs. Silsbee,
The cold of Moscow to Bonaparte was nothing to the cold of Rome to my bony part—the fact is that for five days my inward woman has been in a state of freeze to which, in point of magnitude, I can compare nothing but the frieze of the Parthenon—this dispensation of a benign providence I take, of course, cooly though I cannot say I receive it as a warm proof of the goodness of him who tempers the wind &c. So I shall be obliged to forego the pleasure of visiting you on Thursday evening. HARRIET HOSMER

Harriet Hosmer of Watertown, New York, and Boston was one of the most colorful American sculptors to settle in Rome in the mid-1800's. Her note written in Rome to a Mrs. Silsbee hints that she was almost as well known for her humor as for her sculpture.

state of luxury—to the vicious state or state of destruction, etc. It will be necessary that there should be the same location in each picture; there must be some striking effects introduced in order to identify the spot. The scene must be so composed as to be picturesque in its wild state and appropriate for cultivation and the site of a large seaport. The first picture must be a savage wilderness—the sun rising from the ocean, the stormy clouds of the night retiring tumultuously over the mountains. The figures must be savage, clothed in skins and occupied in the chase. There must be a flashing chiaroscuro and a spirit of motion pervading the scene as though nature was just waking from chaos.

One of the rare disappointments in Cole's career came when he agreed to paint "The Architect's Dream" for Ithiel Town of New Haven, an art collector and bridge-builder-turned-architect. Unlike other Cole patrons, Town presumed to dictate to the painter. In a letter of May 25, 1840, written to Town from Catskill, New York, Cole justifies his conception of this elaborate work:

I have received yours of the 20th inst., and am surprised and mortified exceedingly at its contents. The picture I have painted for you was as fine as lay in my power, executed in such a manner as to meet your expressed desires. I have taken the utmost pains with it and it is one of immense labor. In fact, I have striven to the utmost to gratify your wishes. You may judge then of the disappointment I have experienced from reading your letter. With respect of the choice of subject I proposed several to you which I felt would be fine ones for my pencil. I feel confident that if you had consented there would have been some probability of pleasing you, but you declined them.

I differ with you in the opinion that modern and ancient Athens would have been fine subjects, and with respect to the former, I should not consent to copy any print. I could not visit Athens, and without visiting Athens and sketching there, there would have been a want of veracity in the thing that would discourage me from proceeding.

Almost any painter can copy a print, and as for introducing a few figures in the picture, these would scarcely give any interest, particularly as I should have to go to prints for them, I not having had an opportunity of sketching Greeks and Turks from nature. But we had discussed this matter before the subject I have painted was suggested or was to paint even what you now suggest—the mixture of ages and styles in the same imaginary picture, the landscape to predominate, the architecture, history, etc. to be various and subservient. The architecture, history, etc. would be in a very miniature form and I am confident that the best I could do on any square of canvas would not be satisfactory.

The picture I have painted is one of the best I have ever painted. It has been as much admired as any single picture of mine. It is painted for a much smaller price than any similar commission for several years and it was painted in full confidence that you would be satisfied. I am grieved and disappointed but I cannot undertake to paint another subject in place of it. I might reasonably expect another to be as unsatisfactory to you as the one I have painted. I might paint a dozen and perhaps not be successful. I am sorry for the circumstances but if I were to paint pictures to be refused at the option of those who give the commissions, my profession would be both anxious and precarious. I would much rather return the books I have had from you every one and consider the commission as null however it might grieve me to do so than attempt another picture in place of this.

I have painted you a picture that I hoped would be creditable to both of us and one which I am vain enough to believe is not fully appreciated by you. Whatever hope I may have that you will yet view the picture more favorably, I

continued on page 113)

Thomas Birch: Mouth of the Delaware, oil, 1828.
The White House Collection, Washington, D. C.

Asher B. Durand: Kindred Spirits, oil, 1849.
New York Public Library, New York.

Thomas Doughty: In Nature's Wonderland, oil, 1835.
Detroit Institute of Arts.

William Sidney Mount: Farmers Nooning, oil, 1836.
Suffolk Museum, Stony Brook, Long Island.

Martin J. Heade: Approaching Storm, Beach Near Newport, oil, about 1860.
Museum of Fine Arts, Boston, M. and M. Karolik Collection.

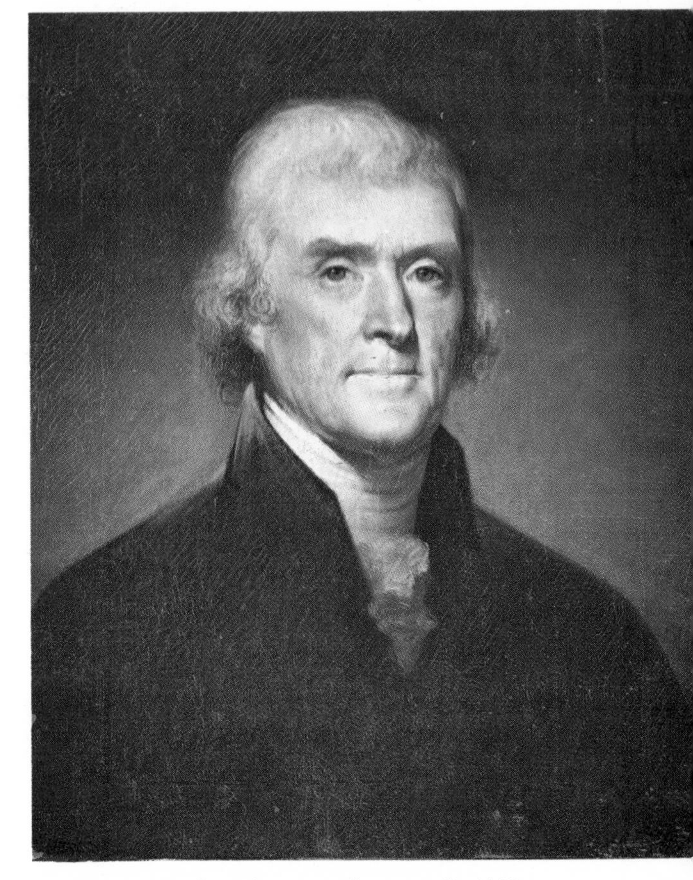

Rembrandt Peale: Thomas Jefferson, oil, 1800.
The White House Collection, Washington, D. C.

John James Audubon: Wild Turkey, watercolor, 1825. New-York Historical Society, New York.

Thomas Cole: The Oxbow, oil, 1836.
Metropolitan Museum of Art, New York.

will not trouble you with any further defense of it or myself and will conclude by saying that I have seldom experienced so great a disappointment when I had made such endeavors or considered that I had taken every means to ensure approbation.

Thomas Cole was the most successful renderer of American scenery in the romantic era, but he had his rivals. One of these was Thomas Doughty of Philadelphia and New York. He could not complain of want of recognition either; a British minister to Washington once offered $2,500 for a landscape. It was only at the very end of his life that Doughty's popularity declined. Writing from Owego, New York, to an unidentified friend on November 21, 1852, Doughty reported:

The Valley of the Susquehanna is truly beautiful even now when Winter is close upon us. In summer it must be magnificent! Fit place for a landscape painter to begin and end his days! It is my intention to commence this winter and execute as well as I can a series of four pictures which shall be characteristic of the scenery and seasons of this country. This is a long cherished intention and I have waited only for a fair opportunity to prosecute the work with vigor. Winter by moonlight will be the first picture, as it will be in season, then Spring, Summer and Autumn. Of course I shall do my best in these pictures, and if I have my health they will probably be finished by this time next year.

If you feel disposed to send me a Guitar, I will be glad to paint you a picture for it. I shall want of course a first rate one, and will endeavor to give you a Quid pro Quo for it.

Neither Cole nor, apparently, Doughty was worried by the threat of foreign art on the American market. But Horatio Greenough was horrified by the thought that any American could purchase a work of art of non-American origin. Writing from Paris on November 8, 1831, Greenough informed Rembrandt Peale, the portrait and historical painter who was the best-known of Charles Willson Peale's numerous artist-sons:

We are all obliged to you. You can take, in consequence of your experience and your acquaintance with European art, a higher tone in instructing our countrymen than perhaps any other living artist. Pray, sir, convince them that one American work is of more value to the United States than three foreign ones, even of superior merit. If they mean that all their pictures should be painted by strangers, they are in the wrong, both in regards economy and praiseworthiness. If they do not, then let them employ us manfully, and not tell us to learn to swim before we venture into the water.

Peale, too, felt that American artists should be encouraged by liberal purchase of their works. In a letter of January 1825 to Senator Elijah Mills, urging that Congress buy his equestrian portrait of Washington, he wrote:

Our Public Edifices have been constructed by native architects & are beginning to do honour to their genius. It is true the costly Sculpture which decorates them is all from foreign lands—but shall not their walls be animated by the pencils of Americans who, otherwise, must look to Europe for a home?

Peale was, however, a more modest man than Greenough. Writing from Philadelphia to Ithiel Town on September 3, 1839, he expressed the hope that his "Court of Death" might find a place in Town's private gallery:

I have the most serious thoughts of going to France and of course with no great confidence of returning to attempt, what has long amused my fancy, to build

Phª March 24th /56

Dear Sir

In regard to the Portrait of Joel Barlow*, I can give you but little information. It was painted when he resided at Washington, under the presidency of Mr Jefferson — & chiefly as the Author of the Columbiad — a Publication, at that time of rare beauty, as being entirely American, except the Plates which were engraved in England from Smirkes Paintings — My father esteemed him the more because he was the friend & Patron of Fulton, who also painted his Portrait.

Respectfully
Yours
Rembrandt Peale.

* by my Father.

In this letter written from Philadelphia on March 24, 1856, Rembrandt Peale, the most talented of Charles Willson Peale's artist-sons, describes the circumstances behind his father's portrait of Joel Barlow, the poet-statesman. Barlow was painted by the elder Peale in 1808 and about twenty-five years earlier by Robert Fulton.

Rembrandt Peale's reputation was based on his fine portraits as well as on the fame of the whole painting Peale family. In 1828, at the age of 50, he did this self-portrait as a gift to his wife before he took a trip to Italy. It is in the Detroit Institute of Arts.

Victor and John Audubon painted this portrait of their father, the famous ornithologist John James Audubon. This was in 1841 when Audubon was 56 years old; he had already spent thirty-eight years studying birds, his observations taking him through Pennsylvania, Kentucky, Ohio, Louisiana, New York—as well as England and Scotland. His original watercolor drawing of The Blue Jay, owned by the New-York Historical Society, appears in his Birds of America. The portrait is, appropriately, in the American Museum of Natural History, New York.

up a gallery of painting. Therefore, in parting with my pictures it is most natural to me to desire that they should find some other honorable situation. With this view I have intended to take my large painting of the "Court of Death" to New Haven, where it has never been seen, and devise some feasible plan by which it may form a part of your public gallery. The idea of this is so agreeable to my feelings, that I shall be induced to be very moderate, if you will not permit me to say liberal, in my expectations of pecuniary compensation. I shall be glad to find you at home, because I know you will be pleased to render me what service you can in this arrangement. Since you saw the picture I have had it up in my painting-room, and think I have much improved it. As it is the first large composition made in America and by an American artist, whose name may be preserved in our future annals—and as it is a composition, certainly unique in its character, and unlike any work of modern times, not being strictly allegorical, but rather a *discourse on life and death,* written or spoken in the language of the picture—I hope it may be considered by the taste and judgment of your city to be worthy of their preservation.

I shall be delighted to see your treasures of art and science in the place of their safe deposit—but must ever regret that they are scattered over the face of our extensive country for want of one capital of our empire, where they might be concentrated.

Ithiel Town failed to acquire the "Court of Death" for his own collection and the picture came to rest in the Detroit Institute of Arts.

Thomas Sully, whose youthful self-portrait is now in the Thomas Gilcrease Institute of American Art and History, Tulsa, Oklahoma, came in 1792 from England (where his parents had been actors) to the United States. He became a successful portraitist in Philadelphia, painting in the decorative style popular in the early 19th-century period of romanticism. This style is apparent in his The Boy with a Torn Hat, right, 1820, now in the Museum of Fine Arts, Boston. Sully was in his late seventies when the photo, opposite page, was taken about 1860. Born in 1783, he died in 1872, the year his detailed manual, Hints to Young Painters, was published.

V Realists and Mystics

Unlike the Revolution, the Civil War as an *event* was of little inspiration to American artists. A new generation of talented painters who joined the ranks of the Hudson River School in the eighteen-fifties modified its literal interpretations of nature and carried the tradition on into the next century. Sculpture continued to flow back from Italy, but it was not until the eighteen-seventies and eighteen-eighties that an improvement was made over the finished neo-classical figures produced by expatriate American sculptors. The vitality of genre painting declined in the second half of the century, but portraiture gained new stature in the period after Appomattox.

The Civil War did, however, usher in a new age of commercial and industrial expansion which had a profound if indirect effect on the conditions of American artists. A class of newly rich who hoped to achieve reputations as men of cultured taste looked upon Europe as the ideal source of their art collections. The result was disastrous for the native painter accustomed to a steady market for his work. "I think the position of American artists a peculiar one," Jervis McEntee (1828–1891) wrote in his diary in 1879. "In all the interest everywhere manifested in art, they seem to be the only ones who are neglected." Three years later, he had to "acknowledge to myself that I paint now what I think will sell. I have to do it and once I did not stop to think of that." The crowning blow was a request made in 1882 by "two well-dressed ladies," who wanted to buy a picture. "Their chief demand was that it should look 'Frenchy.' I advised them to get a French picture, but if they wanted an American landscape, not to get one that looked like a French one."

The despair felt by McEntee's generation was followed by a growing opposition among many artists to all innovation. After 1870 a reactionary mood set in at the National Academy of Design, the powerful artists' association which had been organized in 1825 as a protest against the clannish attitude of the old

American Academy of the Fine Arts. Dealers ignored American art, and membership in the National Academy meant security, respect, and an assured opportunity to exhibit and sell paintings at annual exhibitions. The Academy was closely tied to the romantic landscape school of the past, and now younger men trained abroad in the schools of Munich, Paris, and Rome felt themselves victims of discrimination. The Society of American Artists emerged in 1877 as a concrete expression of dissatisfaction with the Academy.

William Merritt Chase (1849–1916), always an elegant and persuasive individual, became the leader of the new Society. Born in Indiana and trained in Munich, he used the dark colors and facile brush stroke associated with the German School. Soon he adapted his style to the lighter tones of the impressionists and became a major influence on young painters eager to break away from an old-fashioned emphasis on reproducing scenes from nature at the expense of technical skill.

Some of the best American artists went abroad to study and remained permanently. James Abbott McNeill Whistler (1834–1903) studied in Paris and settled in London. His witticisms were famous, but it was his delicately sensitive interpretations of nature which give him a place in art history. He possessed a superlative gift for composition and subtle tone, and in his quest for a lyrical beauty, he made innovations analogous to elements of post-impressionism. Mary Cassatt (1845–1926), daughter of a rich and cultivated Philadelphia banker, followed Whistler to Paris and became a disciple of Degas. She was the most accomplished of the American impressionists, and her many paintings of mothers and children are full of charm and sentiment.

The most fashionable portrait painter in the English-speaking world at the turn of the century was the son of expatriate Americans living in France and Italy, John Singer Sargent (1856–1925). Sargent possessed a remarkable facility for drawing and composition, but although his work is often brilliant, it displays more dash than subtlety or insight into the characters of his sitters.

His opposite was Thomas Eakins (1844–1916) of Philadelphia. A portrait painter of enormous force and honesty, Eakins was far more concerned with scientific anatomy than with esthetic principles. His uncompromising naturalism and his feeling for character make his work the culmination of a tradition begun by Copley and Stuart.

Eakins's name is often coupled with that of his contemporary, Winslow Homer (1836–1910), a caustic semi-recluse who lived in a remote studio on the Maine coast. Homer's lonely seascapes, hunting scenes, and Caribbean watercolors are powerful successors to the old Hudson River School's concern with the grandeur of nature. Criticized in his own time for his unpolished severity, Homer is today very highly regarded.

Another solitary figure was Albert Pinkham Ryder (1847–1917), who was born in New Bedford, Massachusetts, at a time when whaling was still a vital part of its life. The memory of the sea followed him to his New York studio where he painted mystical visions of nature as well as his own brooding interpretations of scenes from Shakespeare and Wagner. His poetic spirit had little relation to the hard-nosed business society in which he lived.

George Inness (1825–1894) of New York and Montclair, New Jersey, began as a superior if conventional Hudson River painter in the eighteen-fifties, but in his maturity he softened objects and brightened colors to create a mood that suggested a personal sensitivity to nature.

A more conscious attempt to paint in an impressionist manner was made by John Twachtman (1853–1902), Theodore Robinson (1852–1896), and Childe

WILLIAM MACBETH,
237 FIFTH AVE., NEW YORK.
TWO DOORS ABOVE 27TH STREET.

PICTURES IN OIL AND WATER COLORS.
THE WORK OF AMERICAN ARTISTS
A SPECIALTY.

ANNOUNCEMENT.

I respectfully call attention to the fact that I have leased the store No. 237 Fifth Avenue for the permanent exhibition and sale of American pictures, both in oil and water colors.

The work of American artists has never received the full share of appreciation that it deserves, and the time has come when an effort should be made to gain for it the favor of those who have hitherto purchased foreign pictures exclusively. As I shall exhibit only that which is thoroughly good and interesting, I hope to make this establishment known as the place where may be procured the very best our artists can produce. An experience of over eighteen years in the picture business will be devoted to the accomplishment of this result.

The location, two doors above 27th Street, is in the immediate neighborhood of the large hotels, and easily accessible from every part of the city.

Visitors will be welcome at all times.

WILLIAM MACBETH.

New York, April, 1892.

The Macbeth Gallery in New York was the first art gallery to deal entirely in American art. As the announcement indicates, it opened for business in 1892. During the sixty years of its existence, the gallery handled the work of major painters of the day as well as earlier American artists. Its most famous exhibit was that of The Eight, held in 1908.

Hassam (1859–1935). The influence of Monet was strong on this group, which brought a natural and fresh approach to landscape.

A more important innovator than the conventional impressionists was Maurice Prendergast (1859–1924) of Boston. His watercolors and oils, with their mosaic-like construction of luminous colors, were looked upon as the most advanced art of the day.

One of the major developments of the late nineteenth century came from a Philadelphia school of still life painting whose masters were William M. Harnett (1848–1892) and John F. Peto (1854–1907). Their fool-the-eye technique of meticulous realism was applied to compositions of hunting gear, musical instruments, and books.

An emerging generation regarded the late nineteenth century as a most uncongenial time for daring imagination or uncompromising honesty. The best and most original spirits of the post-Civil War era were viewed with disfavor by the genteel public, who were influenced by rich new collectors and dealers oriented toward European salon painting. Later, men who fought against the conservative attitudes of the National Academy drew inspiration from artists such as Eakins, Homer, and Ryder.

H*enry Adams, who liked everyone to imagine that he was a failure, and who insisted that success was a tainted commodity in the years after Appomattox, may not be the most reliable guide to the decades between Abraham Lincoln and Theodore Roosevelt, but his bewilderment, when he and his father returned in June 1868 from the latter's diplomatic mission to the Court of St. James, is worth remembering. Said Adams of the Adams family's settling down once again in Quincy, Massachusetts: "Had they been Tyrian traders of the year 1000 B.C., landing from a galley fresh from Gibraltar, they could hardly have been stranger on the shore of a world so changed."*

He was correct that America had changed. True, there had been millionaires long before the Civil War. John Jacob Astor, to cite only one example, left something like twenty million in 1848. But he was to be dwarfed by those who came after him. In 1877 Commodore Vanderbilt was worth one hundred and five million when the end came on Washington Place. This had swelled to two hundred million when his son, William Henry Vanderbilt, suffered a fatal apoplectic fit in 1885. Nor were the Vanderbilts the only family to pass the hundred-million mark. If J. P. Morgan bequeathed only seventy million in 1913—his rival, Frederick H. Price, claimed that he was too fond of art to leave a proper estate for his children—Marshall Field in Chicago had piled up one hundred and twenty million by 1906.

In such a world the relations between artists and their patrons was not so close as in the comfortable years when Luman Reed staked Thomas Cole. But it would be foolish to overlook the fact that there were millionaires who recognized the best of American art. Charles Freer of Detroit, to cite one instance, was one of Whistler's close friends, and he was present in Whistler's London house when the artist's mistresses and models came for their last look at the dead man. Nor should we forget the devotion which many men of wealth lavished on our museums. These were the years when the Havemeyers were laying the foundation of the glorious collection that eventually went to the Metropolitan, when Martin A. Ryerson was buying the Renoirs and Monets now in the Art Institute of Chicago, and when J. P. Morgan was building the collections of both the Morgan Library

William Merritt Chase, well known for his wit and charm as a host—his lavish, flamboyant soirées in the historic Tenth Street Studio Building, New York, were the sensation of the 1880's —painted his friend James A. McNeill Whistler, left, in 1885. The Metropolitan Museum, New York, owns the Whistler, whose Mother is in the Louvre, Paris.

This 1907 photograph shows Winslow Homer at age 71. Homer began his career as a lithographer in Boston, where he was born, and in 1859 moved to New York, where he worked as a free-lance artist for Harper's Weekly. Among his most famous illustrations for Harper's were Civil War studies of the Union army. It was during this period, in 1862, that he did his first oil. After brief post-Civil War trips to France and England, Homer settled on the Maine coast at Prout's Neck; there his concern with romantic aspects of nature inspired extraordinary and powerful seascapes.

and the Metropolitan.

In 1967 we may smile at the $55,500 paid in 1887 by Cornelius Vanderbilt for Rosa Bonheur's "Horse Fair," but collectors would not be worthy of the name if they did not make mistakes. Our artists were not forgotten, no matter if a supercilious traveler like Matthew Arnold despaired of our future. "I asked a German portrait painter, whom I found painting and prospering in America, how he liked the country," reported Arnold in Civilization in the United States in 1888. " 'How can an artist like it?' was his answer. The American artists live chiefly in Europe; all Americans of culture and cultivation and wealth visit Europe more and more constantly . . ." It is true that Jervis McEntee, the landscape painter from Rondout, New York, who was the intimate friend of most New York artists of the day, might have agreed with Arnold. In his diary entry for December 15, 1880, he noted:

All I hear about the condition of American art is most discouraging. A man called to see me about getting a picture to help him start an art room or brokerage, but there is too much borrowing pictures and too little buying . . . December 17. Eastman Johnson came and I had a long talk with him on many things. He recognizes the necessity of doing something to keep our art from falling into utter contempt and neglect. I think something will be done for we are all feeling the absurdity of the situation.

From his Prout's Neck, Maine, studio, Winslow Homer could not be so easily discouraged. Sending his "Fog" to M. Knoedler & Co. on December 1, 1900, he made plain that he knew his own importance:

I hope you will pardon me if I explain to you why I put this price of $2,000 inclusive of frame on this picture. It has taken me a long time and much careful study. Quite different from posing a successful lawyer in one studio light and rattling him off in a week's time to the tune of $3,000. If you want more sentiment put into this picture I can whisk [in] one or two touches—in five minutes time—give it the stomach-ache that will suit any customer.

Homer expresses his strong feeling for realism in an equally uncompromising letter of January 14, 1902, to the same dealer:

That Santiago de Cuba picture *is not intended to be "beautiful."* There are certain things (unfortunately for critics) that are stern facts but are worth recording as a matter of history as in this case.

This is a small part of Morro Castle and immediately over the Harbor entrance which is only about 400 feet wide and from this point were seen all the stirring sights of June and July 1898. I find it interesting.

Nor was he unduly modest when a month later Knoedler asked him for a description of his "Gulf Stream":

I regret very much that I have painted a picture that requires any description. The subject of the picture is comprised in its title and I will refer these inquisitive schoolmarms to Lt. Maury.

I have crossed the Gulf Stream *ten* times and I should know something about it. The boat and sharks are outside matters of very little consequence. *They have been blown out to sea by a hurricane.* You can tell these ladies that the unfortunate Negro who now is so dazed and parboiled will be rescued and returned to his friends and home, and ever after live happily.

George Inness shared Homer's independence. In a long autobiographical letter which was requested by Ripley Hitchcock, the writer on art, Inness wrote from Virginia in March 1883:

A deeply sensitive landscape painter whose father intended him to be a grocer, George Inness worked in Italy from 1870 to 1875 and evolved a style of muted, shimmering color. This photo was taken in his Montclair, New Jersey, studio about 1885. In 1873 he painted The Monk, below; the painting is owned by the Addison Gallery of American Art, Phillips Academy, Andover, Massachusetts.

THE
COPLEY-PLAZA
BOSTON

Jan. 14

Dear Ladies both
Many thanks for
your pork [illegible] –
I always thought you
had a wonderful cook;
knowing my birthday
is one of her triumphs.
Yours sincerely
John S. Sargent

John Singer Sargent was photographed in his Paris studio in 1885. Although he was born in Italy and lived most of his life in England, Sargent maintained his American citizenship and painted portraits of many prominent (and usually wealthy) Americans, including that, opposite page, of Mrs. Adrian Iselin. Dated 1888, it is in the collection of the National Gallery of Art, Washington, D. C. The letters of this fashionable portrait painter were numerous and often illegible. The World War I period note, left, thanks two Boston hostesses for their cook's remembering his birthday.

John S. Sargent
1888

. . . In 1850 I was married to my present wife. Mr. Ogden Haggerty, who had already greatly assisted me, allowed me a certain sum for study in Europe. I was then twenty-five. Spent about fifteen months in Italy returning through Paris and seeing the Salon. Rousseau was just beginning to make a noise. A great many people were crowding about a little picture of his which seemed to me rather metallic. Our traditions were English, and French art, particularly in landscape, had made but little impression upon us. Several years before I went to Europe, however, I had begun to see that elaborateness in detail did not gain me meaning. A part carefully finished, my forces were exhausted. I could not sustain it everywhere and produce the sense of spaces and distances and with them that subjective mystery of nature with which wherever I went I was filled.

I dwelt upon what I saw, and dreamed in disgust at my inability to interpret. I watched, though and fought pre-Raphaelitism. I gave way to my impulses and produced sentiments the best I could, always finding myself in a hobble as I tried to make them look finished. Gradually, year after year, I discovered one truth after another until I had formed a scientific formula of the subjective of nature. My whole aim for twelve or fifteen years has been to apply this. Vast difficulties have lain in the way. A living to make involving the necessity of gratifying a false conception of nature and my own subjective being to answer, induced a continuous internal turmoil. . . . Long before I ever heard of impressionism, I had settled to my mind the underlying law of what may properly be called an impression of nature, and I felt satisfied that whatever is painted truly according to any idea of unity, will as it is perfectly done possess both the subjective sentiment—the poetry of nature—and the objective fact sufficiently to give the commonest mind a feeling of satisfaction and through that satisfaction elevate to an idea higher—that is more certain than its own. Just as I have fought pre-Raphaelitism I fight what I consider the error of what is called impressionism. They both appear to me to be an attempt to reach the negation of mind which consists not of thought alone or of feeling alone, but of both, the compound being will and understanding . . .

Above photo of Thomas Eakins was taken when he was in his twenties and about to start a career as both painter and teacher. A Philadelphian, Eakins studied in Paris in 1866 with Gérôme, Bonnat, and A. A. Dumont, and, on returning to the U. S., taught art at the Pennsylvania Academy of the Fine Arts in Philadelphia. There, his anatomy lectures and insistence on a study of the human figure brought him censure but profoundly influenced American artists of the early 20th century. Not until late in life—see his self-portrait, opposite page, painted about 1902—did he gain recognition for his portraiture. His Miss Van Buren, 1889–91, below, is in the Phillips Collection, Washington, D. C. The self-portrait is owned by the National Academy of Design, New York.

Perhaps the most independent of all American artists in the late nineteenth century was Thomas Eakins. While teaching at the Pennsylvania Academy of the Fine Arts he insisted on the use of nude models. His determination to pursue this method of teaching aroused so much antagonism that, anxious to avoid a scandal, the authorities asked him to resign. On March 25, 1886, he explained the circumstances in a private statement written out for his friend Emily Sartain (1841–1927), another Philadelphia artist:

In pursuance of my business and professional studies, I use the naked model.

A number of my women pupils have for economy studied from each other's figures, and of these some have obtained from time to time my criticism on their work.

I have frequently used as models for myself my male pupils: very rarely female pupils and then only with the knowledge and consent of their mothers.

One of the women pupils some years ago gave to her lover who communicated it to Mr. Frank Stephens a list of these pupils as far as she knew them, and since that time Mr. Frank Stephens has boasted to witnesses of the power which this knowledge gave him to turn me out of the Academy, the Philadelphia Sketch Club, and the Academy Art Club, and of his intention to drive me from the city.

Eakins's views on art are reflected in notes made in 1887 from his class lectures. They were written down by Charles Bregler, a student at the Art Students League in New York:

This oil in the collection of Mr. and Mrs. Lawrence A. Fleischman is the only known self-portrait of Albert Pinkham Ryder. It was painted about 1883. Born in New Bedford, Massachusetts, Ryder spent most of his life in New York, where he lived as a semi-recluse in a cluttered ten- by twelve-foot studio. His subjects, based on his memories of the sea and his own imaginary world, are painted with glazes of thick pigment in a poetic style.

I cannot urge you too much to paint little simple studies. Take a lump of sugar, or a piece of chalk and get the texture. These things can be got with paint, to get these things is not dexterity, or a trick, no—it's knowledge. . . .

All the sciences are done in a simple way; in Mathematics the complicated things are reduced to simple things. So it is in painting, you reduce the whole thing to simple factors, you establish these and work out from them, pushing them toward one another. This will make strong work. The old masters worked this way. Don't copy, feel the forms. Feel how much it swings, how much it slants. These are big factors. The more factors you have the simpler will be your work. Strain your brain more than your eye. . . .

There is too much of this common ordinary work. Respectability in art is appalling. . . .

A chair is constructed with a great deal of common sense, it has been arrived at by long experience. A chair and all common things are hard to draw. Think of the weight, get the portrait of the light, the kind of day it is, cold or warm, grey or sunny, and what time of the day it is. Think of these separately and combine them in your work. These qualities make a strong painter.

Another Philadelphian who exerted a powerful influence on a rising generation of realists was Thomas Pollock Anshutz (1851–1912), Eakins's student and later the teacher of Robert Henri, William Glackens, George Luks, and others at the Pennsylvania Academy. His views on the advantages of a close association among artists are expressed in an August 1884 letter to a student:

Men in our line feel more than others the need, it is a need, of being occasionally with their own kind. This comes about so naturally in a city, especially in a school, that it is not felt.

They meet and fall into talk when some disputed point is apt to arise, which brings on an argument which may convince neither side and often ends in a wrangle. But still many good points are brought out and these are thought about afterwards in cooler moments and are beneficial.

They often see that the end in view by both sides was the same but was approached in different ways or looked at from different standpoints.

Albert Pinkham Ryder of New Bedford and New York, the most solitary of our painters in this period, refers to two of his paintings in a characteristic letter written from New York in April 1885 to Thomas B. Clarke, the major collector of American art in the second half of the nineteenth century:

Many thanks for your kind remembrance of the first hundred for the "Temple of the Mind." So sorry not to have seen you, as I think you may have bought it personally.

I am in ecstacy over my "Jonah": such a lovely turmoil of boiling water and everything. Don't you think we should try and get it in the A.A.A. [American Artists Association, an exhibiting agency] If I get the scheme of color that haunts me, I think you will be delighted with it.

On February 9, 1906, Ryder was confiding from New York to Charles Erskine Scott Wood (1852–1944), an artist and writer:

I am getting the "Lorelei" into shape. I think she was to perpendicular on the rock; reclining more as I have her now, seems [to] help the feeling of the picture very much: of such little things painted dreams are made . . .

The "Tempest" seems to want but little; but oh how much that little may be; however, I really believe if anything happened to me, if the blue of the sky in [the] upper left hand corner was matched, it would be about as valuable as

(continued on page 137)

James A. McNeill Whistler: Lady of the Lange Lijsen, oil, 1864.
John G. Johnson Collection.

Winslow Homer: The Gulf Stream, oil, 1899.
Metropolitan Museum of Art, New York.

Thomas Eakins: William Rush Carving the Allegorical Figure of the Schuylkill, oil, 1877. Philadelphia Museum of Art.

Albert Pinkham Ryder: The Tempest, oil, undated.
Detroit Institute of Arts.

William Michael Harnett: After the Hunt, oil, 1885.
California Palace of the Legion of Honor, San Francisco.

Mary Cassatt: Lady at the Tea Table, oil, 1885.
Metropolitan Museum of Art, New York.

Maurice Prendergast: Cinerarias and Fruit, oil, 1915.
Whitney Museum of American Art, New York.

Maurice Prendergast: Umbrellas in the Rain, watercolor, 1899.
Museum of Fine Arts, Boston.

John Singer Sargent: Daughters of Edward D. Boit, oil, 1882.
Museum of Fine Arts, Boston.

finished. Judging from the work of Millet and others, it is so nice in color and other good things.

My fault is: I cannot some way go at a picture cold; I have to have a feeling for it; perhaps I shall better some.

The expatriate artists of the post-Civil War era were an important group chiefly because of their success in capturing the respectful attention of European artists and critics. Mary Cassatt, the daughter of the banker, Robert S. Cassatt, a gentleman who retired to spend his income in France, was one of the most effective. There was never a financial worry on her horizon—her brother Alexander Johnston Cassatt was, after all, the president of the Pennsylvania Railroad. Living in France with her parents, she spent her passion on learning the technique of the impressionists and on making her own contribution to impressionist history.

Regarding Mary's life in Paris, her mother wrote from Paris to Mary's brother A. J. Cassatt on April 9, 1880:

The exhibition of the "Independents" is now open. It is not such a success financially as it was last year, but as the *Figaro* has opened on them, it may do them good in that way. Mary had the success last year, but this one she has very few pictures and is in the background. Degas, who is the leader, undertook to get a journal of etchings and got them all to work for it, so that Mary had no time for painting and as usual with Degas when the time arrived to appear, he wasn't ready. That *Le Jour et la Nuit* (the name of the publication) which might have been a great success has not yet appeared. Degas never is ready for anything—this time he has thrown away an excellent chance for all of them. As I said, they have not had such a success financially, but nearly all of the exhibitors have sold, which shows that the school is beginning to succeed even with the public.

By December 10 of that year Mary's mother was hoping to interest her son in a Degas:

I don't know whether Mary has written you or not on the subject of pictures. I didn't encourage her much as to buying the large one, being afraid that it would be too big for anything but a gallery or a room with a great many pictures in it, but as it is unfinished or rather as a part of it has been washed out and Degas imagines he cannot retouch it without painting the whole over again and he can't make up his mind to do that, I doubt if he ever sells it. He says it is one of those works which are sold after a man's death and artists buy them not caring whether they are finished or not. It is the same with a picture of *danseuses* which Mary would like to buy for you. He says he must repaint it all merely because a very small portion has been washed out. You know he is famous for his *danseuses*. He has painted them in every imaginable way. Mary is keeping a lookout and whenever she sees anything . . . which she thinks you would like at what she thinks respectable prices, she will buy them. She says she is afraid to order anything from Degas, as he might make something so eccentric you might not like it.

The Cassatts had their oysters imported from America, but they were careful about the Americans they cultivated in France. Mrs. Cassatt makes this clear in a letter from Paris to A. J. Cassatt, written in December 1881:

We jog along as usual, make no acquaintances among the Americans who form the American colony, for as a rule they are people one wouldn't want to know at home and yet they are received as specimens of the best society in America. This morning's paper mentions that Mrs. Mackay, the wife of the California millionaire, and her mother and father and sisters (the Hungerfords) have just

The Vision of Life was painted about 1895 by Ralph Albert Blakelock, whose own life (1847–1919) was a nightmarish struggle against poverty and insanity. Crushed by his failure to provide for a family of nine children and by the rejection of his landscapes, he was declared insane in 1899. When he was released from the asylum in 1916, he never painted again; by then, recognition had come too late. The Vision of Life is owned by the Art Institute of Chicago.

In a New York studio full of "fixings," Francis Coates Jones did mostly figure paintings. He belonged to several art associations, including the National Academy of Design. This photo was taken about 1900.

dined with the ex-queen of Spain in company with the minister from Spain and other dignitaries. Now they say that the Hungerfords are as low and common as it is possible to be. Mrs. Mackay, I suppose, has learned something, and besides is young and pretty.

On May 13, 1883, Mary's mother was writing to A. J. Cassatt's wife of their latest brush with Whistler, who had just executed a picture for A. J. Cassatt's collection:

[Whistler] seemed extremely well pleased with your portrait. He has some landscapes and a full-length portrait in the international exhibition now open at [the dealer] Petit's rooms at the rue de Saxe which are very good but old. Degas says that he gave him [Whistler] more rubs when he was here, and that he went off saying there wasn't an artist in Paris.

On October 14th of that year Mary was writing to her brother of Whistler's progress on the portrait destined for his collection:

The portrait is not done yet. I thought it a fine picture, the figure especially beautifully drawn. I don't think it by any means a striking likeness, the head inferior to the rest. The face has no animation, but that I believe he does on purpose. He does not talk to his sitters, but sacrifices the head to the ensemble . . . Sargent said to Mother this afternoon, it is a good thing to have a portrait by Whistler in the family.

Ohio-born John Quincy Adams Ward (1830–1910), one of the best American sculptors of the 19th century, is shown in his New York studio around 1880. Ward moved to New York from Washington, D. C., in 1861. He specialized in portrait busts and life-size figures. Among his famous works are George Washington, in front of the Subtreasury Building, New York, and Indian Hunter and The Pilgrim in New York's Central Park.

Nor did Mary's mother fail in her duty to remind her son that he should be a collector of the best in modern art. Writing to him from Paris on November 30, 1883, she said:

Your father is anxious to know if any of your friends appreciate the Monets you took home. We have one here which Mary admires immensely. It is a view in Amsterdam. Your father has allowed Mary to exchange our "Trouville" for a seapiece. It is certainly one of those which it would take an artist to appreciate, or maybe a sailor. It is a boat tossing on a great wave . . . Monet's pictures are to be exposed at the Académie des Beaux Arts in a month or two and then sold. As the executors have arranged the whole thing badly, it is thought something may be picked up cheap.

A. J. was never allowed to miss an opportunity. His mother wrote him from Paris on December 10, 1886:

You know you are going to have Durand-Ruel in New York this winter again. He is in money troubles as usual, I think but a New York house has a partner or agent here who says there is no danger but he will make money in America. He owned two or three of Mary's pictures which she didn't think much of and she asked him to exchange one of them for a new one. He took the new one and agreed to give her one back, but it was one he hadn't intended taking. She was very glad to get it, but as he seemed to like the others very much, she let him take them. I hardly think she did right, for it is a good while since she painted them, and Degas thinks she has improved much, especially in drawing. Everybody concerned says there is absolutely nothing doing here in pictures, and all the dealers are looking to New York to save them.

Should Mary get Degas's advice on her latest work? She was not sure this would be wise, as she indicates in a letter written in December 1892 to Mrs. Potter Palmer:

I have been half a dozen times on the point of asking Degas to come and see my work, but if he happens to be in the mood, he would demolish me so completely that I could never pick myself up in time to finish for the exposition. Still he is the only man I know whose judgment would be a help to me.

Of the same Durand-Ruel showing of French impressionists mentioned by Mrs.

Childe Hassam, a Boston painter of impressionist interiors and landscapes, painted this vivid city scene, Allies Day—May 1917, which is in the collection of the National Gallery of Art, Washington, D. C.

Cassatt, Jervis McEntee wrote with a scorn that characterized a typical American academician's attitude at the close of the nineteenth century:

[Worthington] Whittredge came in and talked a while and at 12 we walked up to the American Art Galleries to see the pictures by the French Impressionists. All that is really Impressionist is to me simply absurd, foolish and unlovely from any point of view. There are a few interesting pictures among the three hundred or more but they are interesting for the absence of what distinguishes the work of these lunatics. I can't imagine sane men showing such work as they expose there, with any serious intention. Manet has some forceful qualities and is entitled to respect for that, but the most of the work shocks all my ideas of art or even common sense, and yet the nice scribblers for the press, some of them, as witness the *Tribune,* try to write them up.

A late 19th-century example of trompe l'oeil painting, with the minute detail and realistic composition that, together, deceive the eye, is John F. Peto's The Poor Man's Store. Oil and canvas on wood, it was painted in 1885 and is in the collection of the Museum of Fine Arts, Boston.

In an all-too-brief life, John Twachtman became known for atmospheric, dreamy landscapes—many reportedly inspired by the countryside close to his home near Greenwich, Connecticut. His Hemlock Pool, left, was painted in 1902, the year of his death; he was 49. It is owned by the Addison Gallery of American Art, Phillips Academy, Andover, Massachusetts.

VI Reaction and Revolution

The story of American painting and sculpture since 1900 is the story of revolution against tradition. The National Academy of Design, representing all that was trustworthy and safe, exercised a stagnating power through its hierarchy of membership, its annual exhibition, and its access to publicity. In the first decade of the century only a few inconoclastic critics like James Gibbons Huneker and Charles Fitzgerald acclaimed three groups of imaginative young artists who had broken with the past.

The first of these groups was led by Robert Henri (1865–1929), whose charismatic charm radiated from slightly oriental-looking features. As a boy in Nebraska he had taken part in the murderous conflict between farmers and cattle drivers, and after his father had shot a man who had attacked him, the family moved east to Atlantic City. Henri studied under Thomas Anshutz at the Pennsylvania Academy of the Fine Arts, toured Europe, and returned to Philadelphia to paint and teach. There his enthusiasm and knowledge of art made him the natural leader and mentor of several young newspaper illustrators, among them John Sloan (1871–1951), William Glackens (1870–1938), George Luks (1867–1933), and Everett Shinn (1876–1953). By 1900 the entire group, led by Henri, had moved to New York. The training they had received on newspapers and Henri's persuasive views on art in relation to life led them to paint the ordinary people they saw around them on the streets and rooftops, in cafes and theaters. What later became known as the Ash Can School had its basis in this down-to-earth or down-to-pavement rendering of New York scenes.

An inspired teacher, Henri established his own school in New York in 1909. "Life and art cannot be disassociated," he told his students, "nor can any artist, however he may desire it, produce a line of sheer beauty, that is, a line disassociated from human feeling."

Henri also urged complete freedom of expression for all artists. When paintings by Luks, Glackens, and Sloan were rejected by the National Academy jury in 1907, Henri, who had been elected to membership that year, withdrew his own entries. A few months later he arranged for the exhibition of The Eight at the Macbeth Gallery. This showing of works by Henri, Glackens, Luks, Sloan, Shinn, Maurice Prendergast, Arthur B. Davies (1862–1928), and Ernest Lawson (1873–1939) was given much publicity, drew thousands of disapproving visitors, and went down in the history books as a very important exhibition of an American school of realism.

While this startling new art was being absorbed, if not bought, by the public, another group, working toward an even more astonishing art, was quietly forming under the leadership of Alfred Stieglitz (1864–1946). An experimental photographer, a dealer, and an enthusiastic promoter of radical new European art, Stieglitz helped and encouraged men like Arthur G. Dove (1880–1946), Marsden Hartley (1877–1943), John Marin (1872–1953), Alfred Maurer (1868–1932), Abraham Walkowitz (1880–1965), and Max Weber (1881–1961)—who represented the esthetic wave of the future in American art. Marin, Maurer, Walkowitz, and Weber had been to Europe before 1910 and returned with news of the exciting new work coming out of Paris. Beginning in 1908 Stieglitz exhibited Rodin, Cézanne, the fauves, the cubists, and their young American counterparts at his Photo-Secession Gallery at 291 Fifth Avenue, New York, but all his attempts to stimulate an interest in this strange new idiom were a mere scratching of the surface compared to the effect of the most shattering event in American art history, the Armory Show of 1913.

The show itself was the work of a third group inspired by the knowledge and example of Arthur B. Davies, a seemingly mild-mannered man who was a rather mystical painter. In 1911, when the power of the National Academy was still undiminished, Walt Kuhn (1877–1949), Jerome Myers (1867–1940), and Henry Fitch Taylor (1853–1925) led a move to form a new organization, the Association of American Painters and Sculptors; they hoped it would become a significant rival to the Academy. The Association soon came under the direct control of Davies who, with an unexpectedly strong exercise of authority, used it to bring to America a vast number of examples of the most advanced European art.

Ultimately, the Armory Show not only severely weakened the Academy but also virtually destroyed the developing school of realism represented by The Eight. These results were, however, delayed by the immediate popular and critical opposition to the radical art on view in the show. The men around Stieglitz were the Armory Show's chief American beneficiaries, and if their general acceptance took place years later, in 1913 they were brought to the attention of many perceptive observers.

A subsequent exhibition which also contributed to the public awareness of American modern artists was the Forum Show of 1916, organized by Willard Huntington Wright (1888–1939), an art theorist and promoter of synchromism. This abstract art, based on spectrum colors in graduated intensities, was the style of Wright's brother, Stanton Macdonald-Wright (b. 1890), and Morgan Russell (1884–1953). Most of the Stieglitz group was included in this exhibition as well; it was designed to show the public that American moderns were not painting nudes descending staircases.

Before the nineteen-thirties, few American sculptors broke away from conventional representation. Those who did were strongly influenced by the Armory Show. Paul Manship (b. 1885) was one of the first to turn from conventional anatomical realism toward a stylized simplification of form. He was followed by Gaston Lachaise (1882–1935), who came to New York from Paris in 1906, worked

While teaching at the School of Design for Women in Philadelphia, Robert Henri, above, befriended four newspaper illustrators: John Sloan, George Luks, William Glackens, and Everett Shinn. With Henri's encouragement, the four began serious careers as painters and with Henri, Arthur B. Davies, Maurice Prendergast, and Ernest Lawson composed the group of painters later identified as The Eight.

with Manship, and by 1913 had begun to develop his own style, which was characterized by a massive but seemingly weightless quality and a refined control of rhythmic movement. William Zorach (b. 1887), a painter in the Forum Show, turned to sculpture in 1916. His carving in stone displayed a geometric style that was related to cubism but retained an idealized representational form.

Dear Mr. Macbeth: Sept. 10, 1900

I have returned to America and should have been in to see you the other day while in New York but for the pressure of train time. I am back bag and baggage and with the full intention of remaining. Have rented a house overlooking the East River at the end of 58th Street. Not the most fashionable quarter I'll admit, but with such a view of the river from both ends of the house that I shall never be in want for something magnificent and ever-changing to paint . . .

Will you kindly remember me to Mr. Davies. ROBERT HENRI

Robert Henri, leader of the Ash Can School and one of the most influential teachers of his generation, here announces to his dealer, William Macbeth, his arrival in New York. Eight years later his leadership of the movement against conservatism and respectability culminated in the exhibition of The Eight at William Macbeth's gallery. Five years after that the Arthur B. Davies to whom he wished to be remembered in his letter to Macbeth made of the Armory Show an event which effectively destroyed Henri's dominance over rising non-academic artists.

In an interview recorded in New York by the Archives in 1962, Stuart Davis (1894–1964), Henri's most successful student, recalled the atmosphere of the time and the stimulating effect of Henri's personality:

The ordinary art student in the days of the Henri school wouldn't think of having a show in a gallery because there weren't any galleries that would admit his type of work. He hadn't been around long enough. The communication of art was a very limited, formalized, and restricted monopoly. So the Independent Show idea developed, and this was Henri's idea, where everyone could show who had done something—a show with no jury and no prizes. You say, "All these things mean nothing now"—but then it was an amazing thing. The first Independent Show was held in 1910 down on West 35th Street. They just hired an office building of three or four stories in the middle of the block between Sixth and Fifth Avenues, hung up all those paintings and charged admission. They got out a catalogue. That was Henri in his response to the general atmosphere of the time, and it was the response of John Sloan, Glackens, Shinn, [James] Preston, George Luks and Rockwell Kent, too. Kent and [George] Bellows were pupils of Henri before I got onto the scene . . . . This kind of contemporary response was going on in Henri—the opening of the school and sponsoring and getting enthusiasts for this exhibition.

Henri came to New York with a tradition of art in the environment, art from the environment, art from your own personal experience as opposed to art as a formalistic tradition that had been passed down through the academies . . . . When Henri opened his school his principle was to draw from your own experience, to look not only at art, but at the people around you as well, at the situation around you and draw them. He didn't have any plaster-cast class. He did have a life class. We worked in the life class five days a week. . .where we were told to draw the model not according to some formula, but in terms of

George "Lusty" Luks, mimic and illustrator-cartoonist-artist, who seldom let work interfere with his practical jokes, was painted, left, in 1904 by a fellow member of The Eight, Robert Henri. Luks was then 37 and living in New York, where he roamed the streets sketching the drab and the dramatic that later were to appear in his realistic paintings of the city.

Everett Shinn, Robert Henri, and John Sloan are deep in conversation in Henri's Philadelphia studio about 1896. All three moved to New York shortly afterwards and, with George Luks, began the revolt against imitativeness pervading the American art scene. They were to assert the value of daily experience as an art theme.

The Docks, New York City, below, now at the Munson-Williams-Proctor Institute, Utica, New York, was painted by Everett Shinn in 1901. This was about the time New York gallery director Eugene Glenzer showed some forty of Shinn's Paris pastels at an exhibition jointly sponsored by actress Elsie de Wolfe and architect Stanford White. One other dockside Shinn painting, The Soft-Coal Nuisance—New York, 1902, a smoky, sooty melange of ferries and tugboats in the East River, is certainly the earliest visual protest against air pollution in American art history.

how it looked to us as a fresh experience. The questions of finish or prettiness were of no importance. The question was whether you could communicate some direct experience with this model in terms of its form. . . . The academic training wasn't just to copy that model, but to make a factual reproduction which was pre-established in a context of artistic values. Whereas Henri said in effect, "To hell with the artistic values. There are all kinds of those. What we want are your own fresh reactions to what you see and in relation to what you read, to what you know and to your general experience."

. . . Henri also had a composition class where in addition to making these life drawings, during the week we would make a painting, or drawings of people, places we had been to, street scenes, landscapes, anything we wanted to. Then on Saturday we would bring in these paintings and put them up on the wall. He would talk about the paintings we brought in for three or four hours, and in the process of talking about those pictures he would criticize them not from the standpoint of some pre-established norm of excellence, but in relation to his own ideas. Or he would talk about some book he'd read and what it meant about life, and how this painting and the attitude toward it were related, or not related to the book. He'd talk about his own interests while he was talking about the painting and in that way, since he had more experience, more purposeful experience with culture in general than the crew of youths who were there, his discussions were very educational affairs. . . .

He was a frequent visitor to Europe. He was a man with an impulse to see and know things, and was able to put that impulse into execution. He had the ability, the talent, and the intelligence to use it. That's what he translated to the students in the school, and that's why instead of just an art school, it was an opening-up type of instruction through the experience and intelligence of Henri himself. . . .

When Henri spoke of writers . . . what he did was to inspire a desire on the part of the listener to go out, to look up all this stuff and to get involved with it. There was nothing like that in any other art school in New York, in Europe, or anywhere else so far as I know. It was a unique thing which inspired the students with the thought that they were somebody, that they were worth something, and that they should go out and try to use this awareness, try to develop it as opposed to just going and learning a certain discipline.

INTERSTATE HOTEL COMPANY OF NEBRASKA
LESSEES

HOTEL FONTENELLE

"BUILT FOR YOU TO ENJOY"

H. EDGAR GREGORY
MANAGER

EVERY ROOM WITH BATH

OMAHA, NEB. July 5/19

Dear Mr Kraushaar:—
Still going! reached here today
spent 3 days in Chicago, nicely treated
by the Institute people

Iowa roads were dry most of the way
but we had a sample of what
they are in wet weather! awful
mud
My best regards to [illegible]
Yours John Sloan
(over)

This July 5, 1919, letter from John Sloan to his dealer, John Kraushaar of Kraushaar Galleries, New York, was written during a three-week-long cross-country trip from New York to Santa Fe, New Mexico, in the summer of 1919. Sloan, the driver, was an early member of the Santa Fe art colony.

Initially the best known of Henri's followers were the Philadelphia newspaper illustrators who had moved to New York around the turn of the century. William Glackens, George Luks, Everett Shinn, and John Sloan formed the core of this group and it was their work which startled the public at the famous show of The Eight in February 1908.

John Sloan, who acted as unofficial secretary of The Eight, acknowledged the success of the exhibition in a letter to William Macbeth written in late February 1908:

The check which settles the account for "Stamps" came duly to hand.

Since it is your kind wish to place the small items against us to account of advertising I accept the favor and in the name of the 'Noble Eight' thank you for all the innumerable courtesies and kindnesses you have shown us in the long-to-be-remembered exhibition of February 3–18, 1908.

My very best respects to you.

The revolt against the National Academy took another form late in 1911 when a few artists mildly antagonistic to Henri's leadership organized the Association

Photo by Peter A. Juley & Son

George Luks was one of several Philadelphia newspaper illustrators who followed Robert Henri to New York in the early 1900's, and continued to live and paint with the exuberance that gave him his nickname, "Lusty." In the letter below he thanks dealer William Macbeth for a check sent but gently asks if Macbeth would be good enough to sign his name. On the right is Luks's Mrs. Gamley, now in the Whitney Museum of American Art, New York, which he finished in 1930—the year after his good friend and mentor, Henri, died.

325 W. 56th St
Feb 27th

Dear Mr Macbeth:

I want to thank you for the check, but, would you mind attaching your signature to same a very small matter— but as Daniel Webster once remarked "but damned important" Will drop in to see you in a few days Thanking you for your interest believe me Sincerely Yours Geo Luks

A member of The Eight, John Sloan painted the everyday life of New York with sympathetic yet distinctly unsentimental realism. In this photo, taken during 1910, the artist is at work on one of his many oils of Washington Square, New York.

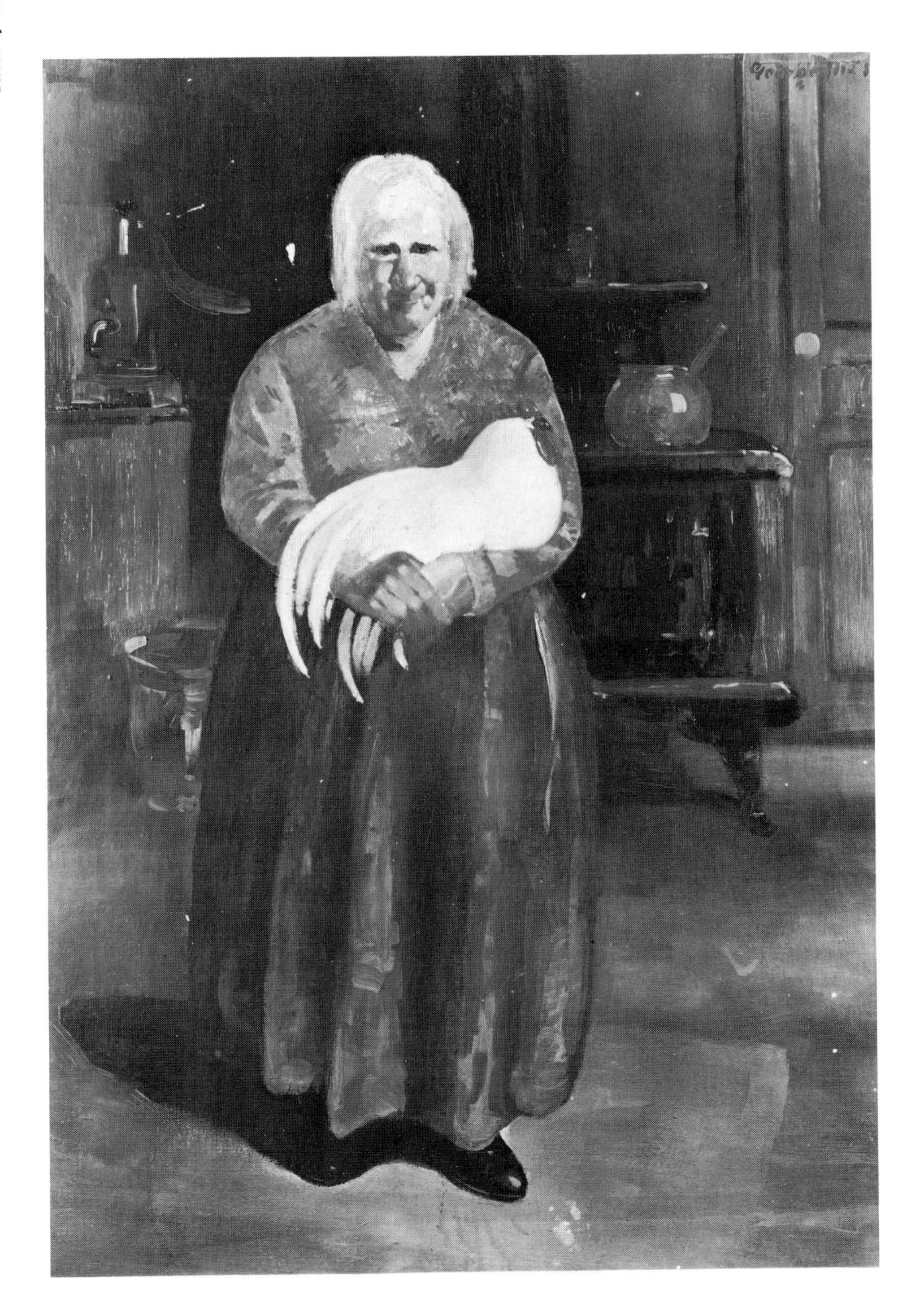

Photo by Peter A. Juley & Son

Rockwell Kent was a former student of Robert Henri who created a stir in March 1911, when he staged the Rockwell Kent Independent show. It represented the first split in the ranks of The Eight, as to representation in an exhibition. Only Maurice Prendergast, George Luks, and Arthur B. Davies were included. Kent painted The Voyagers, above, in 1923. It is in the Phillips Collection, Washington, D. C. The mountainous locale is assumed to be Alaska; Kent, an enthusiastic traveler, had just returned from there.

Arthur B. Davies's A Line of Mountains, below, is known to have been painted before 1913. It was included in the Armory Show of that year but, more significantly, it has the lyrical approach characteristic of Davies's work before he became excited about the new trends from abroad. It was Davies's involvement and interest in modern art that induced him to organize the Armory Show which in 1913 gave Americans their first look at works by the European masters. The painting is in the Virginia Museum of Fine Arts, Richmond.

of American Painters and Sculptors. Walt Kuhn, a rising painter who possessed enormous organizational ability, was the major figure in the Association's initial stages. In letters of December 12 and 15, 1911, he describes his plans to his wife, Vera:

Walt Kuhn, whose role in the mounting of the 1913 Armory Show included gathering many of the European works in the exhibit when he was sent to Germany and France for that purpose by Arthur B. Davies, is best known for brightly colored portraits of circus figures, painted in broad brush-strokes that seemed rough in their day. This photo was taken about 1905.

. . . Beginning the first of January, I am going to organize a new Society. The plans are still in embryo state but clear enough in my mind's eye to spell positive success. No one is in on it except [the critic, James Frederick] Gregg, and he's "mum," and the best advisor I could get.

As soon as I have it thoroughly planned we are going to give it to all the papers, and they'll jump at it. Of course Henri and the rest will have to be let in—but not until things are chained up so that they can't do any monkey business. He's so wrapped up in the McDowall club that he is off guard, and I'll put it over before he knows it, *and* in such a way that he can't make a single kick. I am as strong now as I will be for two or three years, and now is the time, for the [National] Academy has been worse than ever in "fireing" the younger set.

It's a case where we must be selfish, publicity must be secured, if the thing only lasts two or three years its purpose will be accomplished. However the thing is safe with Gregg and me until I get ready to spring it. And I'm going to take my time thinking out every detail . . .

. . . My idea about the new Society is about this: A big broad-liberal organization embracing every kind of art, even that which I do *not* like, one that will interest the public. The soft boys must be there too—the thing must be started so that it can grow and be as big or bigger than the Academy within 2 or 3 years . . . I don't want to be the president of the thing, if I can work it, it will be Glackens. Of course I may take a minor office, such as secretary, which although involving labor—will pay in publicity. Don't worry, I'll be the real boss—but it will be under cover. I'm not looking for the title of impressario. I now feel, that I can stand on the record of the *merit* of my work and believe that any honest method which will foster the publicity of it and my name is legitimate. Why shouldn't I use my talent as an organizer? Now that my work has made good, they will all fall in line with my idea. Henri queered himself with the Independent Show, and everybody is on his guard. The way to get the confidence of the artists is to give the opposite type a chance. I will retain the exclusive privilege of doing the talking to the press—which will be short but to the point. I want to get a reputation for absolute liberality and broadmindedness.

We may not be able to have a show this year but must be organized as a body, before we can expect any outside interest or assistance.

Expect that [John] Quinn [the collector and patron] will be our legal advisor (gratis) when the time comes.

Have made up my mind not to touch the thing unless it can be big enough to prevent people calling it a certain group, which would injure my "stand alone" attitude. If it's big enough, it will be just as though I had a picture hanging in the Pittsburgh or Phila Show and would not affiliate me with any bunch.

More about this when we get together. I feel absolutely certain that the thing can be done, and just think of the publicity! They wouldn't dare fire me from any show in the country. I've shown them that *I can paint;* now I'll show them that *I can fight.*

As it happened, Arthur B. Davies became the president of the Association. Few men in America could match his knowledge of art history and his deep interest in the latest currents from Europe. Determined to introduce these new perceptions to New York, he sent Kuhn to Europe to gather a great show of post-

impressionists and moderns. In a series of letters written in October 1912 Davies kept Kuhn abreast of Association affairs:

[John Frederick Mowbray] Clarke (1869–1953), a sculptor, has promised to work on the second circular, but I am inclined to work with Glackens on it. He has more horse-sense than any of the other fellows, even with the shadow of the "Blackest Henri" over him.

I am gently working a millionaire friend and must say I have big hopes for his help on our show—he still insists I am a bigger man that old Cézanne, and I shrink at such possibilities, that being the same *damned* provincial loyalty which has hurt us so long.

Yesterday we had a little gathering in Meyer's studio to decide on the contents of the second circular and to settle if possible our attitude with the newspapers and general public. The latter has been forced a little by the Academy and another opposition article. They seem to be anxious to "agitate"—for their own advantage. The feeling with us all is to sit tight for the present and saw wood. However, the "better painters" of America are not of the slightest interest to any serious artist. . . .

I presume I shall have your Cologne letter on Monday, your card came yesterday by an earlier boat. I wish I were seeing what you are. I feel free to get away now since the matters above referred to have been postponed. I shall leave things in Clarke's and Glackens' hands. If matters of the domestic character clear up this week I shall be on the briny soon.

Clarke received a note and signed card from Henri from Paris, Hotel de Portugal, which Clarke considers a complete backdown so don't rub it in now, he is weak artistically, God knows! and his faculties are not for art by any means. Dabo is back but have not seen him. All men are highly encouraged by our work of the summer. I enclose a ground plan for the arrangement of the Armory. Please make suggestions and practical improvements. It has made some eyes bulge . . . . Do not forget we want a roomful of Futurists and another of Cubists.

Photo by Peter A. Juley & Son

Brooklyn-born Guy Pène du Bois, shown about 1920 in front of one of his oils, studied painting in New York with William Merritt Chase before going to Paris. On his return to New York in 1906 he was a reporter and then art critic on the New York American and was the assistant of the art critic Royal Cortissoz, who admired his work. Du Bois also studied with Robert Henri and was associated with the Ash Can School, but his work usually had a sophistication and stylized quality reminiscent of European painting. His favorite subjects were wealthy figures at theaters, cafes, beaches, and gala evening parties.

A sense of the rising excitement felt by the organizers of the Armory Show is vividly conveyed in a December 14, 1912, letter from Kuhn to his wife:

Young [Guy Pène] du Bois was in today and tells me all the writers are crazy for stuff—Expect to be busy all day Monday giving interviews, our list of European stuff stupefies everybody. I'm simply in heaven with delight at the coming certain success. This show will be the greatest modern show ever given anywhere on earth, as far as regards high standard of merit. So far I have only seen [Jerome] Myers and [Henry Fitch] Taylor. Everybody is loyal and willing to leave it in the hands of Davies and W.K. Clark is like a faithful dog, but very slow and draggy, however I shall shake him up. The loyalty of the men is almost touching. The meeting next Tuesday will be o.k. We have decided to have booze and lunch for the boys, tell them what has been done and what is to be done and let it go at that. Give them a good time and not have any formal meeting at all. . . . We have adopted an emblem—Taken from the old pine tree flag of the revolution. I got the idea one morning in bed. Davies made the drawing and we'll have it on stationary, catalogues, posters and every where. We are also going to have campaign buttons—here is the design.

We are going to get them by the thousands—give them to everybody—from bums to preachers—art students—bartenders—conductors, etc. Ought to make an immense hit, and get everybody asking questions. This button business is a secret, and will have to be pulled off on the quiet, as some of the fellows might kick. After they are out it's no use to kick. Going to send buttons and posters to

Mouquin's, a New York restaurant (at Twenty-eighth Street and Sixth Avenue) that during the early 1900's was a favorite rendezvous for artists and art critics, was the setting for Chez Mouquin, above. Painted by William J. Glackens in 1905, it is now owned by the Art Institute of Chicago. Illustrating Glackens's photographic memory for details (he became famous for this, back in his days on the Philadelphia Press art staff) is his Curb Exchange No. 2, painted a few years later; it is the collection of Mr. and Mrs. Arthur G. Altschul.

When Robert Henri "resigned" from the New York School of Art (Director Douglass Connah used the word "fired"), he set up his own Henri School of Art in the Lincoln Arcade Building at Sixty-sixth Street and Broadway; date, January 1909. The existence nearby of Tom Sharkey's Athletic Club proved fortuitous for Henri's star pupil, George Bellows. Bellows found in Sharkey's the setting and details for his paintings of pugilists. His Both Members of This Club, right, 1909, is now in the National Gallery of Art, Washington, D. C.

The Dream, 1917, is by Louis Michel Eilshemius, many of whose paintings—moody fantasies in a style both simple and strange—were produced during some thirty years of complete non-recognition. During his lifetime (1864–1941) his work was alternately hailed briefly, rejected, then rediscovered. Two canvases were shown at the National Academy in 1887; his work seen at the Armory Show in 1913 impressed other artists; after 1926 there was wider acceptance, and his imaginative landscapes were much sought after. The Dream is now in the Phillips Collection, Washington, D. C.

[Maurice] Prendergast—Boston; [James E.] Lamb—Washington; [Morton] Schamberg—Philadelphia; etc. I have convinced Davies that owing to the short time of the show, one month, we must advertise. May also advertise in the street cars. He's right with me and tickled to death . . . .

Davies and I will be the only two men known as authorities in America on modern art, when this show is over. Pach deserves a lot of credit, and I shall see that he gets it too. They all say that D[avies] and I were the lucky combination. Pardon my immodesty, but you've said that yourself.

The Henri group, effectively blocked from the Association's inner circle, took little interest in the approach of the Armory Show. References in John Sloan's diary, however, reveal his understanding of cubism's implications:

January 4, 1913.

Notices from the American Association of Painters and Sculptors of which I am, no thanks to me, a member—continue to come but I can't feel interested enough to attend meetings lately. They are going to show what they think "good in art"!

January 16, 1913.

A Miss Merrick representing *American Art News* called and I showed her a few pictures. We had an interesting talk on the subject of the new movement—Matisse and the "neo-Impressionists" and Cubists etc. I think these a splendid symptom, a bomb under conventions. Some of the painters are nothing but flying splinters imagining themselves highly explosive forces but the explosive force is there—revolution it is.

The shattering effect which the Armory Show had on Henri's followers was recalled by Stuart Davis in 1962:

After the Armory Show, the fact that I was impressed by all this new work, and talks with the other students about it left me with the realization that the Henri school, the Sloan school, the Luks school—this American free naturalism wasn't the answer, that all kinds of new areas were opened up. I wasn't the only one in the school who reacted to the Armory Show—there were others. He [Henri] had heard about it and probably I had said something that hurt him—some student told him. So that afterward when I went to see him he said, "I didn't know you were interested in this type of thing anymore."

Davis also speaks of the subsequent failure of the converts to modern art to follow up their temporary victory over the traditional view of art:

There was a period after the Armory Show when a kind of enthusiasm about modern art was reflected in different ways. And then there was a sort of reaction to it which set in, so that the criticism of no content, no contact with the people, no message, no standards of values, nobody knew how to draw, and so forth—that attitude which is going on in a modified way today. These things go on, I guess, just automatically. . . .

During the period of Henri's ascendancy, an altogether different coterie had been coming together at Alfred Stieglitz's Photo-Secession Gallery. In 1958, seven years before he died, [Abraham] Walkowitz recalled for the Archives the atmosphere at 291 Fifth Avenue:

Hartley brought me to Stieglitz, and I had an exhibition at Stieglitz's in 1911. I was with him until 1917 . . . [when] the building came down. It was 291, a little brownstone. And that was the smallest gallery, but the biggest gallery. Small in size, but big in activity. He was a live wire. Stieglitz was Stieglitz . . . .

Alfred Stieglitz, the great pioneer photographer and protagonist of experimental art in the early 1900's, held radical exhibitions at his Photo-Secession Gallery at 291 Fifth Avenue in New York. This poster of a Photo-Secession show is from around 1908. Stieglitz studied in Germany and on his return to the U. S. in 1890 lent his influence to young artists struggling for recognition. In 1902 he published the first issue of his magazine Camera Work, and in 1905 opened "291," where he was to show the work of Cézanne, Matisse, and Picasso several years before they were exhibited in the Armory Show. Charles Sheeler, John Marin, Alfred Maurer, and Georgia O'Keeffe (later Stieglitz's wife) were among the avant-garde American artists that were displayed at "291."

Publicized by the pine tree flag symbol (of the Revolution) and a button—both shown in sketches drawn by Walt Kuhn in his December 1912 letter to his wife, Vera—the Armory Show opened February 17, 1913, in the 69th Regiment Armory, New York. Above is a partial view of what crowds pressed in to see: some 1,600 paintings, sculptures, drawings, and prints by both American artists and the European masters—realists, impressionists, cubists, fauves, post-impressionists. It was the Americans' first look at modern European art and it altered the course of American art history.

i have adopted an emblem—
green
Blue
white
Blue
Blue
Taken from the old
pine tree flag of
The revolution— I got the
idea one morning in bed—
ories made the drawing and will have
t on stationary, catalogues, posters and

3

INTERNATIONAL EXHIBITION of MODERN ART—1913—N.Y.
THE NEW SPIRIT
it will be about this size
and very neat
you are going to get them
by the thousands— give them to
any body— from bums to preachers—
art students— bartenders—conductors

And I stayed with him. I used to come into the Gallery at 10:00 o'clock and stay until 10:00 at night.

I used to stand and advise him. He was a good fighter, but he didn't know too much about inner things. But he was like a good lawyer, he could fight.

Stieglitz's place was an organization where all the artists, musicians, critics, would come together to the Holland House, to a table, and sit all together, eight or ten, and he would pay all the bills. It was an outlet for all ideas. And Stieglitz was of course very sympathetic to all those people. He would make modern art exhibitions, Rodin, Cézanne, Brancusi, all the best artists started with Stieglitz. He was the pioneer of modern art. Weber had an exhibition there. Many of the best exhibitions of that time were held by Stieglitz, up until 1917.

This is New York's 69th Regiment Armory (at Lexington Avenue and Twenty-fifth Street) which housed the famous Armory Show of 1913. Rarely used was the full name, as hung over the armory entrance: International Exhibition of Modern Art.

The Armory Show was a vindication of the men around Stieglitz, but their acceptance by the public would be long delayed. Two who apparently gained little from exhibiting were painter Louis Michel Eilshemius and sculptor Eli Nadelman. That artists suffered from a reaction to the new tendencies is indicated in a 1917 letter from synchromist Stanton Macdonald-Wright to Dr. John Weischel:

For us there seems no kind of help or sympathy except the ridiculous plaudits of third-rate dilettantes and these only after we have suffered the rebuffs that no lackey even would put up with and have forced ourselves on a suspicious and uninterested public. By "us" I mean men who are seriously trying to push the boundaries of our art into realms yet untrod and who are really achieving something en route. . . . Why damnit it is a fact that artists, not merely painters, have no more esteemed place in their friends' and public's hearts than whores and that society treats both classes as pariahs with the obvious preference for the whores. (At least they travel in automobiles and have charge accounts!)

In 1921 another member of the Stieglitz group, Oscar Bluemner (1867–1938), a German immigrant and color theorist, argued the subject in a letter to the rather conservative Macbeth Gallery:

From 1900 to 1910 I was often in your rooms, when I was painting quietly (being then professionally an architect) in order to see how others paint. And it all was, then, art to me and to my own clients.

And I liked Mr. Macbeth and we talked together sometimes. Your place is still the same. And it is nice. And *Art Notes* [the Macbeth Gallery house organ] is clever. Neither is wrong, since Art is very wide and embraces the old and the safe and sane and the nice and the mere artistic and sentimental and with all of this, of course, goes the general larger moneyed home decoration church-going American public. And I have no business to quarrel with them all. Thus far, *you* are right. . . .

In my various ways, of business or personally, I have met and still meet my share of the moneyed public (people able to like and buy art). Very few buy my work. And I have no grudge whatever.

However, I do know, and know for sure, that what is in The Modernists work, not mere "copying Renoir, Cézanne, Gauguin" . . . has in Europe and here with especially the professional class ("rich" doctors, engineers, actors, etc.), and with alive business men, in increasing number, that assured place of pure art interest (love of art and acquiring it), devoid of photographic sentimentalism or of mere decorating or of mere vanity, which it deserves critically.

And you are wrong in your attitude toward it. And toward the public. . . .

American art is, to my critical mind, and has been, absolutely European. The European critics are nothing here. But the fundamental elements for an American art are here, of course. The Art will come, of course. The Modernists are no more right than the "old fogies," they only try a different way, mostly again borrowed in Europe. Not in every case . . . however.

Some of the advanced artists express a poetic sensibility and humor in their writings which are often reminiscent of their paintings. John Marin's letters reflect his own individual style to a marked degree, as his letter from Maine of September–October 1948, to his friend, Charles Duncan, shows:

Dear Duncan,
Well that much's done—any way—its a start—
To continue—what???—Item—its blowing
out there—The seas are piling in-
Its breaking over a Sunken ledge out there—ordinarily
one is not aware of—what does one see—one get glimpses a
repetition of glimpses—and that—I would say is a multiple
that we Critters call Seeing—which has—I will say—nothing
to do with—*Mr. Camera*—The nerve of them with their Mr.
Cameras well—maybe—the nerve of me with my paint pots— . .
I in a way envy the few people here—they
don't have to go to the mixing places
. . . . and . . . .
they don't have to paint pictures. I
have to paint pictures—Oh yes I have
to—Some Cuss inside me forces me
to paint—those things they call
pictures—The thing to do is to paint
the perfect pictures then you are
through—you don't have to paint—
more—
One would be a *damn fool* to
do so—
. . . . but . . . .
startling things that can occur on canvas—
the adventures—come with me—just look out of this door—
Holy Moses—look out of that door—Holy holy Moses—now come
and look out of this other door—Holy Holy Holy Moses—and—
there be other doors—many many more—Hundreds of canvases—
many many paint pots—a great stack of brushes and—an extended
extended extended life.—

Georgia O'Keeffe's letters to the New York Sun critic, Henry McBride, reveal a similar strain. Responding to a review in January 1927, she wrote:

Thanks for the notice in the Sun.
I like what you print about me and am amused
and as usual don't understand what it is all
about even if you do say I am intellectual.
I am particularly amused and pleased to have
the emotional faucet turned off—no
matter what other ones you turn on.
It is grand.
And all the ladies who like my
things will think they are becoming intellectual

This picture of Edward Steichen, the great pioneer photographer, Charles Sheeler, the precisionist painter of industrial subjects, and John Marin, the sea- and city-scape painter, was taken by Sheeler's wife, Musya, at the Sheeler home in Irvington-on-the-Hudson, New York, about 1950. The three men had been close friends since the days of Alfred Stieglitz's "291" Gallery.

...... Its wonderful.
And the men will think them much
safer—if my method is French.
I will phone you to spend an evening with
us sometime soon—if you would like to.

sincerely
Georgia O'Keeffe

It is a grand page. I really feel much relieved because
I am terribly afraid of you.

In May of 1928 she describes to McBride her feeling about the country:

Everything is very green—soft spring yellow
green—the grass is soft and tall—waving—
we only cut it for hay later. The grape shoots
are velvety pink—The paint is coming off
the porch in huge pieces where I took off
the roof last year—We must put on a new gutter.

Charles Demuth (1883–1935) of Lancaster, Pennsylvania, was another member of the Stieglitz circle. When Marcel Duchamp, the French expatriate in New York, sent a urinal, signed R. Mutte, to the first Independents Exhibition in 1917, Demuth tried to persuade Henry McBride to publicize the incident:

My Dear Mr. McBride:

A piece of sculpture called: "a fountain," was entered, by one of our friends for the Independent Exhibition now open at the Grand Central Palace. It was not exhibited.

"The Independents," we are now told, have a committee—or jury, who can decide, "for the good of the exhibition."

We think that show called "The Super-Independents—or Salon des Refusés" is the next move.

If you think you could do anything with this material for your Sunday article we would appreciate it very much.

Yours Sincerely
C. Demuth

Eli Nadelman (1882–1946) was a Polish-born sculptor who settled in America in 1917. Four years earlier he had exhibited in the Armory Show and, later, at Stieglitz's "291" Gallery. A 1948 retrospective at the Museum of Modern Art, New York, which owns his bowler-hatted Man in the Open Air, a bronze of about 1915, directed attention to his work, which has the simplicity and strength reminiscent of the early American folk artists whose works he collected.

P.S. If you wish any more information please 'phone, Marcel Duchamp, 4225 Columbus, or, Richard Mutte, 9225 Schuyler. C.D.

On August 19, 1927, Demuth wrote to McBride after a visit to New England:

In Boston, which I did alone, I found that the Museum had cleaned their Washington Allstons. They are grand. The Sargents on its walls are not grand—indeed they are not in any way grand. They also have all their Blakes hanging. They are grand. . . . How is your garden—ours seems thin. Have painted no flowers, which means that I'll have less money next winter. How the collectors love flowers.

The sculptor Gaston Lachaise expressed his credo in an article published in Creative Art in August 1928:

In answer to numerous requests that I explain my sculpture I avow that I am a portion of the creative forces which are constantly reincarnated throughout the march of time. Protoplasm haunted by the spectre of man realized mankind . . .

Now, as a fragment of creative impulse, here I am. Born in Paris in 1882 I began my apprenticeship, at thirteen, in the national art schools of France. After years of schooling I had found to express only sweet-nothing compositions and soulless reminiscences of classics. At twenty, in Paris, I met a young American person who immediately became the primary inspiration which awakened my vision and the leading influence that has directed my forces. Throughout my career, as an artist, I refer to this person by the word "Woman."

For a time I remained in France lazily contemplating masterpieces of the past. Then in 1906 I left for America. "Wake up," the interjection of a street-car conductor, inducing me to act, should illustrate what I mean when I say that the New World is the most favorable place to develop a creative artist. Especially is this true, once one admits the street-car was headed neither for Athens nor Rome. No more indolent dreams but clarified and new values and "Woman," the sky and the land were mine.

"Woman," as a vision sculptured, began to move, vigorously, robustly, walking, alert, lightly, radiating sex and soul. Soon she came to forceful repose, serene, massive as earth, soul turned toward heaven. "La Montagne"! The feet almost disappeared. Mountains neither jump nor walk, but have fertile rolling pastures, broad and soft as fecund breasts.

Then "Woman" rose again, upstanding, noble, bountiful, poised on her toes, with closed self-absorbed eyes, nearly detached from earth. Still later, after communion with the universe and cosmic realization, "Woman"—spheroid, planetary, radiative—was entirely projected beyond the earth, as protoplasm, haunted by the infinite, thrust forth man, by means of art, toward the eternal.

Arthur Dove, another Stieglitz protégé, wrote out his feelings about art in a 1933 letter to Elizabeth McCausland:

Have studied Latin, Greek, French, Spanish, some German and Italian, also farming, and how to make money. Succeeded with most of them and seem to have forgotten them all successfully with the interest that grew with painting.

That has been the main interest to the point that all ideas became young growing facts, and it is the growing of ideas into facts that is the sort of agriculture that interests me most. One so seldom gets a good breeder idea. Two or three in a lifetime would be enormous.

That goes toward what is meant by modern painting. It is the human laboratory making research into life and all human thought and emotion to find young

(continued on page 169)

ohn Marin: Wave on Rock, oil, 1937.
ollection of Mr. and Mrs. John Marin, Jr.

John Sloan: Backyards, Greenwich Village, oil, 1914.
Whitney Museum of American Art, New York.

Robert Henri: Fifty-seventh Street, oil, 1902.
Yale University Art Gallery, New Haven, Connecticut.

Charles Demuth: I Saw the Figure 5 in Gold, oil, 1928.
Metropolitan Museum of Art, New York.

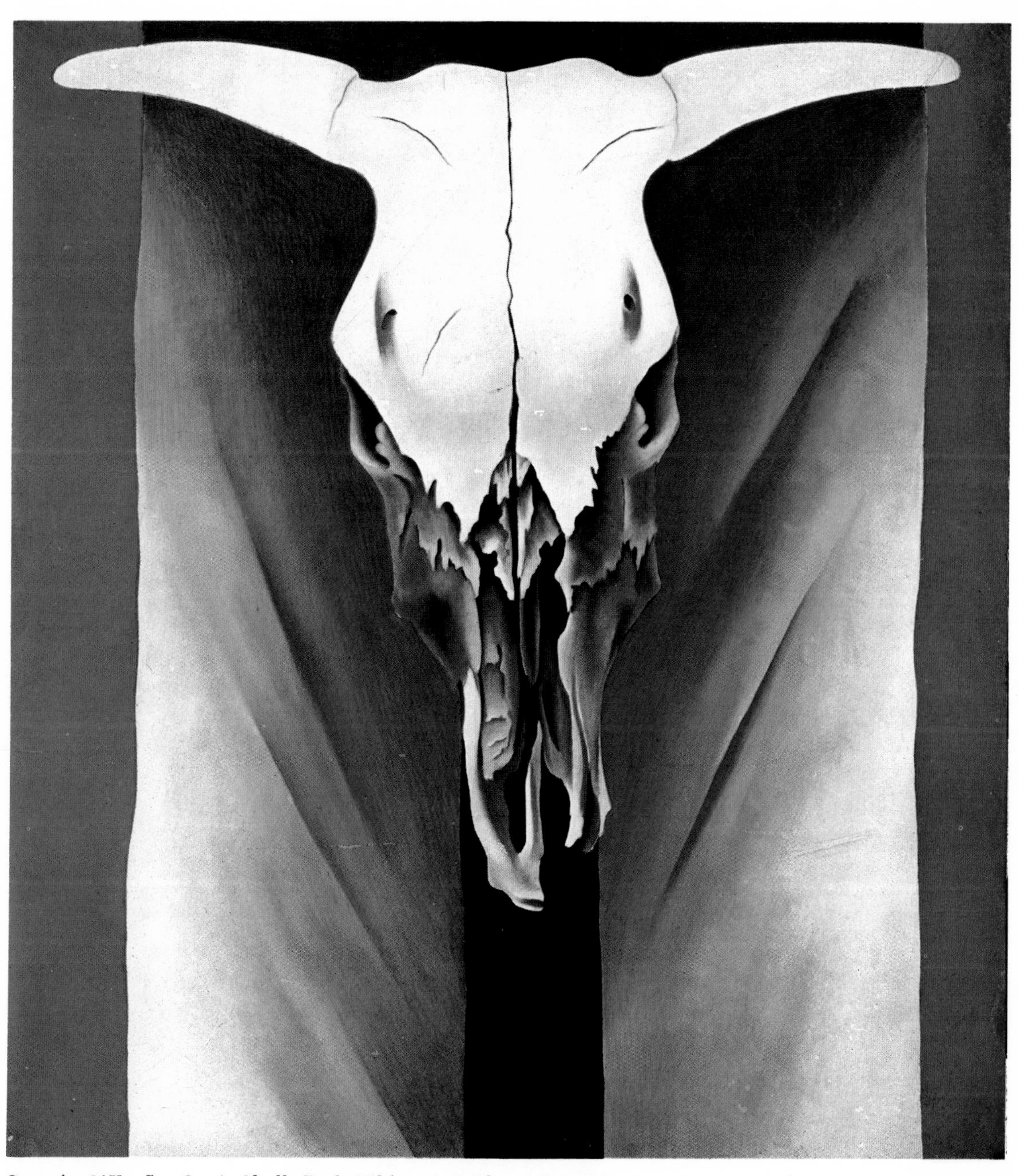

Georgia O'Keeffe: Cow's Skull, Red, White, and Blue, oil, 1931.
Metropolitan Museum of Art, New York.

Arthur Dove: Ferry Boat Wreck, oil, 1931.
Whitney Museum of American Art, New York.

Stanton Macdonald-Wright: Oriental Synchromy in Blue-Green, oil, 1918. Whitney Museum of American Art, New York.

Marsden Hartley: The Lost Felice, oil, 1939. Los Angeles County Museum of Art.

healthy plants that can stand the test of growing among the things that are lasting through the ages.

The making of objects "that please the eye" will always continue as will talent. The real breeder one is genius, the great sire. A great sire can make a whole section of the country fruitful and productive and the same is true of ideas.

To save the finest and breed from it is better than saving all. That is what "Modern" in the real sense means.

It is the elimination of the accumulation that gathers in attics.

The critics who do not realize this and look at paintings for their looks in terms of the past have no sense of responsibility.

So many ideas have been rejected because they may have offended a certain good taste when they contained as many vitamin A's as cod's liver oil.

Just at present I have come to the conclusion that one must have a flexible form or formation that is governed by some definite rhythmic sense beyond mere geometrical repetition, to express and put in space an idea so that those with sensitive instruments can pick it up, and further that means of expression has to have grown long enough to establish itself as an automatic force.

The play or spread or swing of space can only be felt through this kind of consciousness.

To build a head and put on it hair and eyes and lips and ears like the handles on a jug is not enough. To make it breathe as does the rest of nature it must have a basic rhythm. In other words I should like to make a painting exist in itself.

Most of these painters communicate a sense of their attachment to their thriving environment. Joseph Stella (1877–1946) expressed this explicitly in a letter to Henry McBride written from New York in November 1937:

. . . I felt that my "New York" or the "Brooklyn Bridge" possessed by the Société Anonyme, would properly fit in the exhibition of the American works to be opened next year in Paris. Especially "New York interpreted"—the five panels that you know so well—Lately acquired by the Newark Museum and now showing to the public (I hope that you will see them again) affirm and exalt the joyful daring endeavor of the American civilization.

Charles Sheeler's Classic Landscape, 1931, is typical of this artist's precisionist painting, with its flawless finish and sharply defined lines and planes. It is owned by Mrs. Edsel B. Ford.

VII Poverty, Politics, and Artists

Until the establishment of the first government art program in the mid-nineteen-thirties, many American artists suffered bitterly from the effects of the Depression. As the economic crisis deepened after the stock market crash of 1929, collectors stopped collecting, galleries went out of business and museums across the country found their sources of money dwindling. Cut off from contact with an interested public and unable to sell their work, unestablished painters and sculptors faced the alternatives of starving or turning to other occupations.

The art subsidy programs which were developed in the first few months of the New Deal established the radical precedent of employing artists as well as other out-of-work Americans. Edward Bruce (1879–1943), a genial administrator who had turned in the nineteen-twenties from law and international finance to a career as a landscape painter, organized the first of the art projects under the Treasury Department, the agency which controlled funds for construction of federal buildings. The fact that Bruce had wide contacts among artists, museum officials, and critics, as well as a highly developed sense of public relations, made him the ideal man to run a program which turned out to be unique in American art history.

The Public Works of Art Project, which lasted for only a few months in 1934, aided artists by putting them to work as mural decorators of new public buildings. Administering the painting of murals on federal walls was later assigned to another agency, the Section of Painting and Sculpture, also headed by Edward Bruce during most of its brief history. An arm of the Treasury Department, the Section sponsored most of the murals painted in post offices, courthouses, and miscellaneous government buildings constructed during the New Deal. A system of jury selection insured that artists commissioned to paint murals were chosen on the basis of drawings submitted anonymously.

Two influences affected the style of these murals. First was the work of the Mexican muralists, Diego Rivera, José Orozco, and David Siqueiros. Americans interested in promoting a mural movement here had visited Mexico and returned full of enthusiasm. Murals executed in this country by Rivera and Orozco further stimulated a consciousness of monumental painting among men like George Biddle (b. 1885), Ben Shahn (b. 1898), and Edward Millman (b. 1907). New buildings planned by the government offered a good opportunity for aspiring mural artists to work out their own ideas and techniques on hundreds of public walls throughout the country.

In some instances the subject matter of these murals was influenced by the social-protest motifs of the Mexicans. The majority of the murals painted in the nineteen-thirties, however, owed a larger debt to the American Scene school of the regionalists Thomas Hart Benton (b. 1889), Grant Wood (1892–1942), and John Steuart Curry (1897–1946). Indians, cowboys, mail carriers, farmlands, and factories, all appropriately tied to a specific local history and economy, appeared in public buildings across the country from Florida to the state of Washington.

One of the numerous art projects sponsored by the New Deal, the Federal Art Project began in 1935 as a Works Progress Administration agency and continued to employ artists until 1941. Several large exhibitions were arranged to show work produced by its painters and sculptors. The M. H. de Young Memorial Museum show in San Francisco, advertised in this poster, was one of the most important of these exhibitions.

The Federal Art Project, unlike the Section of Painting and Sculpture, was established in 1935 (as a division under the Works Progress Administration) solely to provide work for unemployed artists and art teachers. It was headed by Holger Cahill, a writer and folk art enthusiast who was on drinking terms with hundreds of American painters. The work of this Works Progress Administration agency is still a subject of much controversy among many of the artists who were involved in it. It was by far the largest of the government art programs and subsidized over five thousand people at its height. Its divisions employed easel- and mural-painters, sculptors, art instructors, photographers, and craftsmen. A community art center program brought art classes and exhibitions to scores of small towns. A picture-history of American design, *The Index of American Design,* was assembled.

The WPA was frequently attacked by Congress for spending public money on something Congress regarded as frivolous—art. There was a widespread suspicion that the Project was a hotbed of left-wingers, and unquestionably the exuberant outpouring of class-conscious painting outraged conservative opinion. Threats to cut the Project's appropriation or even to eliminate it altogether were met by the formation of the Artists' Union, an organization which was devoted to protecting the rights of artists employed by the government.

Many artists resented having to sign the pauper's oath, testifying to a destitute condition, which the Works Progress Administration programs required. Many also felt that undue pressure was applied to them to produce social-protest art which showed strikes, unemployed workers, and examples of injustice. Still others regretted the constant political strife which was a feature of the era. Certainly, many painters and sculptors felt both sympathy for and empathy with victims of the Depression and tried to express their indignation in satirical or bitter scenes of breadlines, police brutality, and industrial strife. A large number of them now regard their activities at that time as having been an exhilarating experience, an opportunity to respond to the then-prevailing social idealism.

Among the major figures whose reputations soared in the nineteen-thirties were Philip Evergood (b. 1901), William Gropper (b. 1897), and Ben Shahn. Their work was closely identified with the social criticism of the time. Boardman Robinson (1876–1952) and Henry Varnum Poor (b. 1888) produced some of the more successful murals under the Treasury Department. Jack Levine (b. 1915) is an outstanding example of a major contemporary artist who began his career with the Federal Art Project.

With the onset of World War II, the government art projects were abandoned and some of the artists employed by them produced service training aids, posters, and other visual propaganda for the Office of War Information. Many painters enlisted or were drafted, and some were employed as official war artists. When the war ended, a fresh approach to painting was well under way, and the social realism of the nineteen-thirties was already a thing of the past.

Grant Wood's Daughters of Revolution, top, greeted with anger upon its completion in 1932, has high approbation now. The Cincinnati Art Museum, which acquired it in 1959, reports that "it has been an important picture in our collection since that time." Wood appears, above, adding some final touches to his ice-wagon home in Stone City, Iowa; during the 1930's he was faculty director of an art school there. With John Steuart Curry and Thomas Hart Benton, Wood led the regionalist painting movement of the mid-1930's.

With the approach of the nineteen-thirties, a new movement, the American Scene, arose with the work of Thomas Hart Benton, Grant Wood, and John Steuart Curry. The grim, satirical qualities of Grant Wood's painting, "Daughters of Revolution," aroused a storm of protest. Wood comments on this in a letter to Edward Rowan, a Public Works of Art Project official, written from Cedar Rapids, Iowa, in February 1934:

The Daughters of Revolution of Baltimore, I am told, are trying to have me investigated by the Immigration Board. They are sure that I go under an assumed name and—if the truth were known—am a red and should be deported.

The Depression decade was dominated by a feeling for social content in art which came in part from the artists' sympathies for unemployed working men. Charles Burchfield (b. 1893) expressed this clearly in his account of the circumstances involved in his "The Parade," written in 1955 to Lawrence A. Fleischman, then a Detroit art collector who frequently solicited comments from artists on their works that he had bought.

This picture grew out of an experience my wife and I had one day during the depression of the early thirties.

We had come into Buffalo, on the bus, on some errand, and as we got off the bus, we found our way blocked by an unemployment parade—a group of men on their way to the city hall to make a protest of their plight—As we watched them go past, sullen and bedraggled (it was a thaw day in winter) we knew that unless something were done, that our society might crumble, and much worse come on us. The mounted police silently watching, seemed to have a cold sinister air about them.

The incident stuck in my mind and I felt I must get it down on paper. The answer came to me oddly enough at a symphony concert—during the playing of Beethoven's Fifth Symphony (which had nothing to do with the mood)—I suddenly saw the scene clearly in my mind. The parade seen through the arches of a concrete bridge. That seemed to give it a tomb-like character. To further heighten the effect I put in the foreground the vapors arising from a sewer-vent, and the crack in the bridge was to symbolize that the foundations of our society were cracking.

The only depression picture I painted. I planned a similar one during World War II, a protest against war—but it never materialized. I felt, I guess, nothing I could do would halt the destruction of young men (I believed in our participation in the war, but hated war itself). I also felt I would get myself and dealer in trouble if I exhibited such a picture—and to no purpose. So the impulse dissipated into nothing.

George Biddle was born in Philadelphia in 1885 and graduated from Harvard, where he got a law degree. Before finishing law school, however, he spent a year painting at the Académie Julien in Paris; later he was one of the first Americans to study the work of Diego Rivera and other muralists in Mexico. Returning to the United States, Biddle wrote to his college acquaintance, Franklin D. Roosevelt, urging the President to begin a program supporting murals by American artists. His plan eventually became a reality. In the photo, opposite page, taken about 1937, Biddle is painting a mural authorized during the late 1930's by the government's Section of Fine Arts.

Depression art in America in some ways represented the fulfillment of Robert Henri's realist school. This development was, in part, an aspect of the New Deal art projects, notably the Section of Painting and Sculpture under Edward Bruce

and the Works Progress Administration's Federal Art Project under Holger Cahill.

George Biddle, a painter whose chief interest was in murals, noted some of the background activities in his diary:

April 23, 1933. Drove over to see Henry Varnum Poor. . . . Discussed with him mine and Gerdt Wagner's scheme to get mural work for artists. Wagner's scheme . . . is to insist that during the depression work must also be given to artists and craftsmen on government buildings, and to defeat the slogan, "Owing to depression, we cannot afford to spend on art." My idea is chiefly that great mural work will never be done until the artists work for nothing. Through contacts in Washington to get government murals for the artists who will work at cost prices.

June 23, 1933. . . . we have the genuine interest of Roosevelt, Tugwell, Walter Lippmann and others; and I believe the movement may be a very important development in American art.

November 7, 1933. Lunch with Ned Bruce. [L. W.] Robert [Jr., Assistant Secretary of the Treasury] has asked him to organize a large committee representing modern and academic artists, the Academy of Design, the New Society, the newspaper critics, the crafts, etc. With their backing he will then have the authority to go ahead. We will then appoint a smaller committee who will have the supervision of mural work and crafts for public buildings.

December 8, 1933. [At a meeting held at Bruce's house to organize the Public Works of Art Project] . . . [Ellsworth] . . . Woodward from Tulane asked if he couldn't from the Hopkins fund buy great works of art 30 feet long from a genius 75-years-old. "No," said Bruce, "but you can set that genius to work next week to paint another at $35 a week." "And can I use my artists to depict the dying scenes of the old South, the Negro shanties, the wooden plows, the stills?" "Yes," said Bruce, "but remember the 18th amendment is repealed. It's a new deal in art and liquor. . . ." The feeling of the afternoon was, I think, that this may be the dawn of an epoch in American Art.

December 11, 1933. The newspaper releases went out yesterday. A wave of angry protest from every academic New York society . . . . They are boiling mad because they haven't been consulted, and because the government has leaned toward modern art and lastly because the government may cut into their swill by allowing starving artists to do murals at $35 a week. I received angry long-distance calls from some of them last night, but I think I reassured them that Bruce felt the importance of presenting every phase and tendency of American art, not just the moderns.

April 23, 1934. They realize that the Public Works of Art Project has given work to 2,500 artists during a cold winter, and that thereby the morale of all artists throughout the country has been immeasurably strengthened. . . . Our thanks are due to the Administration.

In 1936 Biddle wrote to Edward Bruce of his enthusiasm for the government mural work he was engaged in:

All goes surprisingly well and I never worked so hard or with such enthusiasm. I get up at 6 o'clock, am on the scaffolding before 7 and always work 10, 11, or 12 hours. I am finishing up the upper portions of the 3 central panels so that when I get down to the figures I shall have had almost a month's experience and I cannot tell you the real passion I have for this lovely medium. I am slowly getting an understanding of its techniques and possibilities.

In 1935 Reginald Marsh (1898–1954) wrote in the Treasury Department's Art Projects Bulletin of the attitudes expressed by some of the individuals who had

Aaron, now in the Pennsylvania Academy of the Fine Arts, Philadelphia, was painted about 1942 by Thomas Hart Benton, a Missourian and midwestern realist. The artist was named for his granduncle, a Missouri editor and statesman who lost his bid for a sixth term in the U. S. Senate because of his antislavery sentiment—an unpopular attitude in his state during the mid-1850's.

This 1938 Children's Festival in Central Park, New York, sponsored by the Federal Art Project of the W. P. A., was one of many outdoor shows displaying art works done under various government projects.

One of the Federal Art Project canvases from the Depression period is Night Pasture, painted by Jackson Pollock about 1936 in a style vastly different from the all-over composition and "drip" technique that was to characterize his work between 1947 and 1956, the year he died in an automobile crash. The whereabouts of the painting (which reflects the influence of Thomas Hart Benton, under whom Pollock studied in 1930–32) are not known.

Ben Shahn, born in Lithuania in 1898, is shown in his studio during the 1950's. Shahn, a socio-political artist, has remarked that "my tropism toward suffering may have become set during the Depression. I'm not sure about that, but it was certainly sharpened during the war. . . . I began to feel that suffering was innate in man." Among Shahn's famous canvases were those done in the early 1930's and based on the Sacco-Vanzetti Case, which ended with the August 22, 1927, execution of Nicola Sacco and Bartolomeo Vanzetti.

been watching him work on a post office mural in Washington, D.C.:

Having mounted the scaffold without a colored smock and a tam-o-shanter resulted in many employees asking when the artist was coming along. This happened even after I had completed full length figures. In all the time I was there, no one asked me my name.

One or two had heard of Kent—three or four had heard of Grant Wood, and about a dozen of a Mexican who had trouble with Rockefeller Center. One had heard of Michelangelo.

Many volunteered to tell me that cubism angered them.

Many wanted to know if there were new jobs in store for me and always looked at me in a pitying way.

Most of them ventured that I must have been "born that way."

Edward Bruce's own view of the first government art project is summed up in The American Magazine of Art, March 1934:

The reaction of the artists to the project . . . has been that while the economic relief afforded them by the project was enormously appreciated and greatly needed, the spiritual stimulus to them in finding that they were recognized as useful and valuable members of the body politic and the government desired their work has been simply amazing. It has, as many of them expressed it, broken down the wall of isolation and brought them in touch and in line with the life of the nation. It has stimulated them to the maximum effort and aroused their excitement and imagination . . .

The lady in an expensive fur coat who told me it was all right to feed the artists, but why make the public look at their stuff, is in for a shock. I think perhaps the outstanding feature of the work which has been produced so far is its honesty and fine quality of naturalness. It is a native product. While, of course, it shows signs of a definite art tradition and an art background, it is amazingly free from isms and fads and so-called modern influences. Ninety per cent of it is modern in the best sense.

It has been a very exciting experience to discover vigorous local art movements all over the country and talent where we did not know talent existed. Artists who were thought of as having only a moderate talent are producing work far beyond and better than they have ever produced before, and artists who were absolutely unknown are producing some of the best work on the project.

If through the project there comes a demand for a beautiful America, the economic as well as the spiritual and esthetic possibilities are very great.

The backers of this project went into it with their eyes open. They didn't expect a hundred per cent quality and they won't get it, but it is quite apparent from the work already accomplished that this country is going to get a great many works of art of high quality which will show the investment to have been very profitable as well as very fine. Masterpieces and geniuses are not produced from isolated efforts; if the history of art is any criterion they come only from large art movements. A large body of work and a large number of artists are necessary to reproduce the Leonardos, the Piero della Francescas, and the Michelangelos.

Many painters remember the period as an exhilarating experience. Ben Shahn, who worked as a photographer for the Farm Security Administration, regards the New Deal projects as a rich and vital development, he told the Archives in a 1964 interview:

There was a strange harmony with the time. I felt very strongly the whole

social impact of the time, and I felt very strongly about the efforts that this Resettlement Administration was trying to accomplish—resettling people and helping them. . . . I felt in complete harmony with the times. I don't think I've ever felt that way before or since. I was totally involved. It was a total commitment.

Burgoyne Diller (1906–1965), a painter and in the nineteen-thirties a supervisor for the New York City Federal Art Project, concurred with Shahn in a tape-recorded interview made for the Archives in 1964:

There's something that's unforgettable about that period. There was a sense of belonging to something, even if it was an underprivileged and downhearted time. It was exciting.

We worked day and night and weekends and believe me, we were not paid well for it, but we thought it was the most wonderful thing that could be happening. We were enthusiastic and we were ready and willing to do anything. It was a madhouse.

I was very much interested in abstract painting. They felt that there was no place for it at the time because they felt the project should be a popular program and while they didn't attempt to invalidate or question the validity of the work, abstract art had no place because you did have a great problem of building up public sympathy and understanding.

Fernand Léger wanted to paint—above all to have a mural in America. He'd never had one in Europe, and they thought there was a wonderful possibility of his doing something in America. No one wanted to take it upon themselves—private industry or anything of the sort. . . . So that Léger was unable to obtain anything. They got in contact with the Project [WPA Mural Division] as a possibility, so that after discussions with Audrey McMahon [New York Project Supervisor], who thoroughly approved of the idea that something might be done on the Project. It was turned over to me to see if it would be possible. We couldn't employ him as an artist on the Project either as relief or non-relief because he was not a citizen. But on the other hand we had an excuse for using him because of his name, and so on, and the fact that a good many American artists might like to work with him on a mural, so it would give them employment.

We decided that if we could find a place where we could do a job that would employ a group of American artists that might take the same theme that he would take . . . he could collaborate with them, and he could more or less establish a theme and then they could do whatever variations on that theme that they pleased. It might make a very interesting project. It was exciting for all of us to do it, and dealing with Léger was a very great pleasure. We got a group of artists to work with him. He came down to the studio area we had at the time. He worked with these artists and then he drew lots at his own studio, until finally we developed this series of sketches for this mural. It had been suggested that perhaps the French Line pier would be good. It was natural for Léger, in collaboration with American artists, to do decorations for the French Line pier. We took the presentation sketches to the Line's office and saw . . . [the director]. I introduced him to Léger, and he said, "I know that man," and started off in a tirade in French . . . [He] practically told him: "You worker, you communist." Léger was terrifically indignant about the thing . . . so we picked up and walked out. That was the end of that project.

We made a rather elaborate model of the work to be done for the [Arshile] Gorky mural in the Newark Airport. We did a rather good one for Gorky's presentation to the Art Commission of the City of Newark. The Commission was made up of rather elderly gentlemen. I'm sure they were of some prestige socially

Atop the scaffolding, Philip Guston, opposite page, and his assistants are working on a mural for the façade of the W.P.A. Building at the 1939 New York World's Fair. Like George Biddle, Guston traveled in Mexico in 1934 and 1935 and was familiar with the work of the great Mexican muralists when he executed commissions for the W.P.A. at a Commerce, Georgia, post office, the Queensbridge Housing Project in New York, and the Social Security buildings in Washington, D.C. After leaving the W.P.A. in the early 1940's, he turned from realism to lyrical abstract expressionism.

Photo by Leo Selzer

Arshile Gorky explains a drawing of his mural for the Newark, New Jersey, airport, to New York's Mayor Fiorello LaGuardia. This was in 1935, at the opening of a Federal Art Project Gallery on Thirty-eighth Street, New York. Installed at Newark, the mural was later removed and is now lost. Below is Agony, 1947, one of Gorky's paintings, which is in the Museum of Modern Art, New York.

Henry Varnum Poor, a ceramist as well as a lyrical painter of landscapes and still lifes, was born in Kansas in 1888. During the 1930's he did frescoes for the Department of Interior and Department of Justice buildings, Washington, D.C., and for years taught art at Columbia University. He is Chairman of the Board of Governors of the Skowhegan, Maine, School of Painting and Sculpture.

and economically. I'm sure they fit into the upper echelons of Newark society—rather cool, forbidding characters. They were the sort of people you would see sitting in the windows of the Princeton Club, or the Yale Club. When we presented the mural I deliberately presented it as decoration so they wouldn't quibble about art. But one of them, probably brighter than the rest, said, "Well, that's abstract art, isn't it?" That unleashed the devil. They started, of course, a tirade of questions and cross-questions and accusations and statements about modern art. Beatrice Windsor, who is socially and economically their equal, shamed them into accepting it.

Something of the philosophy behind much of the mural painting of the nineteen-thirties was expressed by Henry Varnum Poor in a 1939 letter to Edward Bruce:

I think that the basis of any great mural, as of all painting, is a sense of the pictorial necessity, a visual freshness and reality which speaks more clearly than any other thing. So a complicated or highly intellectual idea is a great drawback—something to surmount rather than a real help.

Examine the purely intellectual content of any great mural and you will find it almost nil. Or a truer way to put it would be to say that what the artist contributes to the original story cannot be expressed . . . in words. When it is accomplished it may be the result of the finest wisdom—endless words and ideas can play over it but they would not help in its creation.

In Massaccio's "The Tribute Money" you will find the simplest possible illustration of the subject. The painter's contribution is just in the air and light which bathes the figures, in their grouping, in their types and in their gestures. These things hold the finest wisdom but it is created out of visual sensibility, not out of ideas.

This would hold true for almost all of the great mural painters.

In a 1964 interview the sculptor Louise Nevelson (b. 1900) remembered the projects as a great contribution to American art:

When I came back from Germany where I studied with Hans Hofmann, and also did some movie picture work at the studios, I got on the WPA. Now that gave me a certain kind of freedom and I think that our great artists like Rothko, de Kooning, Franz Kline, all these people that have promise today and are creative, had that moment of peace, even if it was in a loft, to continue with their work. So, I feel that that was a great benefit, a great contribution to our creative people and very important in the history of art. And not only in the visual arts but in the theater, and the folk arts, there wasn't a thing that they didn't touch on. The wonderful buildings that came up, and the highways. At that period, people in our country didn't have jobs and the head of the government was able so intelligently to use mankind and manpower. I think it's a highlight of our American history. . . .

A great many other artists managed to struggle through the Depression with little assistance from the government. One of them was John Flannagan (1895–1942), the stone carver, whose controlled, organic forms made a very personal kind of expressionism. He described his approach to art in a letter applying for a Guggenheim Fellowship in 1939:

My aim is to continue the purpose of twenty years of working in sculpture—to create a plastic idiom alive as the spoken word; sculpture as direct and swift in feeling as a drawing, sculpture with such ease, freedom and simplicity that it hardly seems carved but to have endured always. Fulfilled, it should mean the

This photograph of the painter Morris Kantor was taken in 1938 by his friend and fellow faculty member at the Art Students League of New York, Yasuo Kuniyoshi.

Yasuo Kuniyoshi, who took the photo of Morris Kantor, above, was himself photographed during the 1930's by Barbara Morgan. The occasion was a party in Kuniyoshi's Woodstock, New York, studio, and the artist was too absorbed in his new still life arrangement to pay attention to the festivities. Kuniyoshi came to the U.S. in 1906 when he was 13, and for twenty years (he died in 1953) was a respected teacher at the Art Students League. His Amazing Juggler, 1952, left, is in the Des Moines, Iowa, Art Center.

42 Washington Mews
April 23 1934

Dear Mr Ames
I just received today the bronze statue — the base is 24 inches by 35 inches 35" is the front of the statue

I am sorry that I could not send this information to you any sooner
I am most sincerely
Yours
Gaston Lachaise

Paris-born and trained, Gaston Lachaise moved to the United States in 1906, when he was 24, and became one of the first truly modern sculptors in America. In this April 23, 1934, note to Winslow Ames of Saunderstown, Rhode Island, Lachaise sketches and writes about one of his typically voluminous bronze standing women.

development of an instrument so sensitive as to record the human psyche in all its various moods and reactions to life instead of the usual banal platitudes and worn clichés.

This is an austere art which compels a clear perception of its scope and limitations. Therefore it seems that it should be of a generalized universal symbolic nature . . . man, woman, child animal. The fusion of abstract design with feeling and representational values is one of the major problems of art expression. The design, the sculptural form is of course fundamental but it is necessary to vitalize this through emotion and verisimilitude else the work becomes cold and remote. Over and above the tactile organization of lines, planes and masses should brood the mystery of a living thing.

And in a 1941 letter to his dealer, Curt Valentin, Flannagan expresses in more personal terms his feeling for his work:

. . . long ago—I had a job, a good one and carved and painted all the nights. That was "amateur." So I quit the job to compel myself to live by art alone. I've done a lot of starving since, but I had always a completely professional point of view and still have—a good one. That's why I speak truly of "turning stones into bread," but alas, no matter how fast one labors, carving by hand is pathetically slow when trying to make at least a bare living by it. So I think of an air compressor to help. After all we must forever do our "thinking by hand." With a compressor I can always make a living, that way it will be "making our bread from (air) wind and stones." At this moment I'm trying to find the best and cheapest way to get one. When I've found the most moderate way I'll let you know. It must be the most inexpensive way as obligations worry me too much. I brought in another little bronze head, please try to do something with it—price $300. Any money that comes from it is not for me, but will *free* me from a lot of worry. A chance to keep working constantly to make just enough money to do so and live and pay off obligations and I'm content. I am content and working hard now and want no more.

"The Stone-Cutter" is timeless and *haunted* by *old human* dreams so old-prehistoric; yet the Artist does *remember*. The Alligator called the "Dragon Motif" carved by a chisel that *thinks* and *feels* fascinated by the *wonder* and terror that must have made the fearsome phantasy that was the "Monster Motif Phantasy." The great longing of the *wishful-rebirth phantasy* that is in "Jonah." These things are not *conscious*, may be *unconscious*, thought only *by hand* and just now I realize the *fish* (as in "Jonah") is the very ancient symbol of the Female Principle so "Jonah and the Whale the Rebirth Motif." Margherita sends her best regards, so do I, of course. Anytime you feel like it please come and see us work.

There were other, younger individuals who were also able to ignore the movements going on around them. Andrew Wyeth (b. 1917) was one. Writing to the Macbeth Gallery in 1941, he refers to the work he has been engaged in:

I have put in the most intensive period at work I have yet experienced. I came up here [Maine] this spring fresh from a winter of vigorous study and close tempera painting. My aspirations were placed high and I have worked hard to approach them.

Results are definitely better I am sure, but it has been very exacting in my selection of the things I am willing to show. I hope to have somewhere around fifteen, but these will be only the best of what I have done.

These watercolors have I believe much more in them in the way of emotional substance, color and pattern consideration than any earlier attempts of mine,

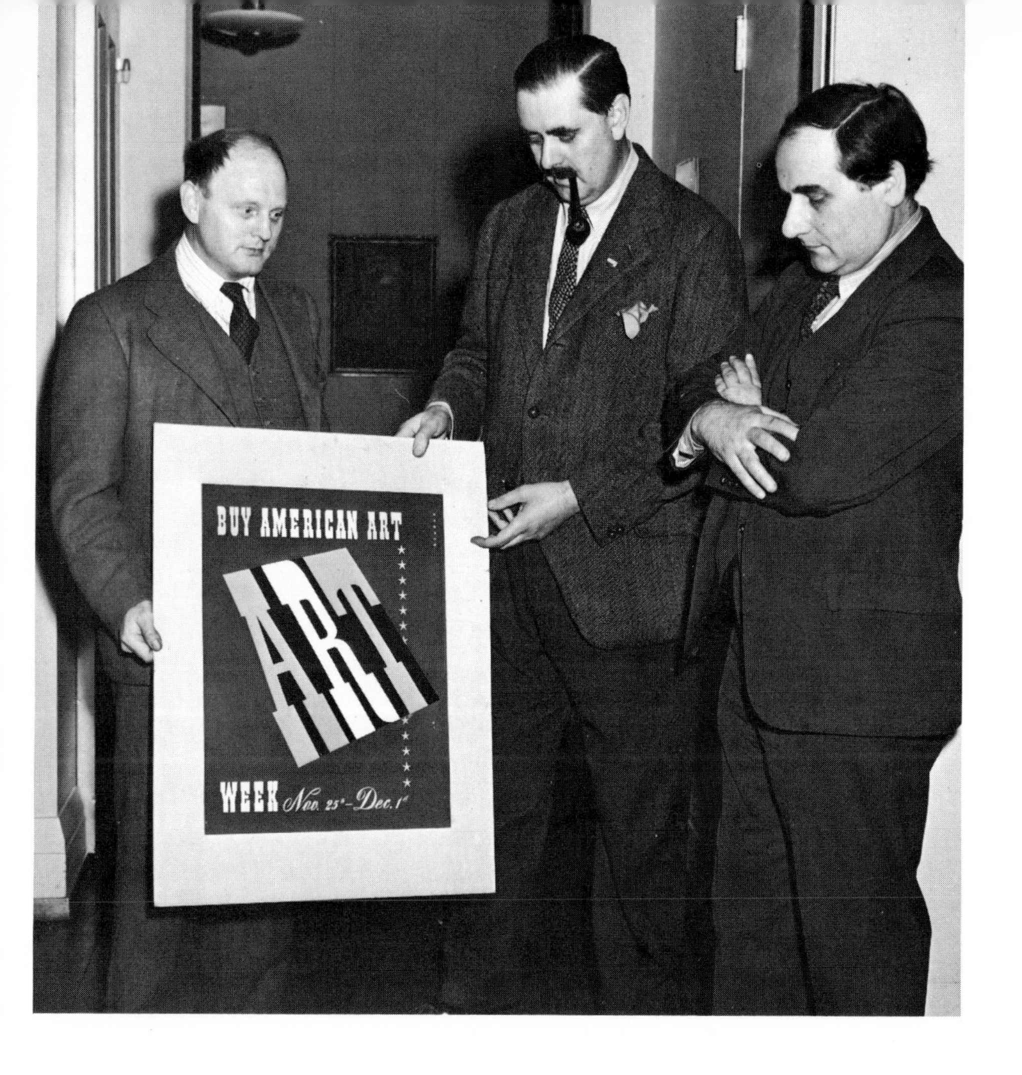

From left to right, painters Reginald Marsh and Louis Bouché and sculptor William Zorach are inspecting a poster for National Art Week, November 25–December 1, 1940. The week was part of a W.P.A. campaign to stimulate a nationwide interest in painting and sculpture.

Edward Hopper, an individualist who attained a stark personal realism, was an important figure during the 1930's. By the time of his death in May 1967 his stature as a painter and the demand for his works were almost unrivaled in America. He was photographed in 1962.

Photo © by Fred McDarrah

This 1939 photo shows I. Rice Pereira with a painting done under the W.P.A. and exhibited at the New York World's Fair in 1939. The problems of light have always been the concern of Pereira's work, and she has been an experimental user of glass, parchment, metals, and a great variety of pigments in her original attempts to achieve new forms.

besides more variety of subject and mood. . . .

I have come to a full realization that I shall never become an annual producer of a great number of watercolors. Rather I shall in all likelihood, produce fewer, but I believe much better ones.

Men from the older generation, too, followed their own earlier means of expression without conforming to the new currents. Charles Sheeler (1883–1965) wrote to Mrs. Elizabeth Navas, adviser to the Roland P. Murdock Collection of the Wichita (Kansas) Art Museum, from New York in 1952:

My work has continuously been based on a clue seen in Nature from which the subject of a picture may be projected. Nature, with its profound order, is an inexhaustible source of supply. Its many facets lend themselves freely to all who would help themselves for their particular needs.

Each one may filter out for himself that which is essential to him. Our chief objective is to increase our capacity of perception. The degree of accomplishment determines the calibre of the artist.

And also in 1952, Edward Hopper (1882–1967) wrote to Mrs. Navas from New York of his 1949 painting, "Conference at Night":

. . . It is going to be difficult for me to make words do much for "Conference at Night."

The idea of a loft or business building with the artificial light of the street coming into the room at night had been in my mind for some years before I attempted it. And had been suggested by things I had seen on Broadway in walking there by night.

The attempt to give a concrete expression to a very amorphous impression is the insurmountable difficulty in painting. The result was obtained by improvisation, and from no known fact or scene. . . .

The sway of social realism in the art of the nineteen-thirties was never absolute. Toward the end of the period the abstract art movement began to gather strength. A few individuals, such as Stuart Davis, insisted on the validity of modern expression. In a letter from New York written to Mrs. Navas in 1940 he refers to his efforts to promote acceptance of what would soon become dominant:

. . . I have fought for recognition of abstract art in various artists' organizations where it had been regarded as an "escape" or an historical curiosity, and I have not been without success in changing this false concept.

I have pointed out that the invention of the process of canning food over 100 years ago in France was something more than a mere example of French inventive ingenuity. Because it was taken up in England and America and developed and perfected and became an international social value. I have drawn an analogy between modern French art and the history of the canning process which I believe to be valid. Modern French art is not merely an interesting example of French genius which happened in the recent past. It is on the contrary a series of real discoveries which have a constructive validity outside the time and place of their creation. At least that is my belief, but in carrying it out in practice by making abstract pictures I have found a curious apathy on the part of the majority of individuals and art institutions. The difficulty doesn't lie in the quality of the art itself but in the mountain of "Americanism" in art propaganda which seeks to isolate American artists from their cultural heritage. . . .

This War Bond poster was based on a painting by Thomas Hart Benton, who is famous for his dramatizations of the American scene.

A great many painters served as Army or Navy artists during World War II. One

(continued on page 193)

Reginald Marsh: Subway Express, oil, 1929. Collection of Lester Avnet.

Ben Shahn: Liberation, oil, 1945.
Collection of James Thrall Soby.

Philip Evergood: The New Lazarus, oil, 1927–54.
Whitney Museum of American Art, New York.

Jack Levine: Welcome Home, oil, 1946.
Brooklyn Museum, Brooklyn, New York.

Gaston Lachaise: Standing Woman, bronze, 1912–27.
Whitney Museum of American Art, New York.

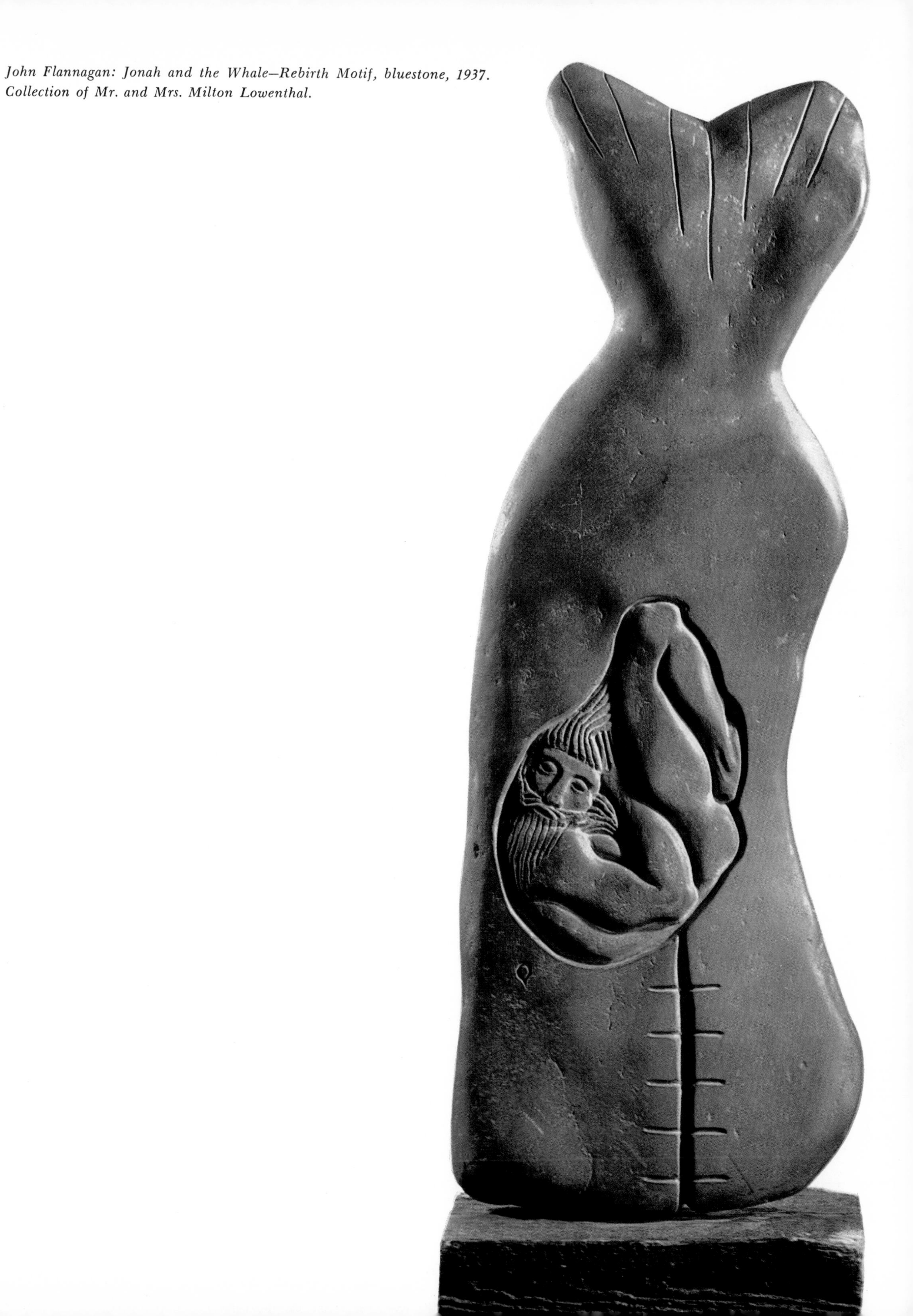

John Flannagan: Jonah and the Whale—Rebirth Motif, bluestone, 1937. Collection of Mr. and Mrs. Milton Lowenthal.

Charles Burchfield: Rainy Night, watercolor, 1930.
Fine Arts Gallery of San Diego, California.

Edward Hopper: Nighthawks, oil, 1942.
Art Institute of Chicago.

Grant Wood: Midnight Ride of Paul Revere, oil, 1931.
Metropolitan Museum of Art, New York.

Stuart Davis: Medium Still Life, oil, 1953.
Mr. and Mrs. William H. Lane Foundation, Leominster, Massachusetts.

Drawn by three artists well qualified to produce such caricatures, this mural dominated the 1943 costume ball of the Art Students League of New York. In the group are Harry Sternberg, a teacher-artist (left rear), and three of the participating artists. Jon Corbino, born in Italy, worked on the Mussolini. Yasuo Kuniyoshi, a native of Japan who was never allowed to become a U. S. citizen, helped with the Hirohito. George Grosz, born in Berlin and noted for his denunciation of the Nazis, worked on the Hitler.

of them, Joe Jones (1909–1963), was sent to Alaska to depict the conditions of the troops there. Writing to Forbes Watson, the critic, in 1944 about a forthcoming exhibition, he refers to his wartime pictures as a new departure in his work:

For myself I would like the Army paintings because so many artists here have been excited about them thinking they were something better than the usual job done and shown here. Also my work approach has changed so much due to my trip to Alaska—such a show would serve as a link between my previous work and what will come in the future.

Jack Levine's description of his feeling in painting "Welcome Home," told to Brian O'Doherty on a Boston Museum of Fine Arts TV program for station WGBH–TV, reflects the attitude of most returning soldiers:

It's a painting really about the army, and I was in the army, fair and square, three and a half years, and I didn't function as an artist. It's the only break in my life. That painting actually isn't so much of an attack on the army as an expression of great joy at getting out of the army. You know Mr. Eisenhower and I were both in the army, and apparently we had different responses to that sort of life. Speaking for myself, I dislike the army as a way of life extremely and the painting although this may be hard for many people to accept was more an expression of joy at my separation from the army. This is what I got away from, I told myself. I don't think it's particularly a grim painting. I don't know how cutting it is, but I think that some people in the army could stand a little bit more criticism of this sort. . . .

In a word, this painting "Welcome Home" is a comic Valentine to the upper echelon of our armed forces.

VIII After World War II

At the beginning of the nineteen-forties the strongest new impulses of American painting were making themselves felt in the area of abstract art. The quality of work done in the late nineteen-thirties and early nineteen-forties by abstract painters like Stuart Davis, Ilya Bolotowsky, Giorgio Cavallon, Burgoyne Diller, Balcomb Greene, Fritz Glarner, George L. K. Morris, Albert Swinden, I. Rice-Pereira, and a few others looks higher now than it did then. The annual exhibitions of the American Abstract Artists group, to which most of these artists belonged, were the most important occasions of those years as far as advanced art in New York was concerned. To these exhibitions the subsequent sophistication of New York painting owed a great deal.

Hans Hofmann's school was another important factor in the situation of advanced art in New York in those same years. It acted as a center for the exchange of experiences and ideas; and through Hofmann himself, painters in general, not just his students, had access to an artistic culture that was uniquely wide and deep. That culture had assimilated Klee, Kandinsky, Mondrian, and Miró at a time when these masters were still being generally overlooked in Paris; and, thanks to Milton Avery as well as Hofmann, it continued to give a large place to Matisse when the avant-garde elsewhere was dismissing him as old-fashioned. The WPA, with its Federal Art Project, had had its part, too, in raising the level of artistic culture in New York. Thanks to the Project, many younger painters had been able to devote themselves entirely to art at a period in their lives when this was most essential. The high seriousness and high ambition which propelled the most advanced American painting in the later nineteen-forties would be hard to account for otherwise.

The war brought famous European artists, and also critics, dealers, and collectors, to New York. For the first time one had the feeling, in that city, of living in the center rather than in a backwater of art. This feeling was far more important than anything American artists learned directly from these visitors. It made for a new self-confidence. And Americans started producing major painting for the first time—painting that defined rather than derived from the mainstream of art in their time—while the war was still on and Paris was still cut off.

Jackson Pollock's first show and Adolph Gottlieb's first show of mature work both took place in 1943; 1944 saw the first shows of Hofmann, William Baziotes, and Robert Motherwell; 1945 saw Arshile Gorky's first show of oils and Mark Rothko's first show. Clyfford Still's first New York show came in 1946. (Pollock, Gottlieb, Hofmann, Rothko, and Still were all more or less introduced by the late Howard Putzel, who was Peggy Guggenheim's assistant at her Art of This Century Gallery before he opened a gallery of his own.) By 1946 abstract expressionism was well under way: the smooth and clearly linear handling that had ruled in abstract painting all through the nineteen-twenties and nineteen-thirties (and which still dominated the American Abstract Artists annuals) was being supplanted by a loose, rapid, *painterly* execution in which the *look* of improvisation and accident had a much larger part. The main influences on all this painting were still, conspicuously, those of Miró and of Picasso of the nineteen-thirties and, far less conspicuously, of Matisse, but this took nothing away from its originality.

In 1947 Pollock went over to his "all-over" composition and "drip" technique in a consistent way. Nineteen hundred forty-eight saw Willem de Kooning's first show and the "joining up" with abstract expressionism of Bradley Walker Tomlin, Jack Tworkov, Philip Guston, and James Brooks, artists who until then had been working in directions relatively distant from painterly abstraction. Nineteen hundred fifty was another year of gathering momentum and at the same time a climax. Barnett Newman and Franz Kline had their first shows in New York in that year, while over in Paris Sam Francis arrived at the manner of his maturity. By this time most of the leading abstract expressionists had been having annual shows regularly in New York for some years, and this practice—which had a lot to do with the crystallizing of an avant-garde art public in New York—was to continue through most of the nineteen-fifties.

As that decade wore along, the hallmark of abstract expressionism became increasingly an execution that involved the smearing, smudging, slapping, and dripping of paint, and this execution became in turn established as the hallmark of advanced painting in general, whether abstract or representational. Hundreds and then even thousands of painters all over this country followed where de Kooning first of all, but also where Kline, Pollock, and Still led. In California Richard Diebenkorn and Elmer Bishchoff, after starting out as abstract painters, in 1955 began applying typically abstract expressionist methods of execution to figure and landscape painting. That year also saw the real beginnings of the public and commercial success of abstract expressionism, which soon became international in dimension. This marked the first time *ever* that American art received widespread and serious attention in Europe; it also marked the first time in over a hundred years that Paris's supremacy as an art center began to be questioned.

In the meantime Gorky (in 1948) and Tomlin (in 1953) had died. Pollock died in 1956, Kline in 1962, and Baziotes in 1964. In the meantime, too, currents running against the tide of abstract expressionism began to manifest themselves.

The first such counter-current to become noticeable in a programmatic way was that embodied in the art of Jasper Johns and Robert Rauschenberg, which represents a culmination of abstract expressionist technique and at the same time

This catalogue cover is from the first show of the American Abstract Artists, a group organized in 1936 by, among others, Ad Reinhardt, Josef Albers, and Alice Mason.

William Baziotes painted The Flesh Eaters in 1952, when the tides of abstract expressionism were still running high. Amoeba-like forms are often found in this artist's work. The painting is in the collection of his widow, Mrs. William Baziotes.

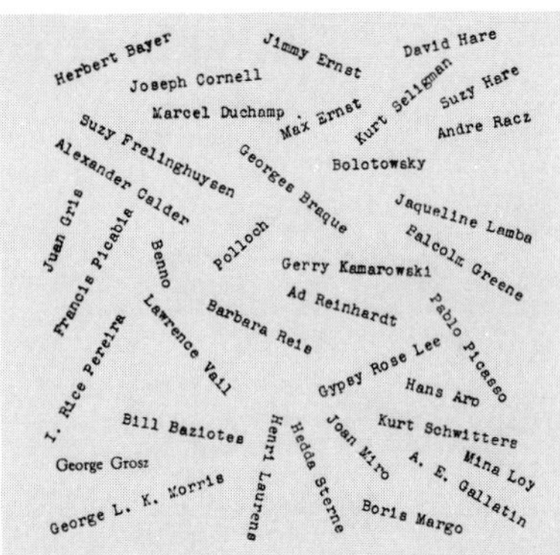

These pages are from a 1943 catalogue of a collage show at the Art of This Century Gallery in New York. In the listing of artists' names, Gypsy Rose Lee is alongside Pablo Picasso, Joan Miró, Hans Arp, and Ad Reinhardt. Owned by the collector Peggy Guggenheim, this pioneer gallery (closed since 1947) gave first one-man shows in the early 1940's to, among other artists, Jackson Pollock, Robert Motherwell, and Mark Rothko.

a canceling-out of the vision of abstract expressionism: the abstract expressionist way of handling paint is preserved and even exaggerated, but it is applied to the representation, both pictorial and sculptural, of man-made objects or signs that are normally produced by mechanical procedures. The smoothly painted pictures, with large simple shapes or divisions of flat color, that Ellsworth Kelly began showing in New York in 1955 break more decidedly with abstract expressionism, while still owing to it all the subtle inflections of color and drawing that differentiate his paintings from geometrical painting of any standard kind. In Washington, D.C., Morris Louis (1912–1962) began doing very thinly painted pictures in 1954 that had more or less of a painterly aspect but which by 1960 had developed almost as far away from abstract expressionism as Kelly's. Likewise in Washington, Kenneth Noland emerged in 1958 with concentric bands and stripes of flat color that moved away from abstract expressionism even more rapidly; and the same is true of Frank Stella's banded paintings, which first appeared in 1959. A painter who is related to Louis and Noland by his vision of color, but who continues and expands rather than breaks with abstract expressionism, is Jules Olitski, who began to show at around the same time as Stella.

In the spring of 1962 there came the sudden collapse, market-wise and publicity-wise, of abstract expressionism as a collective manifestation. The fall of that year saw the equally sudden triumph of pop art, which, though deriving its vision from the art of Rauschenberg and especially Johns, is much more markedly opposed to painterly abstraction in its handling and general design. Assemblage art came along almost simultaneously, and now optical art and kinetic art have appeared, to swell the reaction against abstract expressionism. To the untidy "handwriting" of the latter, all these tendencies—including the ones mentioned in the previous paragraph—oppose clarity, flatness, openness, linearity, the renunciation of thick paint and turbid color. This nominal stylistic consensus covers up vast differences of quality, however, which should not go unnoticed.

Nor have the achievements of the original generation of abstract expressionist painters been diminished by recent events. Those achievements seem, on the contrary, to grow all the larger as they recede in time—this, aside from the fact that some members of that first generation are working as well as they ever did.

American abstract sculpture ran more or less parallel, stylistically, with American abstract painting in these same twenty years. But it hardly matched painting in point of qualitative achievement. By 1940, Isamu Noguchi (b. 1904), who spent 1927–1929 as an apprentice to Constantin Brancusi, and Alexander Calder were on the scene as mature artists, and David Smith was entering on it. (Gaston Lachaise truly a major sculptor, had, in effect, just left it.) Calder's reputation grew enormously in the next two decades, but his role as an influence has never been commensurate with that reputation. It has been almost the reverse with Smith, the only American sculptor whose art has attained a resonance like that of leading abstract expressionist painters.

Smith's sculpture grew out of synthetic cubism, with its clean drawing, and it never forgot synthetic cubism. But by the mid-nineteen-forties it had loosened up in what can be called an abstract expressionist direction, and it was doing so independently of painting and perhaps even earlier. It was left, however, to Ibram Lassaw and Theodore Roszak to carry sculpture all the way into abstract expressionism. More or less geometrical vocabularies gave way in both cases, in the late nineteen-forties, to exuberantly calligraphic plant- and insectlike forms with worked-over, "painterly" surfaces. Similar forms and similar surfaces emerged at around the same time in the abstract sculpture of Herbert Ferber and Seymour Lipton, but with a relative restraint that makes their art "baroque" as against the "rococo" of Lassaw and Roszak. Richard Lippold's constructions in wire, as strictly geometrical as they are, likewise deserve to be called rococo.

All this sculpture belonged to the new tradition of open, draftsmanlike, three-dimensional art born out of the cubist collage and bas-relief construction in which the alternatives of carving and modeling seemed to be transcended. All significant abstract sculpture does not belong in this vein; good abstract sculpture has been made in the old monolithic tradition; yet in this country that tradition has practically died out for the purposes of abstract art. The younger abstract sculptors who came to the fore in New York in the nineteen-fifties worked in the new open tradition, and this has continued to be the case in the nineteen-sixties. Yet there has been a singular lack of continuity in other respects. Hardly any of the newer sculptors (and the same seems to be more or less true in Europe and elsewhere) have shown staying power, the capacity for sustained development. There have been many bright beginnings, but only scattered, isolated realizations. That the spell of abstract expressionism has now worn off, in sculpture as well as in painting, seems to make little difference. Geometrical or near-geometrical shapes and smooth surfaces again prevail in abstract sculpture, but achievement remains spasmodic for the most part. The rise of *assemblage*—which can be defined as three-dimensional art in a two-dimensional or pictorial context which yet escapes the confines of bas-relief—has not changed this situation either, although it has made the name of Louise Nevelson prominent. Nor has the rise of pop art, which has promoted a revival of figurative art in sculpture as well as in painting, changed it.

The American Revolution, the Civil War, and World War II each brought an end to an old way of life and ushered in a new one. By 1945 the Depression and the New Deal had become historical events. Prosperity and a new feeling of internationalism in America inspired a hopeful vigor and a sense of impending opportunities.

Many artists who wanted to turn away from the social-content expression of the nineteen-thirties were affected during and after the war by the presence of several European masters in America. Léger, Mondrian, Lipchitz, the poet Breton, and others brought to New York a direct contact with the advanced art of Europe and a proud spirit that deepened appreciation of abstract art.

This interest had already been provoked by earlier immigrants, for example, Arshile Gorky (1905–1948) and Hans Hofmann (1880–1966). Hofmann came to New York from Germany in 1932, established a school in Greenwich Village, and exerted a profound influence on young painters seeking a new approach. In a 1941 symposium at the Riverside Museum, Hofmann stated his beliefs about abstract art:

. . . Abstract art is, in my opinion, the return to a professional consciousness—a conciousness which controls the emotional accumulations in the process of creation. Such a control is only possible within the limitation of the medium of expression. I think there cannot be doubt that every artist attempts to say what he has to say, and he will say it within the limitation of his personality. Every art expression is rooted fundamentally in the personality and in the temperament of the artist. . . .

Every work of art is esthetically a failure when it is not executed on a plastic basis. But besides the plastic qualities, there exists another quality of equal importance—it forms finally the psychological content of the work. . . .

There are as many possibilities in every medium of expression as there are creative artists. Abstract art does not, however, exclude representation—as long as the representation is the result of the functions and of the activities of the means of expression. We witness this and we admire this in the old masters.

A plastic work has always, however, a decorative quality, but not every decorative work has a plastic quality. There are, therefore, two kinds of decorative qualities. The one, which I call negative, is without a pictorial substance. The one—which is negative—furnishes only a flat pattern in design as well as in color.

The other—which is positive—is not only the effect of the resulting tensions in the correlation between form and color, but the result of the *relationship under the created tension.*

American and European moderns were closely allied in the early nineteen-forties in their struggle for public recognition. The American Abstract Artists, a group including George L. K. Morris, Alice Mason, Ad Reinhardt, and Josef Albers, was organized in 1936. It held its first exhibition the following year and added works by the European refugees Mondrian, Léger, and Moholy-Nagy to its Fifth Annual exhibition in 1941. In their 1941 manifesto, the American Abstract Artists attack the concept of nationalism in art:

. . . Even after more than fifty years of its development, the habit is to allude to the advanced phases of modern art as merely European idioms, and to fail to see that art is not merely the expression of nationality. The falsification of the facts is also often based upon the attempt to foist confusion upon the public under patriotic and traditionalistic disguise. Such fallacies presuppose a split, a separation of content and form, or, in other words, they oppose the intuition of esthetic emotions with emphasis on the colloquial descriptive, naturalistic aspects of expression. This is the consequence of the failure to perceive that the real expression of art is always and everywhere profoundly the same: universal. Esthetic values do not change with latitude and longitude; the cultural significance of art does not change with geographic movement. It is the concept of art that changes.

To understand Abstract Art is in reality the problem of understanding any and all art from a qualitative viewpoint. "Abstract" signifies a direct, untrammeled relationship of the elements of plastic expression. The abstract artist is concerned with the universal values, the real expression of art. Because it is the clearest effort to represent these values, Abstract Art is in the forefront of esthetic development.

Another group of artists interested in abstract work but not associated with the American Abstract Artists organization met in Greenwich Village during and after the war and formed an informal association to discuss modern art. This was the nucleus of what later became the Eighth Street Art Club, an uninhibited center of abstract expressionist thought. In a series of fiercely argumentative panel discussions, members of what came to be known simply as The Club hammered out their views on the nature of modern art, technical procedures, European influences, and the American contribution to abstract painting and sculpture. The early days of The Club were recalled by one of its founders, the New York sculptor Phillip G. Pavia, in a lengthy taped interview conducted in January 1965 by the Archives of American Art:

Just before the war ended a lot of us who had not served in the army would

Photo by John D. Schiff

In a photo taken about 1959, Fritz Glarner is seated in his Long Island studio in front of his work-study for a ground-floor mural for the Time-Life Building, New York.

Milton Avery's March in Green Hat, 1948, is an early canvas by this artist, who painted in the tradition of Matisse. His skill in achieving subtle relationships of color thinly applied in large areas, and his loyalty to the figurative, set him apart from the action painters who dominated the 1940's and 1950's.

Franz Kline, a leader of the abstract expressionist movement, had his first New York show in 1950. His Painting No. 7, 1952, is in the Solomon R. Guggenheim Museum, New York. Kline died in 1962.

meet in the Waldorf Cafeteria, which was a bleak place with a lot of odd characters. At that time there were about seven or eight artists who met there quite regularly every night. First on the list was Landes Lewitin, then Aristo Kaldis. The others were Franz Kline, Bill de Kooning, and myself. Later there were others but we were the regulars. Once in a while Gorky would come into the Waldorf. Jackson Pollock would come in drunk or sober and give us a big ranting speech. This was the first stage of the Waldorf in the war years when it was bleak and quiet. Right after the war came the big change. This is what people have to remember about American art, 1946 was the big year. It was quite noticeable, our little table at the Waldorf started to get bigger and bigger. Lutz Sanders, Milton Resnick, Lewitin and Kaldis and myself were there and [Conrad] Marca-Relli came into the group about this time. Then came all the ideas from Europe back again. It's hard to describe the evenings but there was a real hunger, we all sought each other's company. Six out of seven nights in the week, practically daily we all sat around and talked. Then as the exhibitions of European art opened there were vast, long hours of criticism. The key show that really opened up the whole Waldorf group was the Dubuffet show.

During the war years we would stand on the corner of Eighth Street on warm days. Zadkine would always come by, Lipchitz, and all the refugees. Léger would be seen once in a while at openings. The refugees were very popular then. Once in a while we'd see Breton. Of course, we'd never say hello, we were just too humble.

The whole breadth of avant-gardism really started after the war when the refugees went home and we were on our own. We opened our club. [Robert] Motherwell, [Adolph] Gottlieb and David Hare were not members until much later. We started with a nucleus of about eight or nine people. But we needed more money so we got more members. They were friends we just pulled in from here and there.

The Club had three important nights, Sunday, Wednesday and Friday. Sunday night we had a sort of social meeting, we danced a little bit. Wednesday nights we had a panel for members only, that was the best part of the Club. Friday nights some of the boys started to have talks.

Stirred by the diverse theories and influences in the air, some American painters and sculptors began to work in a new manner which came to be called the New York School or abstract expressionism or action painting.

Jackson Pollock, who came from Cody, Wyoming, where he was born in 1912, became the unrivaled leader of this art form, the first American school of art to achieve international fame. Pollock had his first one-man exhibition at Peggy Guggenheim's Art of This Century Gallery in 1943, when he was thirty-one. Thirteen years later, killed in an automobile accident, he was still without financial security in spite of a worldwide reputation.

In a taped interview conducted at his house in Springs, Long Island, in 1950 by William Wright, a neighbor interested in developing a radio program, Pollock discussed modern art:

Modern art to me is nothing more than the expression of contemporary aims. The age that we're living in . . . All cultures have, have had means and techniques of expressing their immediate aims. The Chinese, the renaissance, all cultures. The thing that interests me is that today painters do not have to go to a subject matter outside of themselves. Most modern painters work from a different source, they work from within. . . .

Referring to the importance of a new technique for a new age, Pollock said:

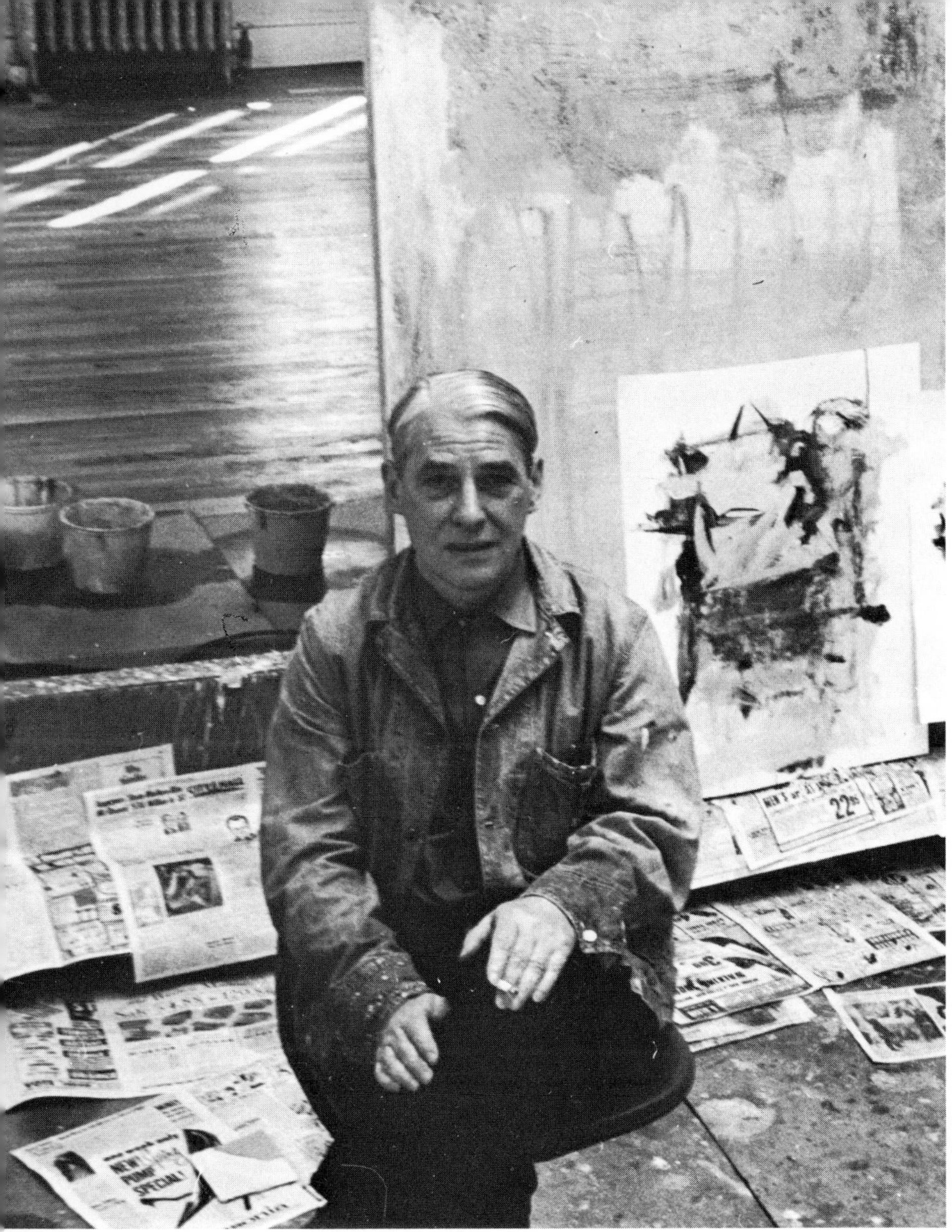

Photo © by Fred McDarrah

An acknowledged hero of the New York abstract expressionist movement, Dutch-born Willem de Kooning is seated in front of two paintings from his Women series in a 1961 photo taken in a studio he once had on lower Broadway, New York.

Photo by Hans Namuth

Jackson Pollock, a painter of enormous talent and explosive moods, was photographed during a pensive moment at Springs, East Hampton, Long Island. He had just come out of his studio, where he had worked to a point of exhaustion.

Photo by Hans Namuth

The first showing of mature works by Adolph Gottlieb, above, in 1943, was an early clue to the drama of abstract expressionism about to unfold across the United States. Jackson Pollock was another painter who had his first show in 1943.

My feeling is that new needs need new technique and the modern artist has found new ways and new means of making his statement. It seems to me that the modern painter cannot express this age, the airplane, the atom bomb, the radio, in the old forms of the renaissance or any other past culture. Each age finds its own technique. . . . I think [people] should not look for but look passively and try to receive what the painting has to offer and not bring a subject matter or preconceived idea of what they are to be looking for. . . .

In response to the interviewer's question on the role of the unconscious in modern art, Pollock replied:

The unconscious is a very important side of modern art and I think the unconscious drives do mean a lot in looking at paintings. . . . [abstract painting] should be enjoyed just as music is enjoyed. After a while you may like it or you may not but it doesn't seem to be too serious. I like some flowers and others, other flowers I don't like. I think at least it gives it a chance. . . .

The modern artist is living in a mechanical age and we have mechanical means of representing objects and nature such as the camera and the photograph. The modern artist, it seems to me, is working and expressing an inner world. In other words, expressing the energy, the emotion, and other inner forces . . . [We are] working with space and time and expressing . . . feelings rather than illustrating. . . .

[Modern art] didn't jump out of the blue, it is part of a long tradition beginning back with Cézanne and coming up to the cubists and post-cubists, to the painting being done today.

Even before Pollock's death, leadership in the abstract expressionist movement was shared by Willem de Kooning (b. 1904), a Dutch-born painter who came to New York in 1926 when he was twenty-two years old. De Kooning was a close friend of the Armenian-born painter Gorky, who had been influenced by surrealism and was a foreruner of abstract expressionists.

In a symposium on abstract art which was conducted at the Museum of Modern Art in February 1951, de Kooning said:

Photo by Anton Kamp

Theodore Roszak—one of his famous works is Whaler of Nantucket, 1952, in the Art Institute of Chicago—is credited with having taken sculpture toward abstract expressionism.

The word "abstract" comes from the light-tower of the philosophers, and it seems to be one of their spotlights that they have particularly focused on "Art." So the artist is always lighted up by it. As soon as it—I mean the "abstract"—comes into a painting, it ceases to be what it is as it is written. It changes into a feeling which could be explained by some other words, probably. But one day, some painter used "abstraction" as a title for one of his paintings. It was a still life. And it was a very tricky title. And it wasn't really a very good one. From then on the idea of abstraction became something extra. Immediately it gave some people the idea that they could free art from itself. Until then, art meant everything that was in it—not what you could take out of it. There was only one thing you could take out of it, sometime when you were in the right mood—that abstract and indefinable sensation, the esthetic part and still leave it where it was.

For the painter to come to the "abstract" or the "nothing" he needed many things. Those things were always things in life—a horse, a flower, a milkmaid, the light in a room through a window made of diamond shapes maybe, tables, chairs, and so forth . . . . At the time they were not abstract about something which was already abstract. They freed the shapes, the light, the color, the space by putting them into concrete things in a given situation . . . .

There *is* no style of painting now. There are as many naturalists among the abstract painters as there are abstract painters in the so-called subject matter

Photo by Ugo Múlas

In her house at the edge of New York's Chinatown, Louise Nevelson stands near one of her wall sculptures. Miss Nevelson's dramatic construction-assemblages originated during the early 1940's when she found on the street a long empty box (in which a carpet had been packed) and, carting it home, filled it with castoff wooden pieces cut to varying lengths and shapes.

In a 1962 photo, Robert Motherwell sits in front of a painting from his Summertime in Italy series. At the right is Motherwell's Elegy to the Spanish Republic No. 70, an oil from another series.

Photo © by Fred McDarrah

school.

While abstract expressionists held the center of the avant-garde stage, many painters were busy with their own personal visions. Andrew Wyeth, Leonard Baskin, Edwin Dickinson, Jack Levine, Raphael Soyer, and Philip Evergood all work in a figurative manner and all continue to command attention.

Jack Levine stated his position in a 1961 interview with Brian O'Doherty presented by the Boston Museum of Fine Arts and station WGBH-TV there.

I think art has reached the point of inarticulateness—and the more cultivated section of the population has embraced more things it doesn't understand and feigned admiration and pleasure which it does not feel. I think things have never stood quite as bad as they are today.

I think that abstract, the non-objective, the modernist movement generally . . . I think these people have really lost themselves in the wilderness. I don't think they can find their way back. I think they have been motivated by a continuous sequence of rebellions, one against the other, so nobody remembers which came first, the why and wherefore of what they are doing. I think most people that have any sophistication at all by now can see that a search for novelty is very characteristic of the present-day art world, and I think that most people with any wisdom would concede that it has gone much too far and it has been so for a long time. It isn't a question of too far in a sense that you have a sense of a norm and there's an extreme and that there's a mean and there's a normal. I don't particularly go along with such reasoning. I just simply think that too many parts, valuable parts of the human mind, even the conscious mind at a fairly low level, have dropped out of the situation. I think that simple cognition, simple reason has been dispelled by the ceaselessness of the rat race. . . .

You might have been against the impressionists if you were living at the time when they made their stand, but you knew what it was that they were breaking away from and what they were trying to do in their breach with the Academy. Things were quite clear. Now you can't tell what has broken away from which and why. There is no thread to this thing, this is a labyrinth that I think most painters, critics, museum directors are lost in.

I have always been interested in the human image, the human countenance, I am a physiognomist, I suppose, I think my work shows this. For example, I would not be in the least interested in painting a picture where the head is simply a diagrammatic oval. I couldn't care less. I am very interested in somehow creating a man . . . or a painting which has some investigation of character and personality.

By the late 1940's, Jack Tworkov had joined the ranks of the abstract expressionists. This more recent photo is taken from a color film, the Americans at Work.

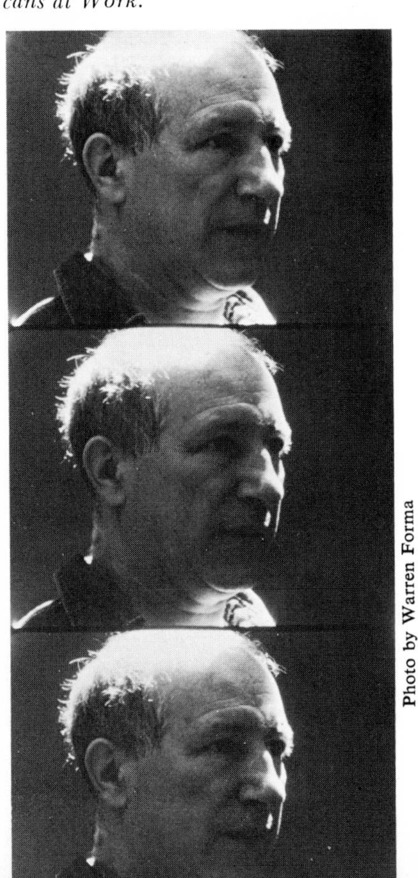

Photo by Warren Forma

While the abstract expressionists held the center of attention through the nineteen-fifties, variations on and reactions to their technique of handling paint were developing. One abstract expressionist, for example, Ad Reinhardt, started in the beginning of the nineteen-fifties to paint red or blue canvases of balancing rectangles that led later to nearly black, square pictures he called "pure . . . neutral . . . bottomless . . . topless . . . colorless . . . disinterested." Jasper Johns and Robert Rauschenberg used abstract expressionist techniques on popular and commercial images, as de Kooning did in his "Marilyn Monroe." It was a return to subject matter that contributed to the rise of pop art. As Reinhardt and also Barnett Newman were moving away from "painterly" abstraction to paintings that shocked with anonymity and perhaps heralded the cool, repetitive bands of paint Frank Stella produced in the nineteen-sixties, Ellsworth Kelly, Jack Youngerman, Morris Louis, Kenneth Noland, and others began making very diverse abstractions that had in common a concentration on bright, flat, luminous color

Photo by Jim Moore

Andrew Wyeth, a traditionalist whose works have set records for prices paid to living American artists, summers in Cushing, Maine, where this photo was taken in 1963. His home is in Chadds Ford, Pennsylvania, in the Brandywine River Valley countryside—the scene of many of his paintings; one of his best known is Christina's World, 1948, left, in the Museum of Modern Art, New York.

Below, Ad Reinhardt, abstract painter, teacher, and writer on art, is standing in front of some of his coolly mysterious canvases that appear to be flat black and on close inspection are seen to contain rectangles with slight casts of, for example, olive or violet.

Photo © by Fred McDarrah

Sculptor David Smith was photographed by Alexander Liberman, one of the guests at his home, the Terminal Iron Works, Bolton Landing, New York. There had been a luncheon prepared with gourmet skill by Smith after a tour of his sculptures installed over acres of his land. About a week later, in May 1965, he was killed in an automobile accident.

and smoothly perimetered forms.

With few exceptions, American sculptors emerged from their concentration on realism only in the nineteen-forties. One notable exception was David Smith, the first American to work with welded metals. He produced his earliest steel construction in 1933 and went on to evolve a monumental style with the use of abstract forms wrought from iron and steel plate and found metal objects. The rugged and dramatic quality of his work made him one of the most influential sculptors of the post-war period. In a statement written for the Walker Art Center in Minneapolis and published in its Everyday Art Quarterly in 1952, Smith talked about his work:

I was acquainted with metal working before studying painting. When my painting developed into constructions leaving the canvas, I was then a sculptor, with no formal training in the sculpture tradition. When the construction turned into metal—lead, brass, aluminum, combined with stone and coral in 1932—nothing technically was involved outside of factory knowledge. The equipment I use, my supply of material comes from factory study and duplicates as nearly as possible the production equipment used in making a locomotive. I have no esthetic interest in tool marks or surface embroidery or molten puddles. My aim in material function is the same as in locomotive building: to arrive at a given functional form in the most efficient manner. The locomotive method bows to no accepted theory of fabrication. It utilizes the respective merits of casting, forging, riveting, arc and gas welding, brazing, silver soldering. It combines bolts, screws, shrink fits—all because of their respective efficiency in arriving at an object or form in function.

In the nineteen-fifties abstract expressionism in painting was paralleled by abstract expressionism in sculpture. A leading abstract sculptor, Ibram Lassaw, saw his work as a continuing evolution of form. At Duke University in 1963 he said:

In the back of my mind is the idea of a process going on, a continuum of forces in space. It seems that a "space field" is at work, a field which comprehends a relationship of forces and interplay of forces. I think also of space densities; thickness and thinness of space, distinction between networks of thin lines and heavy bold shapes. In many ways it's a matter of handling polymorphism—relating many objects and many shapes one to another. . . .

My work is moving toward a sculpture that is more mobile, a motion sculpture. I want to begin to add movement to parts, to achieve a kind of space dance. These must be irregular movements, free of repetition, not machinelike in any way. The motto is "No repetition whatsoever." This covenant is consistent with what I understand of reality and nature: nothing occurs in nature in the same way twice.

One of the most noted individualists among sculptors whose style was formed in the nineteen-thirties is Alexander Calder, inventor of the mobile. His ingenious wire figures had won him a reputation in Paris in the nineteen-twenties, and in 1930 he began to experiment in abstract forms which evolved into his hanging, air-driven constructions. He described his concept of abstract art in a statement in the Museum of Modern Art Bulletin for Spring, 1951:

My entrance into the field of abstract art came about as the result of a visit to the studio of Piet Mondrian in Paris in 1930. . . .

I think that at that time and practically ever since, the underlying sense of form in my work has been the system of the Universe, or part thereof. For that

(continued on page 226)

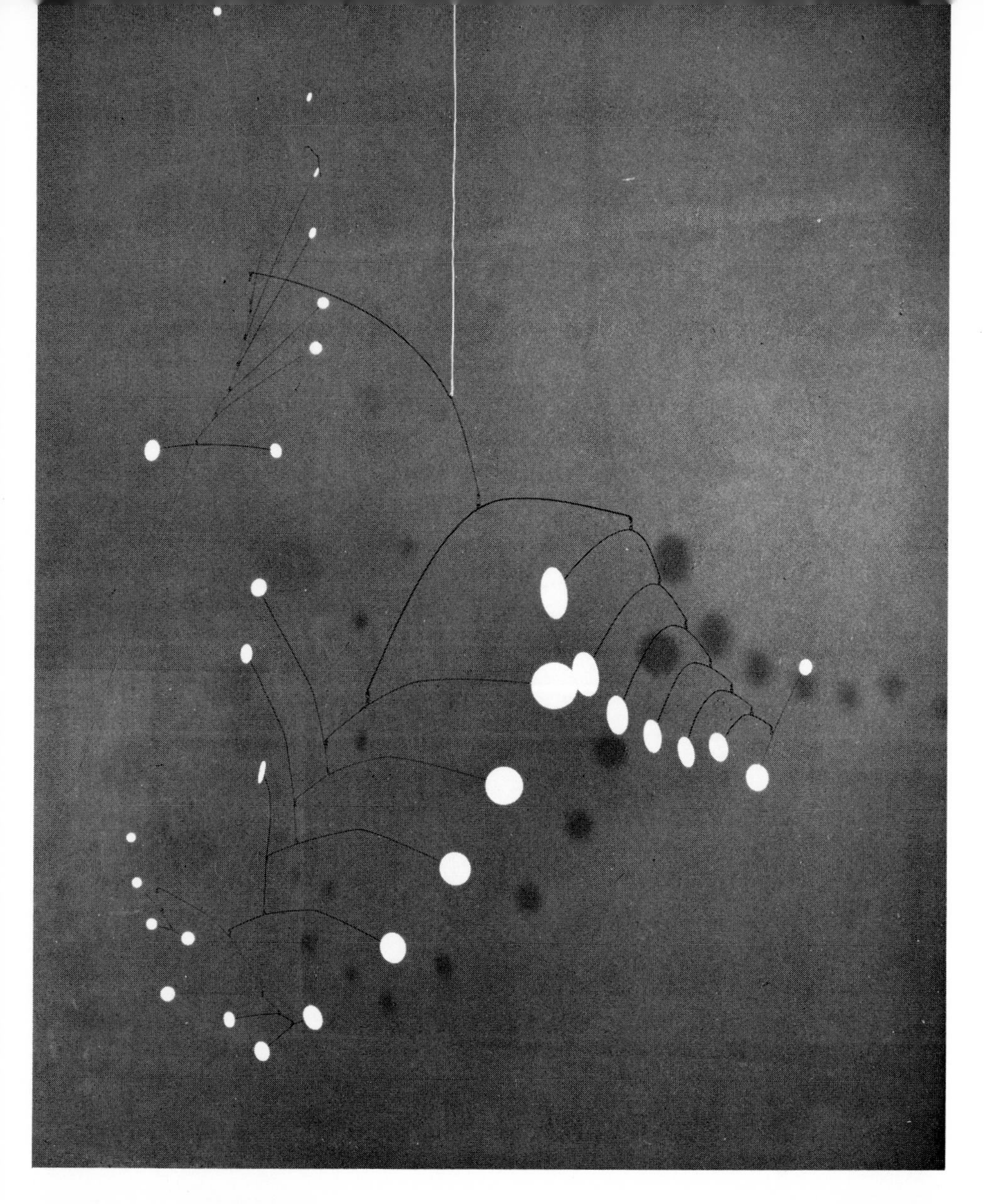

Searching for a floating movement which he feels "approximates freedom from earth," Alexander Calder created his air-driven, suspended mobiles. He was photographed in 1962 by his New York dealer, Klaus Perls, standing by his stabile, Disconnected. An early Calder mobile, Snow Flurry I, 1948, left, is in the Museum of Modern Art, New York.

The photo of Ibram Lassaw, left, a welder of delicate expressionist sculptures, was taken in 1963 when Lassaw was artist-in-residence at Duke University, Durham, North Carolina.

Leonard Baskin, in his drawings, prints, and sculpture, adheres to the figurative style. His Seated Man with Owl, 1959, is in the Smith College Museum of Art, Northampton, Massachusetts. Baskin's longtime interest in fine typography and graphic design led him to start his Gehenna Press now located in Northampton.

Photo by John D. Schiff

In this 1955 photograph, Richard Lippold, the sculptor, is at work on his intricate metal construction, The Sun, now in the collection of the Metropolitan Museum, New York. His Variation No. 7: Full Moon, 1949–50, right, is in the Museum of Modern Art, New York.

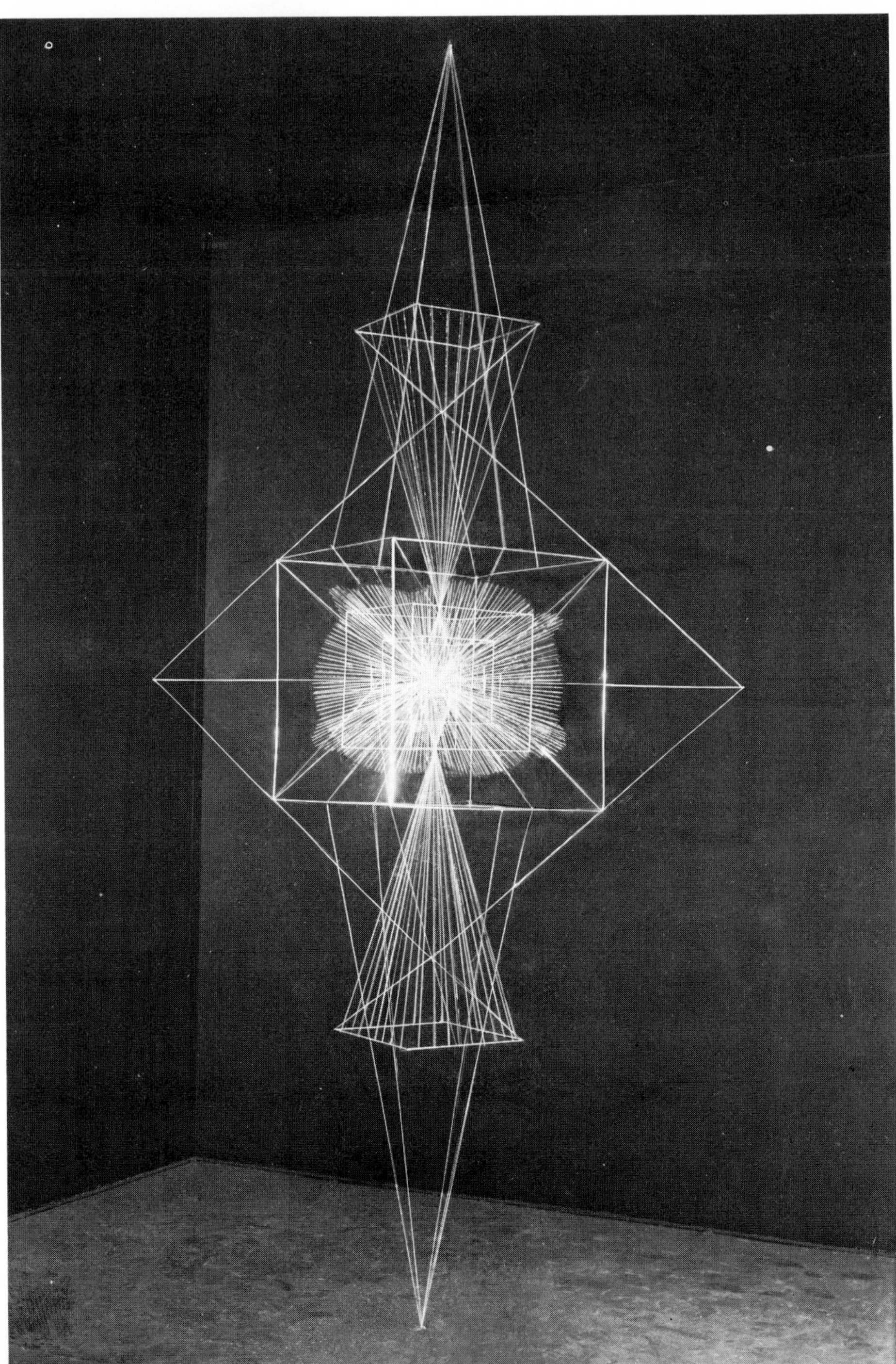

Frank Stella: Gran Cairo, oil, 1962.
Whitney Museum of American Art, New York.

Mark Rothko: No. 10, oil, 1950.
Museum of Modern Art, New York.

Adolph Gottlieb: Aureole, oil, 1959.
Private collection.

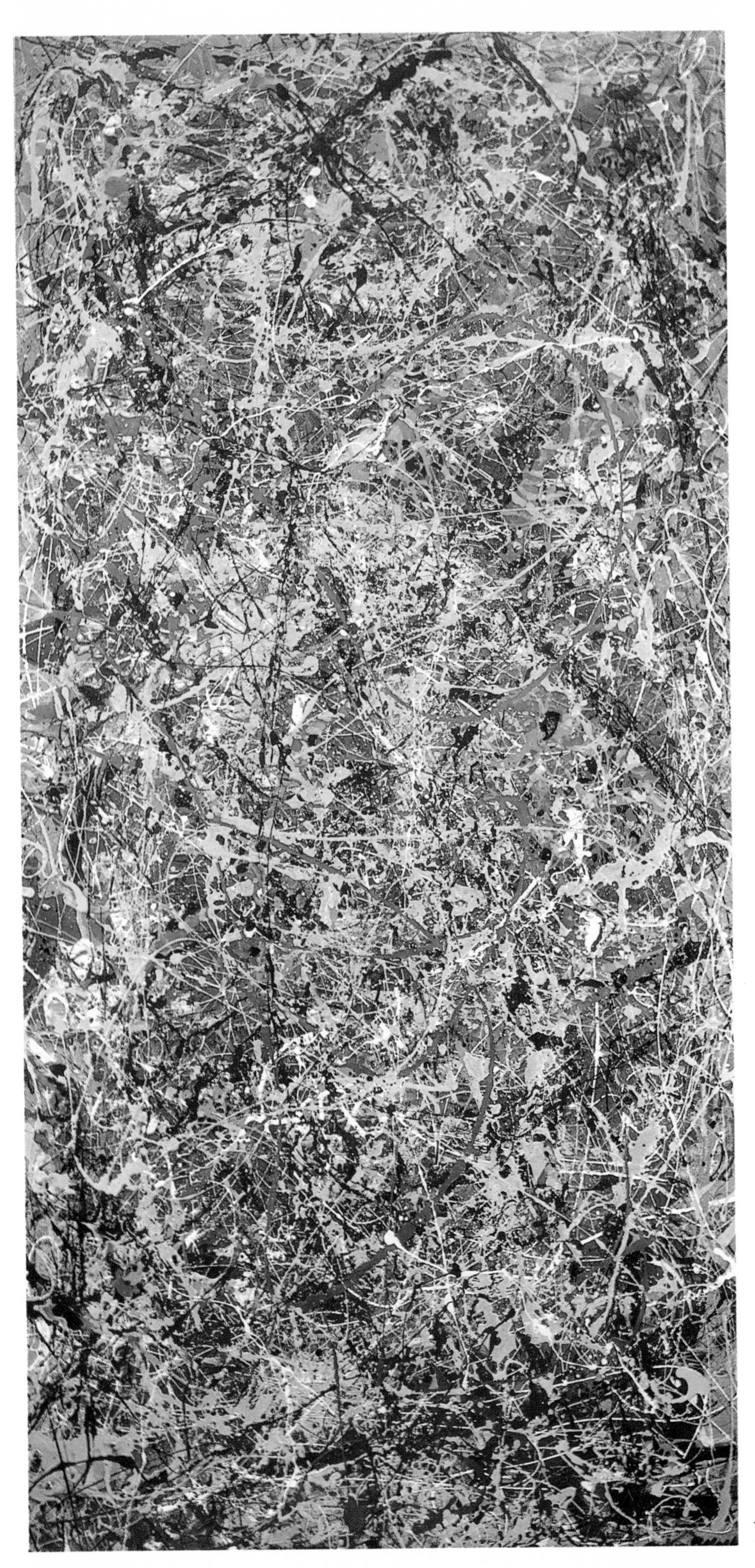

Jackson Pollock: No. 5, oil, 1948.
Collection of Alfonso Ossorio.

Clyfford Still: Number 2, oil, 1949.
Collection of Mr. and Mrs. Ben Heller.

Josef Albers: Homage to the Square—Gobelin, oil on board, 1963. Sidney Janis Gallery, New York.

Morris Louis: Lambda, acrylic, 1960–61.
André Emmerich Gallery, New York.

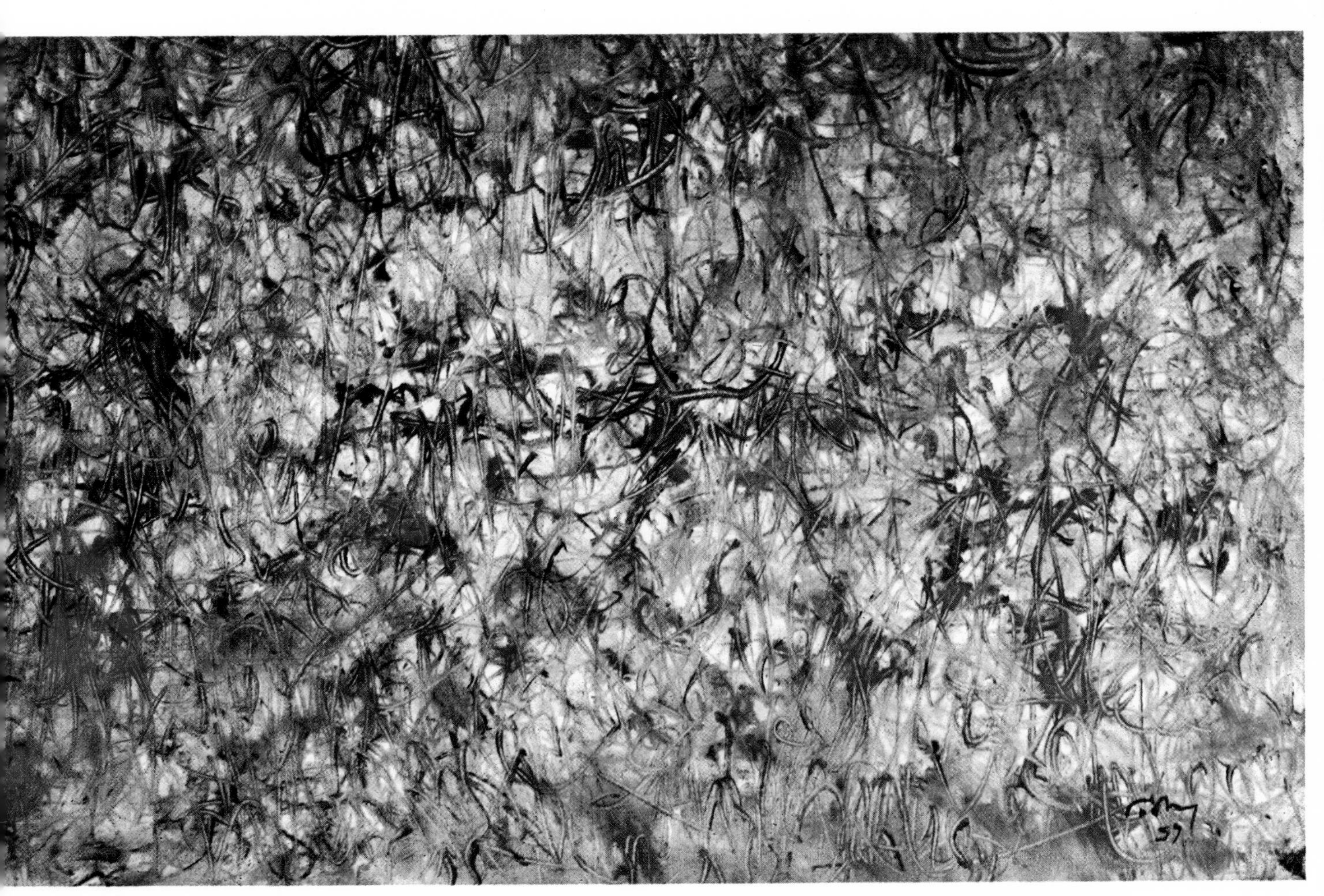

Mark Tobey: Sleep, oil, 1957.
Collection of Arthur Dahl.

Ad Reinhardt: Abstract Painting—Red, oil, 1952. Woodward Foundation, Washington, D.C.

Robert Rauschenberg: Canyon, combine with eagle and pillow, 1959.
Collection of Ileana Sonnabend.

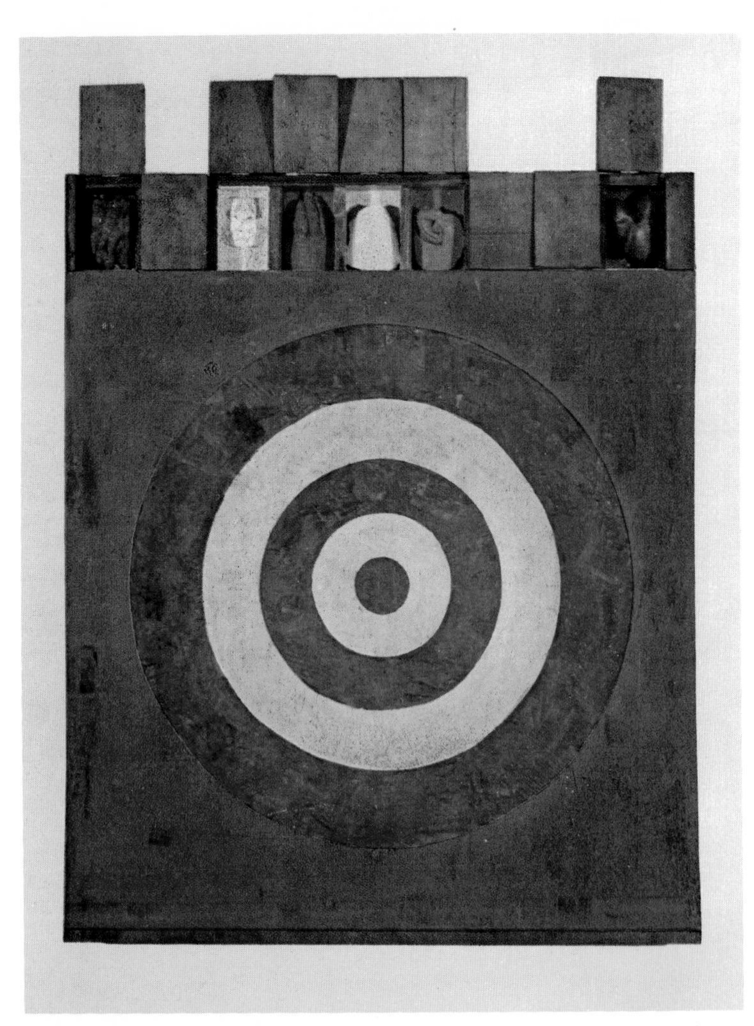

Jasper Johns: Large Target with Plaster Casts, encaustic and collage on canvas, 1955. Collection of Mr. and Mrs. Leo Castelli.

Robert Motherwell: The Voyage, oil and tempera, 1949. Museum of Modern Art, New York.

as Hofmann: In Upper Regions, oil, 1963.
lection of David N. Marks.

Willem de Kooning: Marilyn Monroe, oil, 1954.
Collection of Mr. and Mrs. Roy R. Neuberger.

Richard Diebenkorn: Girl on a Terrace, oil, 1956.
Private collection.

Louise Nevelson: America—New York Blue, wood in plexiglas case, 1965. Private collection.

'hoto by Irving Penn

)avid Smith: (Circles) 2 CI.IV, painted steel, 1962.
:state of David Smith.

Andrew Wyeth: Far from Needham, tempera, 1966. Knoedler, New York.

Andrew Wyeth: May Day (detail), dry-brush drawing, 1960. Collection of Mrs. Andrew Wyeth.

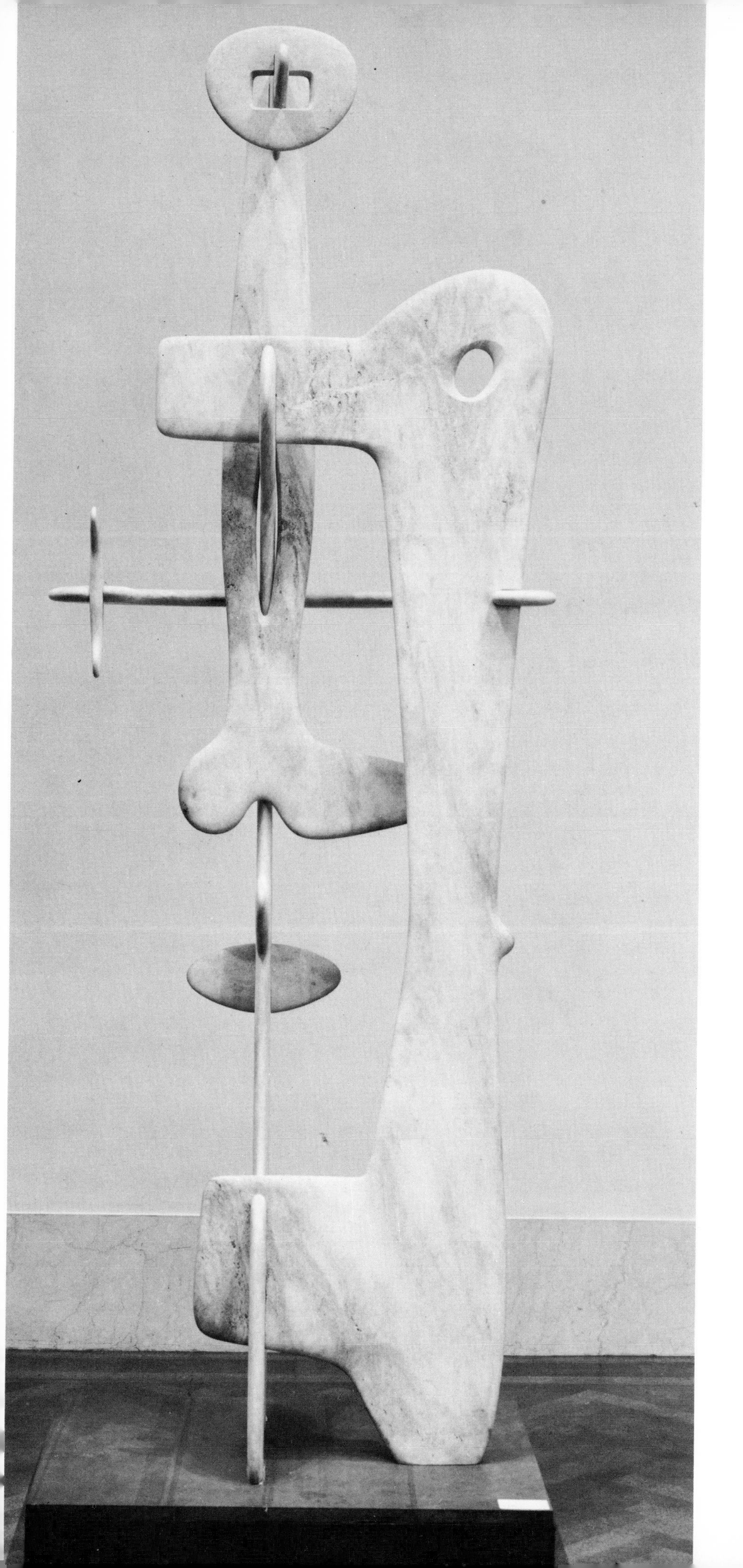

Isamu Noguchi's Kouros, a large, nine-part sculpture of pink marble, is in the Metropolitan Museum of Art, New York; it was carved in 1944–45. Noguchi was born in Los Angeles; he studied under Gutzon Borglum and, awarded Guggenheim Fellowships, had two years of study in Paris with Constantin Brancusi.

Texas-born (1925) Robert Rauschenberg, whose "combines" command enormous prices in today's art market, is considered the pioneer of pop art. As early as 1955 he presented as a work of art a canvas to which he had attached everyday objects, some painted, some not, and this dramatization of the commonplace subsequently flourished as pop. An expert in the silk-screen process used for multiple images, Rauschenberg won first prize at the 1964 Venice Biennale; and he has been described by some French critics as the most important artist since World War II.

Photo by Ugo Múlas

is a rather large model to work from.

What I mean is that the idea of detached bodies floating in space, of different sizes and densities, perhaps of different colors and temperatures, and surrounded and interlarded with wisps of gaseous condition, and some at rest, while others move in peculiar manners, seems to me the ideal source of form.

I would have them deployed, some nearer together and some at immense distances.

And great disparity among all the qualities of these bodies, and their motions as well . . . .

When I have used spheres and discs, I have intended that they should represent more than what they just are. More or less as the earth is a sphere, but also has some miles of gas about it, volcanoes upon it, and the moon making circles around it, and as the sun is a sphere—but also a source of intense heat, the effect of which is felt at great distances. A ball of wood or a disc of metal is rather a dull object without this sense of something emanating from it.

When I use two circles of wire intersecting at right angles, this to me is a sphere and when I use two or more sheets of metal cut into shapes and mounted at angles to each other, I feel that there is a solid form, perhaps concave, perhaps convex, filling in the dihedral angles between them. I do not have a definite idea of what this would be like, I merely sense it and occupy myself with the shapes one actually sees.

Then there is the idea of an object floating—not supported—the use of a very long thread or a long arm in cantilever as a means of support seem to best approximate this freedom from the earth.

Calder's moving pieces pointed toward, although they did not strongly influence, a new development in sculpture, kinetic art, which is becoming a significant force on the art scene in the present decade. George Rickey and Len Lye were two experimenters in this vibrant art form before its current growing popularity. This moving sculpture was described by Rickey, a scholar as well as a creator in the field, in an essay written in 1962 for Gyorgy Kepes's book, The Nature and Art of Motion (New York, Braziller, 1965). In a statement relating to his 1962 account, Rickey explained to the Archives in 1965:

I commented in my article for the Kepes book on the adolescent condition of kinetic art and the confusion between experiment and mature expression. I also wrote of unrecognized possibilities and listed some unexplored but promising territories: water-driven sculpture (corresponding to the air-driven work of Calder and others); objects supported in space by columns of water or air; pulsating membranes; polarization of light passing through stressed material; "feelies"; the use of chance; and the effects of huge scale on rates and periods of movement.

Confusion as to what is experiment and what is art continues and is, perhaps, increasing. As in new fields of science it is rather easy to reach a frontier. The number of people working in kinetic art and the amount and variety of work being done have increased enormously in the last three years, but mostly in extending and subdividing the more obvious areas of study, which I have suggested are: (1) Optical Phenomena, (2) Transformations, (3) Movable Works (audience participation), (4) Motor Driven Machines, (5) Light Play and (6) Pure Movement itself. The first, often combined with some of the others plus some chance and one example of polarized light, was reported in The Responsive Eye exhibition at the Museum of Modern Art in February–March 1965.

What might be considered technical extensions are the work of Len Lye with steel ribbons in varying magnetic fields, the levitation in fixed fields of various objects by Takis and Collie, the water sculptures of Kosice, Goodyear's superimposed swinging lattices, the prism projections of Gruppa N. and vibrations in the mini-constructions of Haese. After the early swaying rods of Takis, however, the great promise of springs has interested only two Germans, Goepfert and Cremer, unknown here.

More important, though, than new experiments is deepening involvement and refinement of existing means. Discoveries are, by definition, unfamiliar. Great art comes, not from novelty, but from intimately understood esthetic and technique. Their development is a ripening process and it goes slowly and ignores fashion.

Clumsy work, having lost its initial impact, begins to look very clumsy; empty work looks empty. A fully controlled and deeply expressive kinetic art may be quietly maturing. For example, the recent and unheralded kinetic light painting of Thomas Wilfred at the Museum of Modern Art in New York is more epic and evocative than its predecessor of thirty years ago; and in the same metier John Healey, an ocean away, showed extraordinarly rich and precisely wrought pictures at the Royal College in London last year. There may be other quiet kinetic masterpieces on their way.

An important change has taken place in the hospitality extended to kinetic art. The Howard Wise Gallery's On the Move show in New York in 1964 was the first kinetic group show in this country. It was followed in the summer by Arte Programmata, sent from Italy by Olivetti and later circulated by the Smithsonian. Subsequently there were Denise René's tenth-year anniversary Movement II show in Paris and group exhibitions at the Hanover Gallery, and at McRoberts and Tunnard in London, Gimpel-Hanover in Zurich, Aktuell in Bern, The Contemporaries in New York, the Albright-Knox Art Gallery in Buffalo and the Stedelijk Museum in Amsterdam. More are coming.

IX Trends of the Sixties

In past decades, artists have been content to cope with, at the most, one major innovation at a time in formal or visual concepts. Even the turbulent twenty years that started with World War II were dominated by only one basic trend—abstract impressionism.

The decade of the nineteen-sixties is a very different story. The general tone is one of searching and uneasy experiment, and the vogue for Marshall McLuhan's theories of media impact and spectator participation has helped to establish an almost total permissiveness in terms of what can qualify as art. It is possible to name at least eight innovations or mutations which have profoundly influenced the vision and attitudes of the contemporary art world.

Although the duration of predominance of the new trends has often been short, they have left an indelible mark on private and museum collections and have drastically influenced the way we look at art. They are: figurative, assemblage, junk, hard-edge, and pop, which flourished in the early nineteen-sixties; and op, kinetics, minimal, and light, which have dominated the scene during the past few years.

Pop art is a term coined during the mid-nineteen-fifties by Lawrence Alloway, the English critic and museum director seduced across the Atlantic by the siren song of American contemporary painting and sculpture. [He taught at Bennington College in Vermont, 1961–62, and was the Curator of the Solomon R. Guggenheim Museum, New York, 1962–66.]

"Pop" defines the artistic process by which American artists have absorbed the detritus of our commercial society—billboards, movies, comic-strips, food cans,

cartons, household appliances—and have transformed them, often by mere assimilation, into works of art. Ramifications of pop are happenings and environments (involving viewers) created by such artists as Jim Dine and Allan Kaprow.

The artists particularly associated with the pop movement are Andy Warhol, James Rosenquist, Roy Lichtenstein, Tom Wesselmann, Robert Indiana, Jasper Johns, Claes Oldenburg, and Robert Rauschenberg—the latter, the most experimental of them all, has stated his sentiments about pop art as follows:

The word "pop" is more Hollywoodian than historian. Pop art decontaminated our art stream-of-conciousness. We have a frontier country—the means to be direct. . . . I think that one of the aspects of my work that I criticize myself for the most is that so many people recognized it as a way of working, as an end in itself, so that the influence the work had on other artists who work in what they would call the same direction is really a weakness in my concept. . . . I think in the last twenty years there has been a new kind of honesty in painting where painters have been very proud of paint, have let it behave openly though they have used it for different reasons. . . . This was opposed to the older way of using paint only to build an illusion about something else or wanting only the color aspect. . . . In this new give-and-take, when an artist sees something exciting that another has done he is likely to say, as Larry Poons (an op artist who scatters dots, ovals, and ellipses over a brilliant color field) has, "Well, now I won't have to do that." . . . which goes far to account for the proliferation of styles.

Claes Oldenburg, one of the earliest and most stylistically consistent pop artists, explains his work:

I'm against the notion that there is a world of art and then a world of real things, and that one thing has to be brought out of the world of real things into the world of art. I'm more inclined to put the things somewhere halfway between the real world and the world of art because nothing is interesting to me unless it's halfway, unless it's very ambiguous. . . . Artists can come in and say, well, this is not art, this is a hamburger and other people will come in and say, well, this is not a hamburger, it's art. . . . I find it very hard to separate my theories from my action. I think what I do is, I take possession of the object and I only allow as much of the object in as I want. . . . I have the feeling that even when I look at an object I'm doing something creative. I tend to regard everything that's seen as subjective; that is, all reality as subjective.

Assemblage, defined by Lucy R. Lippard in her book Pop Art (published by Frederick A. Praeger, New York, in 1966) as "a broad term for three-dimensional collage or collage sculpture, using objects instead of pasted paper," should not be confused with pop art, to which it often bears a strong resemblance. The movement has its roots in dada, and its spiritual father is Marcel Duchamp, but it has branched in several new directions. The Art of Assemblage exhibition organized in 1961 by William C. Seitz for the Museum of Modern Art in New York, included works by, among others, the ubiquitous Robert Rauschenberg; Louise Nevelson, whose monumental wood sculpture was shown, March 8–April 30, 1967, in a retrospective exhibit at the Whitney Museum of American Art, New York; Edward Kienholz, a West Coast artist with a flair for the shocking; and Alfonso Ossorio, whose brilliantly colored assemblages, which include such varied items as beads, shells, antler's horns, metal strips, glass eyes, and wood, completely defy classification.

Louise Nevelson tells of her involvement with box forms, after her 1948–49 trip to Central and South America. She describes her work in the following terms:

It doesn't matter where you begin because each form calls for another; you may start with organic forms and they call for intensification and contrast. I always depend on the eye. It's like those wonderful pyramids in Mexico—they're valid and they're right. They have these heavy stones—they never connected them—but these slabs, just lying down as they have for thousands of years, have the dimension of gravity and weight. Anyone that says they were made by a primitive race makes me laugh, because they left for us to see this high development, this high order. . . . I've lived so much with forms that I might go to bed and these forms would take on a life of their own. It's as if you plugged in the electricity and they'd all move.

Optical, or op, art are terms used to describe works with a primarily visual emphasis—paintings and constructions whose repetitive designs achieve perceptual effects that create after-images with seeming movement and focus changes. Poons, Richard Anuszkiewicz, and Gerald Oster are among the noted op painters. In 1965 the Museum of Modern Art staged a vast exhibition of op art, The Responsive Eye, which dramatized the objectives and achievements of optical art.

The tags affixed to art movements and tendencies are seldom precise. Josef Albers, one of the early and best known leaders of perceptual abstraction, objects to the terms "optical" and "retinal" because the responses they denote are "psychological and thus happen behind our retina, where all optics end." Either at school or in their own studios the optical painters have learned that no color, and even no shape, has an invariable identity: that a given mixture of pigment can appear lighter or darker, warmer or cooler, brighter or duller; that a line or a shape can appear long or short, large or small, straight or bent, depending on the elements among which it appears.

Hard edges can be made to soften, wave, and fluctuate, flat bands can be modeled perceptually to appear like Doric fluting; and, because of periodic fatigue, or "bleaching" of color-sensitive cones in the retina, luminous shapes, purer and more brilliant than the painted shapes that generate them, can be made to appear, disappear and reappear at another location in a rhythmic cycle.

One wonders why the variability and vital propensities of flat surface colors were harnessed so late in the history of art. There are two reasons: first, the advent of abstract painting was essential to the full liberation of color as an autonomous means; second, extensive experimentation with modern pigments and such materials as colored papers was necessary before a perceptually functional art could develop.

Minimal art, still the dominant current trend, is simplified, devoid of emotion, uninflected, reductive, and seemingly empty of content. It is the antithesis of the figurative or action painting that antedated it. Among its many practitioners are Robert Morris, Tony Smith, Donald Judd, Leo Valledor, and Ronald Bladen. Art critic Barbara Rose has described it as "an art whose blank, neutral, mechanical impersonality contrasts so violently with the romantic, biographical abstract expressionist style which preceded it that spectators are chilled by its apparent lack of feeling or content . . . one has the sense that form and content do not coincide [and] that, in fact, a bland, neutral form is the vehicle for a hostile, aggressive content. . . . Why, for example, are the pastel tints so unpleasant? Why is surface tension stretched to the breaking point? Why do we feel, in the end, vaguely deprived or frustrated? That such matters crop up, and that they are ultimately unanswerable, is part of the elusiveness and ambiguity that seem to be the prime qualities of the new art. Of the sculptors one might ask similar questions: Why is it so big, so blunt, so graceless, so inert?"

But the apparent simplicity of the minimal art is an illusion; actually, the empty look is attained only after the minimal artist, through a series of complicated rationalizations, has decided to make it so, has eliminated whatever he feels is nonessential. Donald Judd, sculptor, art critic, and one-time philosophy student, commented in 1965:

One of the important things in any art is its degree of generality and specificity and another is how each of these occurs. The extent and the occurrence have to be credible. I'd like my work to be somewhat more specific than art has been and also specific and general in a different way. This is also probably the intention of a few other artists. Although I admire the work of some of the older artists, I can't altogether believe its generality. Earlier art is less credible. Of course, finally, I only believe my own work. It is necessary to make general statements, but it is impossible and not even desirable to believe most generalizations. . . . It is silly to have opinions about many things that you're supposed to have opinions on. About others, where it seems necessary, the necessity and the opinions are mostly guess. Some of my generalizations . . . are about this situation. Other generalizations and much of the specificity are assertions of my own interests and those that have settled in the public domain.

Hard-edge abstraction, a style of the early sixties based on sharp definition and immaculate color and surface, may have a remote kinship with minimal art, if only in its over-simplification of line, its compression of content, its rejection of all but the bare essentials. Among the representative hard-edge artists are included Ellsworth Kelly, Edwin Ruda, Lorser Feitelson, and Al Held. Answering a questionnaire sent out by Barbara Rose and Irving Sandler (the results of which were published in the January–February 1967 issue of Art in America), Al Held wrote:

The surrealist sensibility has been rejected by the artists I'm interested in today. The artists who interested me in the fifties considered themselves alone, tormented, tortured. Their emphasis was on an internal monologue (surrealist). Now, there's a different emphasis, more on the formal and esthetic aspects of art. The slogan of the fifties was the old art slogan: Art and life. The slogan of the sixties is the old art slogan: art out of art. I like both slogans. . . . If by avant-garde one means a reaction against action painting, O.K. Most of the ideas advanced in the sixties are based on the premise that art began in 1945. . . . The shaped-canvas and the painting-sculpture combine are avant-garde concepts only if one conveniently ignores a centuries-long medieval tradition. The idea of avant-garde has to do with process, method and materials. But these have always been given in twentieth-century art. Why raise them as issues now?

Edwin Ruda has a defense and forecast of hard-edge art:

What began as hard-edge art has now reversed course and is treading a new kind of poetry. At times it even shows a soft profile. Reflections of smooth metal or plastic surfaces liquefy the hardness of the object. The use of a single color and color vibrations break down the definition of the edge. Simultaneous shifting space introduces the idea of pure motion rather than a stable, resistant object. The pendulum is swinging toward energy rather than matter. In my mind this suggests dematerialization and technical lyricism. . . .

Words like reduction, logic, mathematical, and technical are frequently used in connection with art of the sixties. As used by critics, "reduction" seems to imply a shrinking cerebellum accompanied by boredom. A nicer word would be "deduction," which means the removal of all excess except "the one that stands for many." . . . Speaking of technology, I just bought a brand new one-half horse [power] compressor-spray unit and threw out all my paint brushes. No nostalgia, just relief. Results were gratifying. I could get the gun-metal finish I wanted, nearly perfect craftsmanship, sensual, groovy, too much, etc. Then I sit back and say to myself, so what? The up-and-coming artist making it in an elevator going down. I still got to hustle and stay invisible with not even a name or color or even Kafka's crutch to prop me up. Maybe this is my tie with the fifties. I mean the fifties B.C.

Minimal, hard-edge, and op are all, in a sense, part of what is now being called the new abstraction, and perhaps the best example of a new abstractionist is the painter Frank Stella, who is a major connecting link between many contemporary styles. His work contains elements of all the trends mentioned above, and his shaped canvases have added still another dimension. He discussed his work in a lecture he delivered at Pratt Institute, New York, in 1960, as follows:

I got tired of other people's paintings and began to make my own. I found, however, that I not only got tired of looking at my own paintings but that I also didn't like painting them at all. The painterly problem of what to put here and there, and how to make it go with what was already there, became more and more difficult and the solutions more and more unsatisfactory. Finally I had to face two problems: one was spatial and the other methodological. . . . The obvious answer was symmetry—make it the same all over. . . . The solution I arrived at —and there are probably others although I know of only one, color density—forces illusionistic space out of the painting at a constant rate by using a regulated pattern. The remaining problem was simply to find a method of paint application which followed and complemented the design solution. This was done by using the house painter's technique and tools.

Kinetic and light constructions have a common denominator in the use of movement. The air-driven mobiles of Alexander Calder were the major—and early—manifestations in kinetics; Len Lye and George Rickey, along with Charles Mattox on the West Coast, and many other artists, have used mechanically and naturally induced movement in their works. Rickey, one of the country's leading kineticists, a critic and author, has been making kinetic sculpture since 1949 and has exhibited widely both abroad and in the United States. In a discussion of kinetics, Rickey points out that optical art (involving retinal disturbance and the illusion of movement) and kinetic art are "two completely different idioms." He writes further:

The idea of "movable" works is now widespread, although their relation to kinetic art is hazy. The participation of the spectator either through manipulation or his own movement is often provided for. . . . This motility is not strictly kinetic art. When the spectator must turn knobs, pull strings or wag his head, the movement is not an attribute of the object, but a momentary attribute of something else—the kinetic spectator. The movement is temporary and promptly subsides. . . . Movement itself, apart from light, sound, water-play, magnetism or any other phenomenon used simply to embellish, remains the essential objective of the kinetic art of our time. . . .

To design with movement itself, as distinct from adding movement to a design, has been my preoccupation for the past fifteen years. Movement reveals itself most clearly in very simple forms, for example in a single line moving through space. Combined with a second line, moving contrapuntally, the two may cut each other; may divide, squeeze, and define space; and, moving at different speeds, may measure time in a surprisingly complex way.

I have thus far worked with lines in combinations up to six. I have also, in another mode, assembled constellations of very numerous parts, sometimes lines and sometimes other forms. These groups exploit a different kind of phenomenon, where the *many* become a new *one,* and complexity and simplicity develop simultaneously.

I have not exhausted linear themes (in fact they seem inexhaustible); but a line has in it to become a plane. Planes do not simply repeat linear themes with one added dimension; they are another world with its own laws and language. With moving lines, space is cut; when it is planes which move, space is compressed, stretched, twisted, and compartmented.

Any material will reflect or absorb light; a line will thus be light or dark. A surface has a greatly augmented response to light; its reflection or absorption almost adds another dimension. If the surface is polished like a mirror it disappears and becomes space instead, as it receives and retransmits, in altered form, the surrounding world.

Mr. Rickey has written that "the artist's use of light, even if embracing both movement and optical phenomena, is a field of such extensive possibilities that it should be examined by itself. . . . Nothing is communicated without light; the use of light is ubiquitous in art; and mere illumination, whether still or moving, is not art. The controlled movement of transmitted light is one of the directions in which much has been done in the last five years." The use of light as a medium is an experiment which artists such as James Seawright, Howard Jones, and many others have been pursuing with an increasing enthusiasm. Stephen Antonakos and Chryssa have been working with neon, Dan Flavin uses fluorescent tubes. Flavin's light art, which he rightly refuses to call sculpture, is much the starkest and most typical of the mood of contemporary art in its effects, rejection of standard esthetic concepts, and liberal use of overtly commercial materials. (Flavin has remarked that any hardware store could easily supply enough exhibition material to satisfy the season's needs of a commercial art gallery.)

Flavin, who is notoriously reluctant to make comments about his working intentions, briefly explained his light art with the curious dedicatory title "greens crossing greens (to Piet Mondrian who lacked green)" as follows:

This room contains two simple segmented barrier channels of green fluorescent light which cut each other's course arbitrarily, each at a different horizontal height over the floor. The length of either channel is variable—restricted by bounds of walls. Green is used throughout because it is a pleasant color at this extent, brilliant as fluorescent light and soft in the total barrier.

Chryssa, a Greek-born artist who is now an American, was among the several participants in the Art in Process exhibition organized in the spring of 1966 by the Contemporary Study Wing of the Finch College Museum of Art in New York. In the show catalogue, she sketches the background of her devotion to light as art:

When I came to New York after my frightening childhood years in Athens during World War II, when it was occupied by the Germans and Italians, I became fascinated with the lights and signs of Broadway and Times Square. It appeared to me like a garden of light and I was unable to capture what I felt or saw in the medium of paint. I realized a more energetic medium was required and came to the conclusion that only neon tubes, with their dazzling combinations, could produce this garden of light. It is Bach who keeps me going and from whom I have learned everything I know about sculpture. It is the music of Bach which made technical structure synonymous with big and powerful emotions. I draw from Bach's music a great deal of courage.

Stephen Antonakos, another Greek who has become an American, is very explicit about the medium he prefers for his work:

Neon—light arresting space/ Neon—programmed movement/ Neon—silent screams of color/ Neon—the rhythm of images/ Neon—the shock of the unexpected/ Neon—is beautiful/ Neon—is aggressive/ Neon—always makes me work harder than before/ Neon—to be seen as never before.

The sculpture of the nineteen-sixties has, though following the same general directions as painting in assimilating the commercial and industrial products of our society, taken the lead in the so-called "fine arts" of our day. The best-known sculptors, among them Richard Stankiewicz, Claes Oldenburg, Marisol, Peter Voulkos, Mark di Suvero, Ernest Trova, David Von Schlegell, John Chamberlain, and Alexander Liberman (who is also a painter), is their various styles—which range from junk structures to the utmost in technological precision—have this in common: they make use of the industrial object, in fact or in concept.

Figurative art is the one carry-over from the past which has been thoroughly assimilated into current idiom, and figurative artists of the nineteen-sixties with widely divergent styles hold an important place on the scene. Among these, Larry Rivers, Richard Lindner, and George Segal have introduced today's attitudes and media into their work while keeping contact with the past. George Segal has expressed his attitude toward the contemporary scene in these words:

There is an avant-garde today, healthily shooting down different extreme directions. Everyone shares a huge stew of ideas. Some of the ideas are pushed to logical extremes or strained through unique personalities, and unexpected jumps are made. I think we're in the middle of an explosion of vitality that has affected all the areas of art: painting, sculpture, music, dance, poetry, film, architecture, theater; we've seen only the beginning of hybrid forms and mutations that can and will be invented. . . . Many people seem to forget that different ideas flowing have subterranean currents and connections. A new hard-edge painter can have affinity with both Mondrian and a musical score by John Cage. A shaped canvas can become fully three-dimensional. If a real object is placed in a room, it's called pop. The same object, abstracted into a geometric shape three-dimensionally, is called a primary structure.

Obviously, styles from past periods still have their place, in almost pristine condition, in today's world of art. Traditional painting—particularly as represented by Andrew Wyeth—draws far larger crowds than even the most sensational of exhibitions in the contemporary mode. Moreover, it is an odd reflection that, apart from Wyeth, probably the most popular American painter is Grandma Moses. Impressionism, post-impressionism, romantic landscape, and almost the whole spectrum of previous styles still have enthusiasts who, outside the inside world of art and the big cities, probably far outnumber the admirers of present-day forms of expression.

What will remain of the tremendous and exciting upheaval of the nineteen-sixties? Which movements will survive, what will be the most significant of the multitudinous trends? Only two things are absolutely certain. First, that the ultimate responsibility rests with the individual artists and that it is he and not the trend that survives. The second is that there is only one ultimate judge of the value of a period in the history of art, and that is time.

Larry Rivers: Washington Crossing the Delaware, oil, 1953. Museum of Modern Art, New York.

Richard Lindner: Los Angeles, oil, 1966. Cordier and Ekstrom, New York.

Jasper Johns: Studio, oil, 1964. Whitney Museum of American Art, New York.

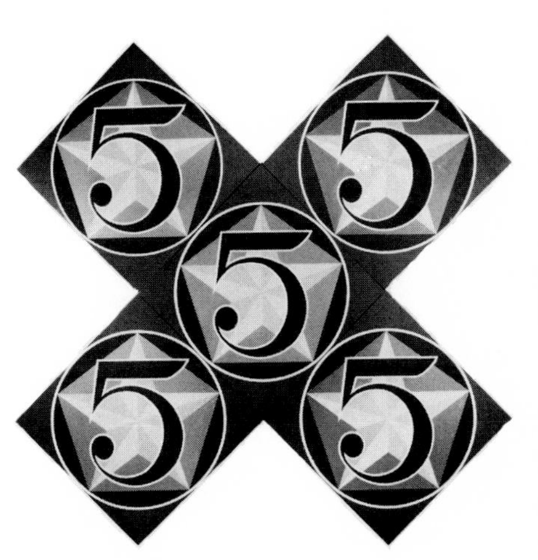

Robert Indiana: The X–5, oil, 1963. Whitney Museum of American Art, New York.

Photo by John D. Schiff

Claes Oldenburg: Dual Hamburgers, painted plaster, 1962. Museum of Modern Art, New York.

Andy Warhol's silk-screened pop art wood constructions, at a 1964 show at the Stable Gallery, New York.

Tom Wesselmann: Bathtub Collage No. 3, mixed media, 1963. Collection of Fred Weisman.

James Rosenquist: F–111, oil, 1965.
Collection of Mr. and Mrs. Robert C. Scull.

Marisol: Women and Dog, wood, plaster,
miscellaneous items, 1964.
Whitney Museum of American Art, New York.

George Segal: Walking Man,
mixed media, 1964.
Sidney Janis Gallery, New York.

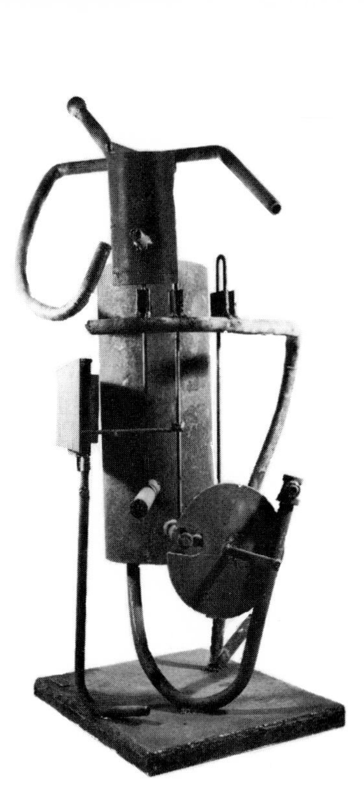

Richard Stankiewicz: Wind Gong III, steel, 1967. Stable Gallery, New York.

John Chamberlain: Miss Lucy Pink, welded auto metal, 1962. Leo Castelli Gallery, New York.

Mark di Suvero: B L T, iron, wood, rubber, 1966. Park Place Gallery, New York.

Richard Anuszkiewicz: One and a Half, liquitex, 1967. Sidney Janis Gallery, New York.

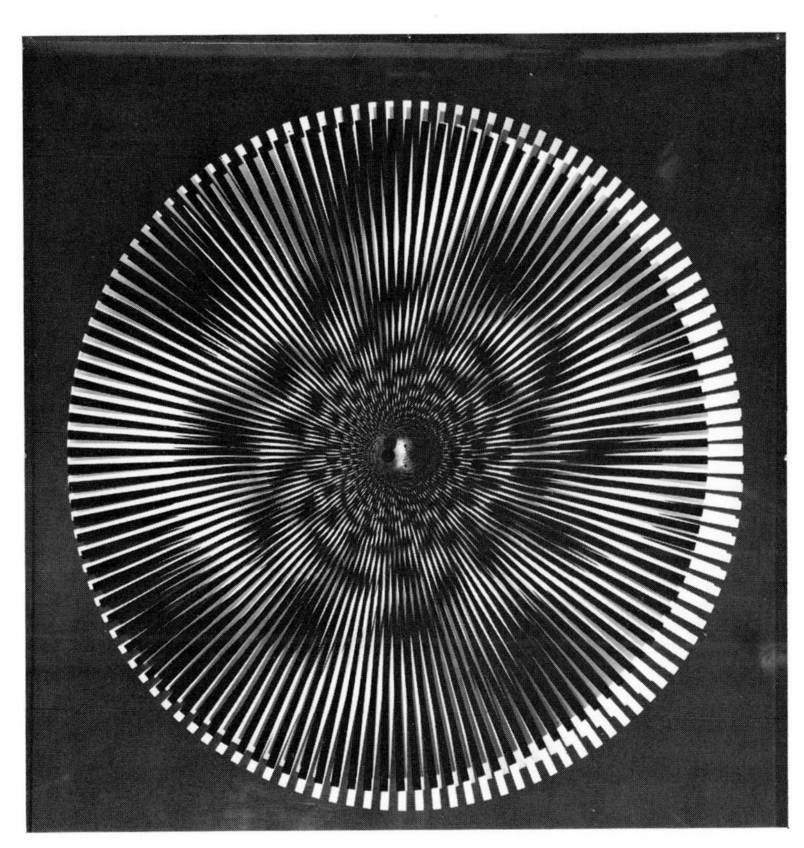

Gerald Oster: Triple Radial, serigraph on plastic, paper, and wood, 1964. Howard Wise Gallery, New York.

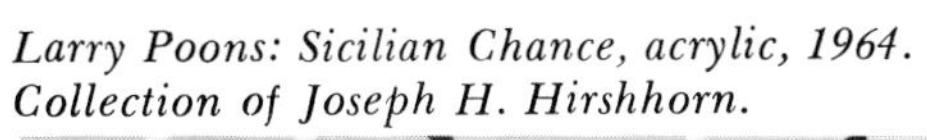

Larry Poons: Sicilian Chance, acrylic, 1964. Collection of Joseph H. Hirshhorn.

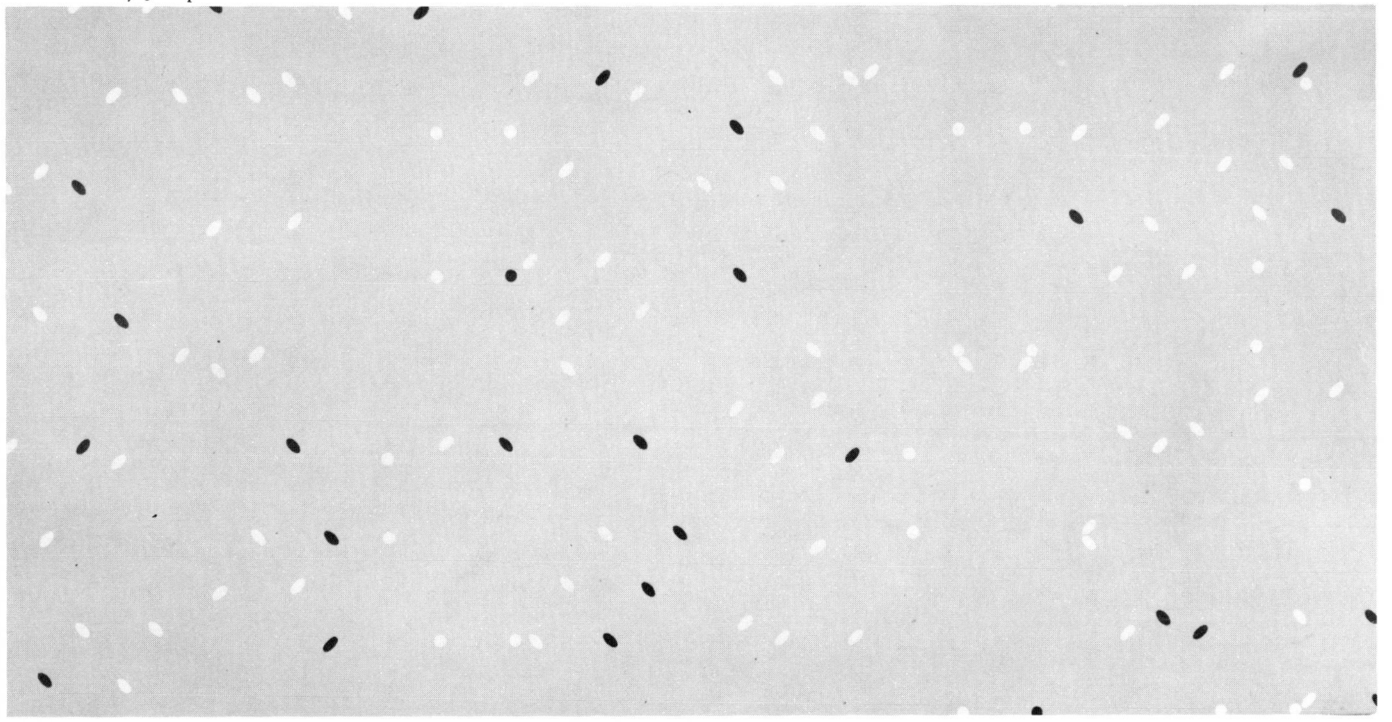

Photo by John D. Schiff

James Seawright: Watcher, electric lights and electronic parts, 1966. Collection of Jean and Howard Lipman.

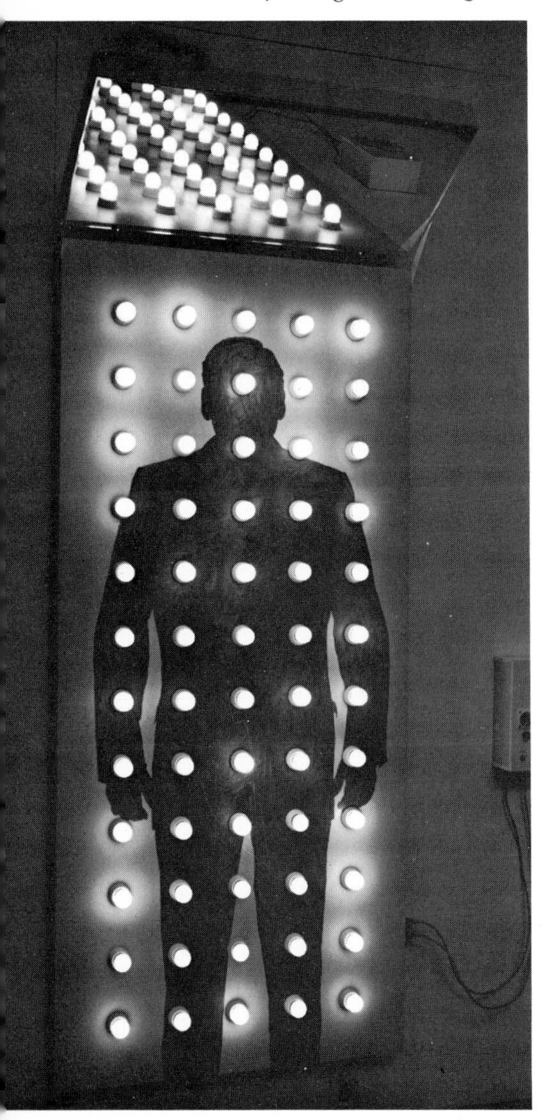

Howard Jones: Solo Two, wood, mirror, and programmed light and sound, 1966. Collection of George Rosborough.

Stephen Antonakos: White Hanging Neon, neon and aluminum, 1966. Fischbach Gallery, New York.

Jim Dine: Self-Portrait, charcoal and paint on canvas with cement, 1964.
Oberlin College, Oberlin, Ohio.

Roy Lichtenstein: Hopeless, magna on canvas, 1963.
Collection of Ileana Sonnabend.

Edward Kienholz: The Wait, tableau, 1964–65.
Whitney Museum of American Art, New York.

Leo Valledor: Red Wing, acrylic, 1965.
Collection of J. Patrick Lannan.

Ellsworth Kelly: Red Yellow Blue, oil, 1966.
Sidney Janis Gallery, New York.

Donald Judd: Structures in galvanized iron and painted aluminum, 1966.
A February 1966 exhibition at Leo Castelli Gallery, New York.

Chryssa: Fragments for the Gates to Times Square II, programmed neon and plexiglas, 1966. Whitney Museum of American Art, New York.

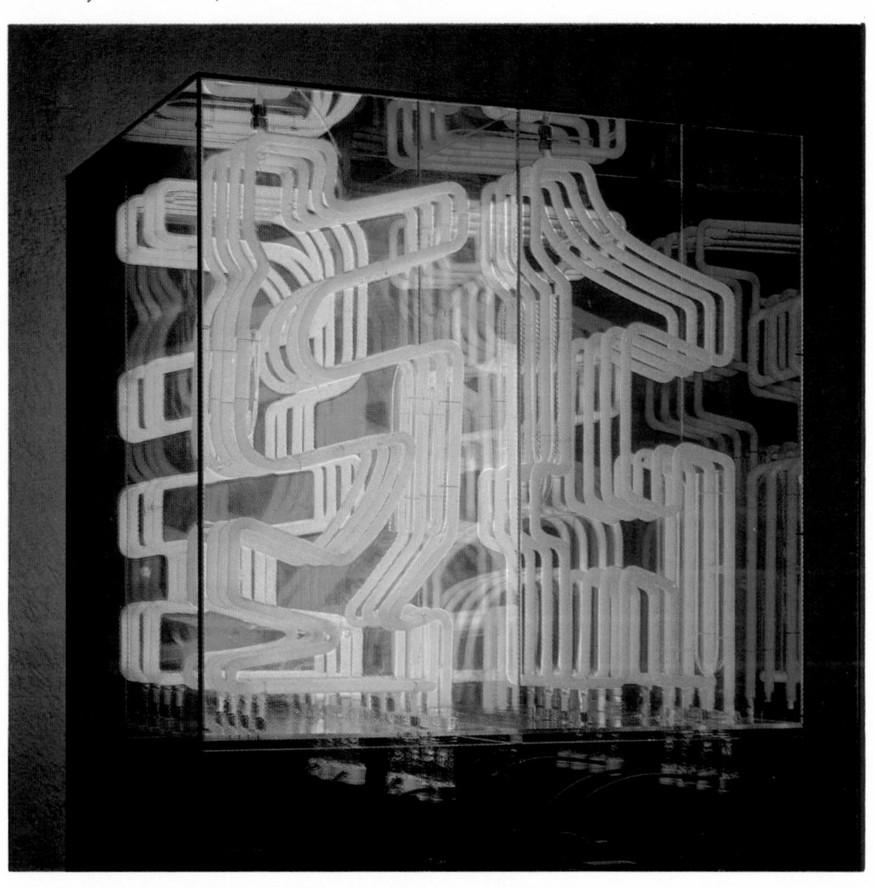

Len Lye: Flip and Two Twisters, stainless steel, 1965. Howard Wise Gallery, New York.

Photos by Hans Namuth

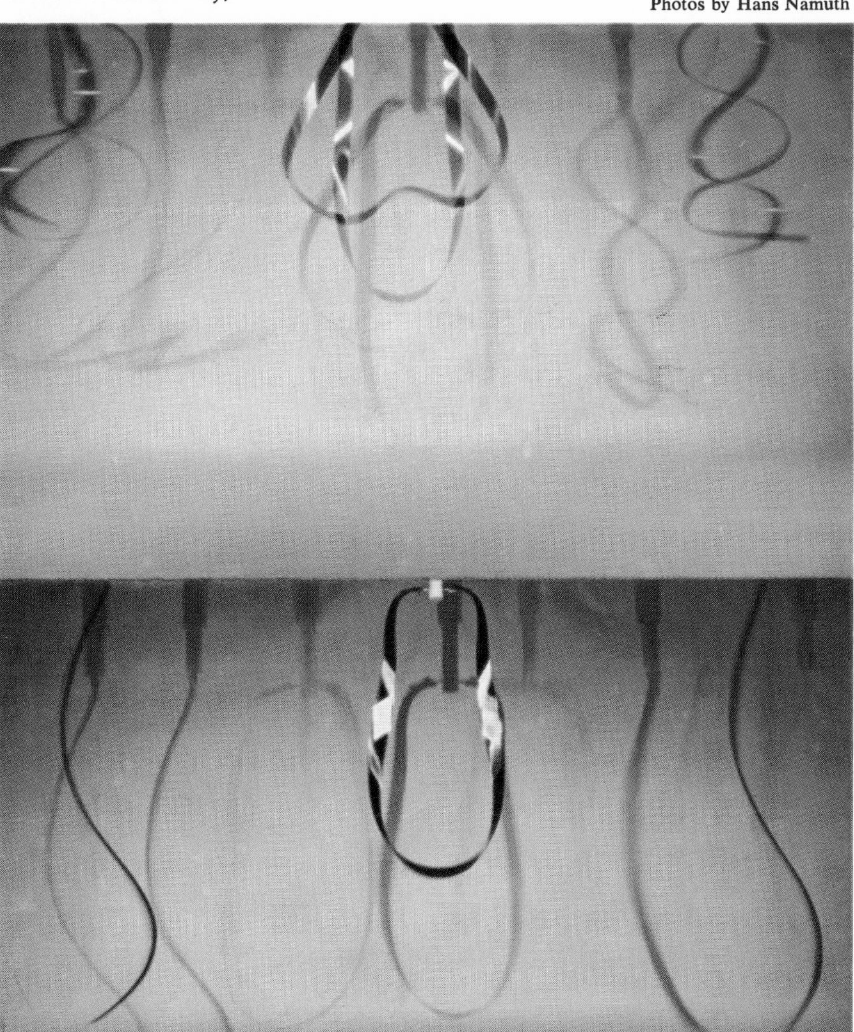

Smith: Amaryllis, painted wood (completed work to be done in steel), Fischbach Gallery, New York.

Dan Flavin: greens crossing greens (to Piet Mondrian, who lacked green), green fluorescent tubing and frosted translucent plastic, 1966. Temporary installation for Kunst-Licht-Kunst exhibition, Eindhoven, Holland.

Photo by Rolf Schroeter

Robert Morris: Untitled, gray fiberglass, 1965.
Dwan Gallery, New York.

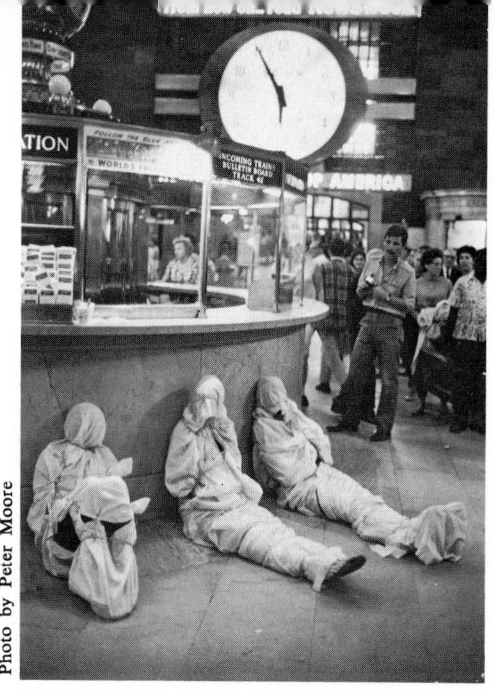

Photo by Peter Moore

Allan Kaprow: Calling, a happening staged at the information counter in New York's Grand Central station.

Ronald Bladen: Three Elements, painted aluminum and wood, 1965.
Fischbach Gallery, New York.

Jack Youngerman: Elegy for a Guerilla, plastic paint, 1965. Betty Parsons Gallery, New York.

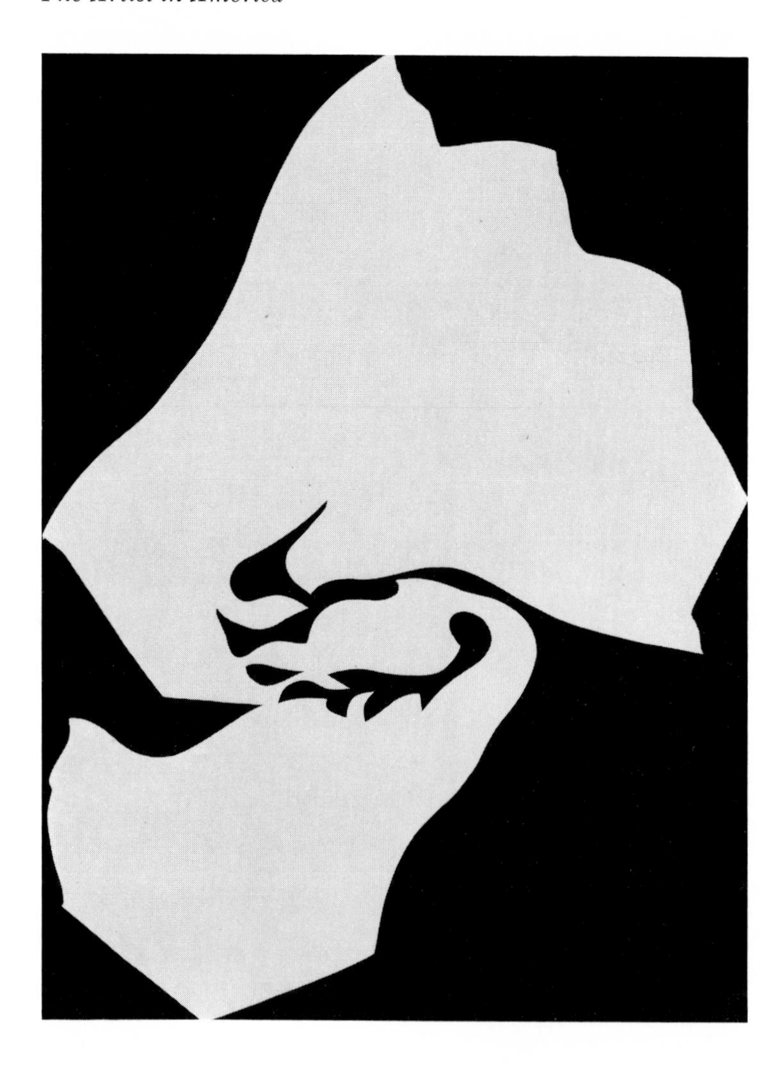

Frank Stella: Empress of India, acrylic and metallic powder on canvas, 1965. Collection of Irving Blum.

Al Held: Untitled, acrylic, 1964. André Emmerich Gallery, New York.

Kenneth Noland: Midmost, acrylic, 1966. Collection of Walter Netsch.

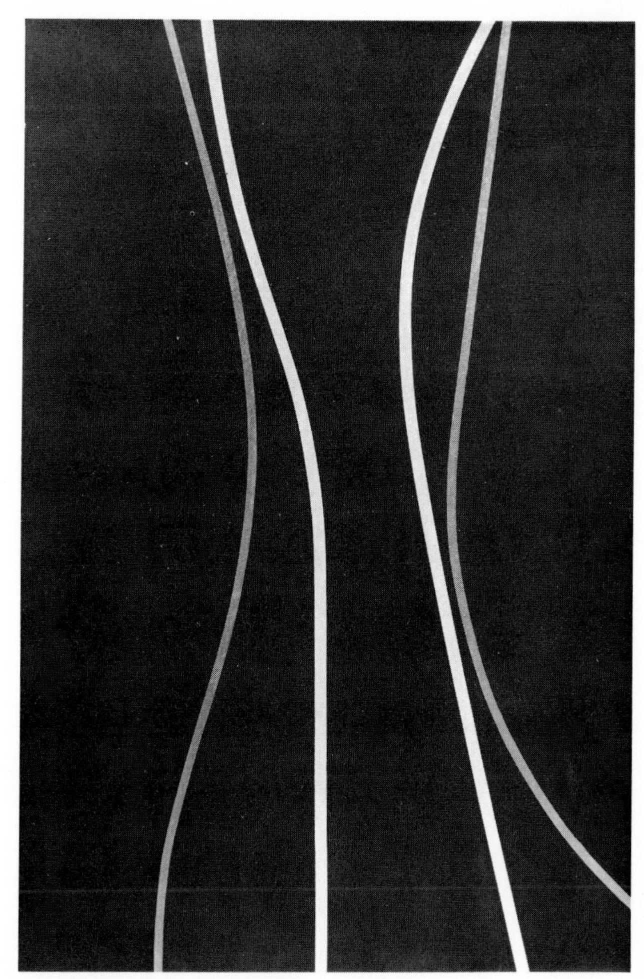

Lorser Feitelson: Hard-Edge Line Painting, oil and enamel on canvas, 1964. Ankrum Gallery, Los Angeles.

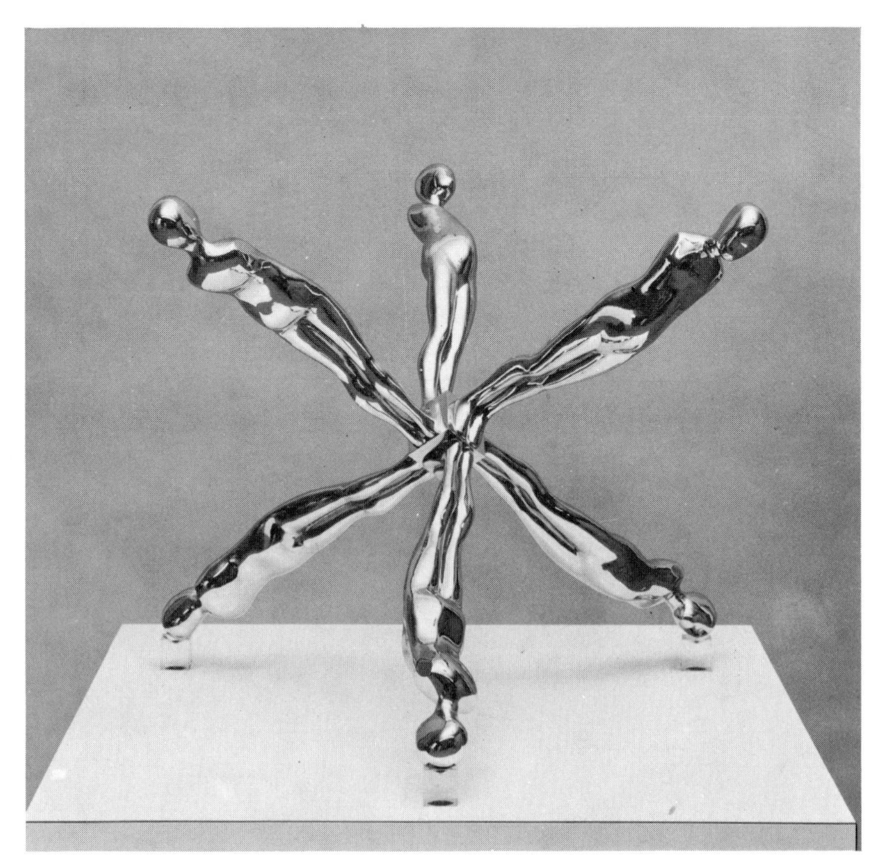

Ernest Trova: Study, Falling Man Series—Six Figures, chrome-plated bronze, 1964. Whitney Museum of American Art, New York.

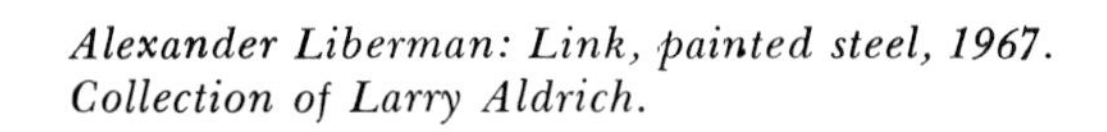

Alexander Liberman: Link, painted steel, 1967. Collection of Larry Aldrich.

George Rickey: Four Lines Up, steel, 1967.
Collection of Robert H. Levi.

David Von Schlegell: Classical Study, aluminum, 1965.
Royal Marks Gallery, New York.

Contributors

LLOYD GOODRICH is Director of the Whitney Museum of American Art, New York, and author of *Winslow Homer's America, Edward Hopper,* and *Three Centuries of American Art.*

RUSSELL LYNES, Contributing Editor of *Harper's* magazine, is President of the Archives of American Art, and author of *The Tastemakers, The Domesticated Americans,* and *Confessions of a Dilettante.*

WAYNE ANDREWS holds the Archives of American Art Chair at Wayne State University in Detroit, Michigan. He is the author of *Battle for Chicago* and *Architecture in America.*

GARNETT McCOY, Archivist of the Archives of American Art, is the author of *Printing, Printers and Presses in Early Detroit.*

JOHN C. EWERS, Senior Ethnologist of the Smithsonian Institution, Washington, D. C., is the author of *Artists of the Old West* and *Plains Indian Painting.*

MARY BLACK, Director of the Museum of American Folk Art, New York, and formerly Director of the Abby Aldrich Rockefeller Folk Art Collection, Williamsburg, Virginia, is the author (with Jean Lipman) of *American Folk Painting.*

CLEMENT GREENBERG, critic, whose articles appear in many art and national publications, is the author of *Joan Miró, Matisse, Art and Culture,* and *Hofmann.*

Acknowledgments

Text and captions acknowledge the ownership of the individuals, museums, and galleries which provided information and illustrations. The Archives of American Art made available documents, photographs, and research material that formed the basis for several chapters. Special acknowledgments follow:

page 41
Letter, John Trumbull to Robert Gilmor, Nov. 14, 1825. Dreer Collection, Historical Society of Pennsylvania, Philadelphia.

page 43
Letter, Charles Willson Peale to President Thomas Jefferson, Feb. 8, 1806. Jefferson Papers, Library of Congress, Washington, D. C.

pages 52, 53
Excerpts from *Journal of Rudolph Friederich Kurz,* edited by J. N. B. Hewitt. Bureau of American Ethnology Bulletin 115, Washington, D.C., 1937, pp. 1–2, 94.

page 53
Excerpt from *The West of Alfred Jacob Miller* by Marvin C. Ross. University of Oklahoma Press, Norman, Oklahoma, pp. 1, 26, 29, 114, 130.

page 56
Excerpt from Letters of George Caleb Bingham to James S. Rollins, edited by C. B. Rollins, in the *Missouri Historical Review,* Vol. XXXII, January 1938, pp. 171–172.

pages 56, 65
Letter from Albert Bierstadt to *The Crayon,* Vol. VI, Part IX, September 1859, p. 287.

page 65
Excerpt (Thomas Moran quotes) from *American Painters* by G. W. Sheldon. D. Appleton & Co., publishers, New York, 1881, pp. 125–126.

pages 65, 66
Excerpt from Frederic Remington's article, "Horses of the Plains," in *Century Magazine,* Vol. XXXVII, No. 3, January 1889, pp. 339–340.

page 66
Excerpts from "A Few Words from Mr. Remington" in *Collier's Weekly,* March 18, 1905, p. 16.

page 66
Excerpt from Charles M. Russell's "A Few Words About Myself" in a brochure, *The Log Cabin Studio of Charles M. Russell,* published by the Russell Memorial Committee, Great Falls, Montana.

page 67
Excerpt from George de Forest Brush's "An Artist Among the Indians" in *Century Magazine,* Vol. XXX, May 1885, pp. 55–57.

page 87
Shem Drowne's copper Indian weathervane is mentioned by Nathaniel Hawthorne in "Shem Drowne's Wooden Image," in Hawthorne's *Mosses From an Old Manse.*

pages 103, 104
Letters, Thomas Cole to Robert Gilmor, Jr., Jan. 5, 1829, Jan. 20, 1829, Jan. 29, 1832. New York State Library, Albany.

page 104
Letter, Thomas Cole to Ithiel Town, May 25, 1840. New York State Library, Albany.

page 113
Letter, Horatio Greenough to Rembrandt Peale, Nov. 8, 1831. New-York Historical Society, New York.

page 122
Letters, Winslow Homer to M. Knoedler & Co., Dec. 1, 1900, Jan. 14, 1902, Feb. 17, 1902. M. Knoedler & Co., New York.

pages 122, 127
Letter, George Inness to Ripley Hitchcock, March 23, 1883. Montclair, New Jersey, Art Museum.

page 127
Statement, Thomas Eakins, written for Emily Sartain, March 25, 1886. Pennsylvania Academy of the Fine Arts, Philadelphia.

pages 127, 128
Quotations from notes on Thomas Eakins' lectures on art, taken by Charles Bregler, April 1887. Maximilian Miltzlaff, New York.

page 128
Letter, Thomas Pollock Anshutz to John Laurie Wallace, Aug. 25, 1884. Pennsylvania Academy of the Fine Arts, Philadelphia.

page 128
Letter, Albert Pinkham Ryder to Charles Erskine Scott Wood, Feb. 9, 1906. Harold O. Love, Grosse Pointe Farms, Grosse Pointe, Michigan.

pages 137, 139
Letters, Mrs. Robert S. Cassatt and her daughter Mary to Alexander J. Cassatt and to Mrs. Alexander J. Cassatt, 1880 through 1886. Mrs. John B. Thayer, Rosemont, Pennsylvania.

page 139
Letter, Mary Cassatt to Mrs. Potter Palmer, Dec. 1, 1892. Art Institute of Chicago.

pages 144, 147, 155
Tape-recorded interview with Stuart Davis in May-June 1962. Copyright 1965 by Roselle Davis.

pages 151, 152
Letters, Walt Kuhn to Vera Kuhn, Dec. 12 and Dec. 15, 1911, Dec. 14, 1912. Miss Brenda Kuhn, Cape Neddick, Maine.

pages 151, 152
Letters, Arthur B. Davies to Walt Kuhn, Oct. 1, about Oct. 15, Oct. 20, all 1912. Miss Brenda Kuhn, Cape Neddick, Maine.

page 155
John Sloan's diary entries, Jan. 4 and 16, 1913. Mrs. John Sloan, New York, and Delaware Art Center, Wilmington, Delaware.

page 155
Photo-Secession Gallery poster, 1908. Museum of Modern Art, New York.

pages 158, 159
Letters, Georgia O'Keeffe to Henry McBride, Jan. 16, 1927, May 11, 1928. Yale Collection of American Literature, Yale University Library, New Haven, Connecticut.

pages 159, 160
Letters, Charles Demuth to Henry McBride, April 1917, Aug. 19, 1927. Maximilian Miltzlaff, New York.

page 169
Letter, Joseph Stella to Henry McBride, Nov. 17, 1937. Maximilian Miltzlaff, New York.

page 172
Letter, Charles Burchfield to Lawrence A. Fleischman, Aug. 14, 1955. Mr. and Mrs. Lawrence A. Fleischman, New York.

page 174
George Biddle's diary entries, April 23, June 23, Nov. 7, Dec. 8, Dec. 11, all 1933, and April 23, 1934. George Biddle, Croton-on-Hudson, New York.

pages 200, 202
Tape-recorded interview with Jackson Pollock, about 1950. Lee Krasner Pollock, New York.

page 204
Statement by Ad Reinhardt, 1962. Typescript in Museum of Modern Art, New York.

Index

Italic numbers indicate black-and-white illustrations (accompanied by text); **boldface** numbers indicate color plates; others are text references.